Shipwrecked Identities

Shipwrecked Identities

NAVIGATING RACE ON NICARAGUA'S MOSQUITO COAST

BARON L. PINEDA

RUTGERS UNIVERSITY PRESS
New Brunswick, New Jersey, and London

Library of Congress Cataloging-in-Publication Data

Pineda, Baron L., 1967–
    Shipwrecked identities : navigating race on Nicaragua's Mosquito Coast/ Baron L. Pineda.
     p. cm.
    Includes bibliographical references and index.
    ISBN-13: 978-0-8135-3813-6 (hardcover: alk. paper)
    ISBN-13: 978-0-8135-3814-3 (pbk.: alk. paper)
    1. Indians of Central America—Nicaragua—Ethnic identity. 2. Indians of Central America—Urban residence—Mosquitia (Nicaragua and Honduras) 3. Indians of Central America—Mosquitia (Nicaragua and Honduras)—Social conditions. 4. Indigenous peoples—Mosquitia (Nicaragua and Honduras)—Ethnic identity. 5. Indigenous peoples—Mosquitia (Nicaragua and Honduras)—Social conditions. 6. Mosquitia (Nicaragua and Honduras)—Race relations. 7. Mosquitia (Nicaragua and Honduras)—Social conditions. I. Title.

F1525.3.E74P56 2006
305.897′882—dc22   2005019946

A British Cataloging-in-Publication record for this book is available from the British Library.

Manufactured in the United States of America

For Gina, Antonio, and little Pablo

Contents

Shipwrecked Identities

CHAPTER 1

The Setting

DON PACO MENDEZ owns and operates a store among
the strings of general stores that line the *calle commercial* (commercial
street) of Puerto Cabezas—the port and capital of Nicaragua's recently
formed North Atlantic Autonomous Region (*la RAAN* as it is known
locally). One afternoon I stopped by his store to do an informal interview with him about his life.[1] He told me that his family was one of the
founders of Puerto Cabezas during the period that is known locally as
"company time"—an idealized period from the 1920s to the 1970s in
which US and Canadian banana, lumber, and mining industries operated on a large scale in the region.[2] His Costa Rican mother and
Nicaraguan father migrated from the Pacific side of Nicaragua to establish a general store in the burgeoning Caribbean port city that in the
1920s was converted from a small Indian village called Bilwi to the
Nicaraguan headquarters of the largest employer in Nicaragua, the Standard Fruit Company.

He was quick to remind me that although he had been born and
raised *en la costa*, on the Mosquito Coast, he was, in an existential sense,
profoundly *del Pacifico*, from the Pacific. Although he referred to himself
as an *indígena* and an *indio*, he explained to me, with more than a trace
of prejudice, the fundamental superiority of the Pacific Indian vis-à-vis
the *Moscos de aqui* (literally, flies from here), as he perjoratively referred
to the Miskito Indians.

Don Paco explained that he had spent some time in the *campesino*
(small-scale agriculturalist) villages of the mountainous Nicaraguan
interior that he regarded as being part of the Pacific Coast, an important distinction in the context of Nicaragua where all Nicaraguans
regard the country as being divided into two fundamentally different

halves: Atlantic (Mosquito Coast) and Pacific. In the Segovian Mountains he had witnessed the vigor and skill with which the Indian campesinos coaxed harvests from marginal and relatively dry lands. In his opinion the land's suitability for agriculture and the climate of the Pacific interior were far inferior to that of the Mosquito Coast, Nicaragua's relatively sparsely populated and heavily forested Caribbean lowlands. Don Paco's perception of the absence of ideal geographical, climatic, and social conditions for agriculture in the Pacific vis-à-vis the Atlantic stood in sharp contrast to his perception of the disparity in productivity between the inhabitants of each region:

> If the Indians [of the Pacific] have a little piece of land, they plant green peppers, onions, tomatoes . . . everything . . . but here the damn Moscos are lazy. They just plant their cassava and banana and then sit back in their hammock, real easy. They just cultivate in order to live and as long as they are eating, they don't worry about getting ahead . . . no progress. In the Pacific they plant corn, beans and bust their asses taking care of the crops . . . they will walk ten kilometers to get water. Every day there they are cleaning and taking care of the crops, but for the Moscos from here that is too much work to do. They don't want to grow corn, the damn Moscos, because they are lazy.

Unfortunately, the sort of prejudice against *Costeños*, people of the Mosquito Coast, reflected in this quotation is not uncommon, even among some natives such as Don Paco.[3] Indeed, more generally, the projection of negative qualities such as laziness and ignorance on marginalized out-groups, however defined, is common throughout the world. What stands out about this particular expression of prejudice is the way in which perceptions of land and geography—in other words, environmental ideologies—intersect with ideologies of race and group difference. Don Paco's belief that the Miskito Indians are lazy was confirmed in his mind by the fact that the agricultural production of the region had historically been low. But he also found this supposed laziness to be particularly disturbing in light of what he perceived to be the distinctive natural abundance of the region. This abundance and the agricultural opportunities he believed this abundance offered stood in contrast to the situation of the relatively arid and more heavily populated Pacific Coast.

In the minds of many Nicaraguans the region's natural abundance serves to explain the human poverty of its inhabitants. This luxuriant natural world is thought to lead to a diminished industriousness among the inhabitants of the region.

Few people in contemporary Nicaragua question the widely held notion that the Mosquito Coast is a rich land with tremendous natural abundance. However, the region is also popularly regarded as the country's poorest and least productive—its people suffering from an acute lack of infrastructure, social services, and employment. Since the late nineteenth century, Nicaraguan governments, while decrying the country's inability to harness the exploitable natural resources, have encouraged foreign companies to operate extractive mining, fishing, and lumbering industries in the region.

From the standpoint of Pacific Nicaraguan nationalism, the historical connection that the Mosquito Coast has had with Great Britain and the English-speaking world provokes suspicion and serves to place Costeño society as a suspect internal other. Throughout the Contra War the opposition of Costeños was viewed as a problem of separatism that was the residue of the hyper-exploitation of the region by British and North American colonialism and neo-colonialism.

In my conversations with Pacific Nicaraguans, many disapprovingly assert that Costeños "*se creen ingleses*" (believe they are English). This perceived insistence on maintaining cultural, linguistic, social, economic, and military (during the Contra War) ties with the English-speaking world and nonintegration with Nicaraguan *Mestizo* nationalism is ridiculed because it is perceived to stand in contrast to the reality of Mosquito Coast poverty and marginalization from both the English-speaking world and the relatively more prosperous Pacific half of the country. In light of the perceived Blackness, poverty, isolation, and corrupted languages of Costeños, Pacific Nicaraguans ridicule the idea that they should carry the torch of the Anglo-American and Anglo-Caribbean world.

Living and working with Costeños, I found that they are well aware of the derision with which many Pacific Nicaraguans regard them. Not surprisingly, they seek to contest or invert, formally and informally, the status hierarchies in which they find themselves in a subordinate position. In many ways Costeños see themselves as cosmopolitans whose continuing ties to the English-speaking world place them above Pacific Nicaraguans. With regard to their presumed over-identification with their British and North American oppressors, they remind themselves and Pacific Nicaraguans, when they have a chance, that the Pacific Coast has a long history of subservience and humiliation at the hands of these same alleged oppressors.

They speak of their successes in finding work in the United States, which they attribute in part to their English skills, western Caribbean location, and social capital (i.e., contact with Protestant churches). Costeño men frequently work on Caribbean cruise boats, and they pride themselves for being regarded as hard workers and being paid in US dollars. In that vein, they take pride in the long-standing fact of the circulation of dollars in the regional economy, in contrast to the troubled monetary history of the Nicaraguan Cordoba. Some Costeños describe themselves as "dollar men"—an expression that refers to their positive identification as cosmopolitans.

With regard to race, Costeños do not outright reject a pan-hemispheric skin-color hierarchy that ranks light skin above dark skin, but they note that Pacific Nicaraguans are themselves often quite dark skinned. Costeños typically construct their own Caribbean Blackness as being an integral part of their cosmopolitanism.[4] In this sense they both invert and contest the negative stereotypes that are applied to them and their region.

Costeños typically derive optimism and hope from their unwavering belief in the richness of the region and its potential for human transformation. For them the natural wealth of the region, far from sapping the energy of the people who inhabit it, represents an underutilized asset that under the right conditions should propel the Mosquito Coast into a particular kind of material prosperity. They share a vision of a dollar-driven and wage-driven prosperity that, in their minds, existed during company time. Costeños feel that in light of their natural environment and its role in their region's history, they should not be materially poor. In other words, they experience a nagging dissonance, what I call "environmental dissonance" (Pineda 2001c), between the abundance of their natural environment and the stagnation of their economies.

Notwithstanding the region's history of armed conflict and cycles of economic boom and bust, *Porteños* (inhabitants of Puerto Cabezas) find the current state of material poverty in the Atlantic Coast to be particularly appalling.[5] They fervently affirm their conviction that given the natural abundance of the Mosquito Coast, they should not be so poor. According to their cosmopolitan framework of viewing the world, the natural resources of the region should translate into their own material well-being. They shouldn't be so poor because their land is so rich. This environmental dissonance that Costeños experience stands in contrast to the way that the inhabitants of the Pacific view their relationship to the environment. The Pacific is a place where, to quote anthropologist Roger Lancaster's provocative title, life is hard (Lancaster 1992).

THE CULTURAL POLITICS OF BLACKNESS AND INDIGENEITY IN THE MOSQUITO COAST

Deprived of their original language, the captured and indentured tribes create their own, accreting and secreting fragments of an old, epic vocabulary from Asia and from Africa, but to an ancestral and ecstatic rhythm in the blood that cannot be subdued by slavery or indenture, while nouns are renamed and the given names of places accepted like Felicity or Choiseul. The original language dissolves from the exhaustion of distance like fog trying to cross an ocean, but this process of renaming, of finding new metaphors, is the same process that the poet faces every morning of his working day, making his own tools like Crusoe, assembling nouns from necessity, from Felicity, even renaming himself. The stripped man is driven back to that self-astonishing elemental force, his mind. That is the basis of the Antillean experience, this shipwreck of fragments, these echoes, these shards of a huge tribal vocabulary, these partially remembered customs, and they are not decayed but strong. (Walcott 1992, 28)

In the mid-1600s a ship carrying African slaves is said to have shipwrecked off the Mosquito Coast. The survivors of the shipwreck are believed to have joined with the inhabitants of the region, eventually leading to the emergence of two new categories of people. In the course of what Walcott refers to above as a process of renaming, and others have termed ethnogenesis, the indomitable Miskito Indians and later the

Creoles emerged at the western edge of the Caribbean Sea on the shores of the Spanish Main in what is today Nicaragua and Honduras.[6] Straddling this boundary between land and water, Central American isthmus and Caribbean Sea, Spanish colonies and English colonies, the inhabitants of the region relatively successfully charted an independent course that spared them much of the human devastation wrought on their neighbors by European rule.

Over time a unique and distinctive society emerged on the Mosquito Coast that was composed of the many fragments that were brought by sea to the lagoons and beaches of this tropical coastal plain. Outsiders, such as pirates, scholars, fisherman, merchants, revolutionaries, drug smugglers, Cuban counterrevolutionaries (briefly), American Indian Movement activists, diplomats, and capitalists have been attracted to the region by its natural resources and geographic and geopolitical position. In the course of history these and other visitors, as well as the local people, have debated and contested the African, Indian, and European constitution of Nicaragua's Costeños.

For example, in the colonial period the English crowned a Mosquito King with a sworn allegiance to Great Britain in an attempt to strengthen their political and economic foothold on the Spanish Main. Spain, and later Nicaragua and the United States, opposed English presence in the area and contested the legitimacy of the Mosquito monarchy on the grounds that its people were Black Africans and therefore lacked grounds for a claim to self rule (Olien 1985). More recently, during the Contra War when Ronald Reagan famously declared himself a Miskito Indian, Costeño leaders and their US allies invoked Miskito indigeneity, in specific and distinct ways, as justification for their opposition to the revolutionary nationalist programs of the Sandinista government.[7]

As illustrated in the case of Pacific-Atlantic rivalry articulated by my informant Don Paco Mendez, Costeños in their everyday affairs form and contest ideas about Indianness and Blackness in regionally specific ways that are rooted in Nicaragua's geography, history, and political economy. These instances are among many moments in the history of the Mosquito Coast in which racial and ethnic identification has been navigated in fascinating, complex, and changing ways. This book tells the story of these voyages.

From an early date Europeans identified many of the inhabitants of the Mosquito Coast as being the product of the biological mixture of Africans, Amerindians, and Europeans. The Spanish and English consistently used terms such as *Zambo* (a Spanish term often used for a person of mixed African and Indian descent that was also used in English, spelled as *Sambo*), *Mulatto* (also used in both English and Spanish accounts), and *Mustee* (primarily in English accounts) to refer to the residents of the area. Their testimonies are full of often-contradictory reports regarding the question of whether the inhabitants were pure Indians, African slaves and their Negro descendants, or mixed Zambos and Mulattos.

In contrast, on the islands of the Caribbean indigenous populations were quickly decimated and subsequently replaced by the uprooted shards of African, Asian, and European peoples whom over time were integrated through the archetypal Caribbean process of creolization—a process that has generated order from radical displacement and disarticulation. Anthropologist Sidney Mintz described the plantation societies of the Caribbean as landmark experiments in modernity, which were populated, often forcibly, by people from other places (Mintz 1994, 295). Precociously multicultural and globalized, the Caribbean islands, when conceived of this way, have been cast as non-indigenous by definition. In contrast, post-conquest Mosquito Coast society has been typified by the persistence of systems of group identification that include both African and Amerindian categories—the use and associations of which have varied widely over time.

In the modern Mosquito Coast the official system of socio-racial categorization recognizes five groups. This system recognizes four groups that are regarded as distinctive to the region. Three of these are officially recognized as indigenous peoples (Miskito, Sumu, and Rama) and one (Creole) is defined as an Afro-Caribbean ethnic group (or *etnia* in Spanish). Mestizo, the fifth category, refers to the population of the dominant Pacific part of the country who reside in the Mosquito Coast. In the popular usage in the region, Mestizos are referred to, anachronistically, as Spaniards. This modern classificatory system took shape in the nineteenth century as inhabitants of the Mosquito Coast, who had formerly been identified by a variety of quasi-tribal terms in addition to the dominant Miskito, came to be identified by a reduced set of terms that included a putatively racially Black category. As opposed to the Miskito

Indian category, the term "Creole" has come to be used to refer to an Afro-Caribbean group whose ancestral ties and contemporary affiliations were with Afro-Caribbean populations of Belize, Jamaica, and the Cayman Islands rather than the Indian populations of the lower Central American coast.

The Mosquito Coast represents a fascinating case of the deployment and change of discourses of being Indian, African, and "mixed" in a politically charged Caribbean context. In the Latin American context scholars have typically studied race and *mestizaje* (miscegenation) on an Amerindian-European axis, whereas in Brazil and the Caribbean they have studied race on African-European axis. Anthropologist Peter Wade notes that this has resulted in a general separation of studies of blacks from those of Indians such that the Black-Indian axis is rarely studied explicitly (Wade 1997, 36). This study builds on the work of anthropologists who have focused ethnographically on the constructions of race in Afro-Indian contexts in the Americas, such as Norman Whitten in Ecuador, Nancy Solien in Guatemala and Honduras, Laura Lewis in Mexico, Peter Wade and Michael Taussig in Colombia, and Karen Blu in the United States (Whitten 1974; Gonzalez 1988; Lewis 2000, 2001; Wade 1993; Taussig 1980, 1987; Blu 2001).

In the aftermath of the destructive Contra War of the 1980s, I conducted fieldwork in the port city of Puerto Cabezas, or Bilwi, as it is known in Miskitu, among people who call themselves, among other things, Porteños (Port People). What had initially brought my attention to the region was the conflict between the Pacific-based revolutionary Sandinista government and the Costeños of the Mosquito Coast. The region received a great deal of international attention in the 1980s as a result of the persistent opposition that many Costeños offered to the programs and policies of the Sandinista government. The most serious manifestation of this opposition took the form of armed Costeño groups incorporating themselves into the ranks of the US-trained and US-supported Contras.

In their international pronouncements during this period, Costeño leaders increasingly couched their aspirations and goals in the language of ethnicity and cultural difference as they appealed to their rights as minorities and indigenous peoples to self-determination. Also, in the deadlocked process of regional autonomy, which started in the mid 1980s and remains at an impasse today, appeals to cultural and ethnic differences have continued to be the very substance of the political discourse in the region. Social scientists and journalists universally interpreted the Costeño-Sandinista confrontation as a prototypical example of ethnic conflict and cultural clash between marginalized minorities and a dominant and ethnically distinct national population. In contrast, the conflict between the Sandinistas and main Contra forces was interpreted as a standard case of the Central America cycle of revolution and counter-revolution that pitted the Right and its allies against the Left.

A standard analysis of the causes of the Costeño-Sandinista crisis emerged. This standard analysis emphasized the deeply rooted cultural differences between inhabitants of the Atlantic and Pacific regions of the country. The idiosyncrasies of Atlantic Coast history and social structure, particularly with regard to the British role in the region until 1894, as well as the so-called enclave economy in which US companies exercised a de facto governmental role until well into the twentieth century, immediately were brought into focus in order to explain the nature of the ethnic and national problems that the revolution faced. Although a great deal of scholarly effort, both academic and otherwise, was dedicated to this problem, not enough attention was given to ways that these cultural differences manifested themselves in everyday practice or how they constituted part of specific regional and national ideological systems. The majority of interpretive energy was directed at positing a direct link between the ethnic particularities formed in the past and the modern predisposition to resist Pacific Nicaraguan governmental expansion.

This standard analysis placed undo emphasis on those differences that could be said to correspond to ethnic categories, while overlooking other kinds of group difference that crosscut these categories, such as those rooted in gender, class, and spatial dynamics. Analysts tended to ignore the historically forged pan-regional features that characterize Costeños as a whole regardless of their situational identification as Miskito, Creole, or Spaniard. This, of course, was understandable in a politically charged context in which Costeños themselves were for geopolitical reasons predisposed to construct and fortify the boundaries between ethnic categories. The trick for me as an ethnographer was to structure a research project that would devote attention to the complexity of Costeño social life while recognizing the undeniable trend of ethnic reification.

I chose to do fieldwork in Puerto Cabezas precisely because it was, according to conventional thinking, the worst place to study one of the region's so-called ethnic groups. Indianness within the Mosquito Coast is associated, on an ideological level, with rural origins and small village life. For this reason I found that when Costeños discovered that I was a cultural anthropologist who planned to conduct fieldwork in the region, they invariably told me that I should choose the smallest and most remote village in order to find the real Indians. Indeed, many people, assuming that as an anthropologist I should be interested in Indians, told me that I should not interest myself at all with the Miskito Indians. They suggested that I study the Sumu Indians (Mayangna) because these Indians were perceived to have most accurately retained their traditions. These suggestions speak to the extremely pervasive idea in the Americas that attributes cultural stagnation and conservatism as essential traits of Indians (Frye 1996).

While I was in Puerto Cabezas, I spent a great deal of my time learning to speak Miskitu. I found that even Miskitu-speakers in Puerto Cabezas encouraged me to go the communities of the Coco River section of the region in order to learn good Miskitu. They regarded the variety of Miskitu that they spoke as inferior because it was too mixed. These reactions that I observed illustrated that in the minds of Costeños, the communities of the Coco River represented the ideological center of Miskito culture.[8] In the same way that the ideological center of the Miskito people was the Coco River, the ideological center of the Afro-Nicaraguan Creoles was the city of Bluefields. Each of the region's indigenous or ethnic groups was conceived of as if it had its own respective center in which each group manifested its own culture in its most pure form. The western half of Nicaragua was commonly regarded as the proper home of the Spaniards, the multi-valent term used by Costeños to refer to Pacific Nicaraguans. In the race-conscious landscape of the Mosquito Coast in which ideologies of group difference are inscribed in complicated ways on the regional geography, Puerto Cabezas is a thoroughly mixed city.

In this book I illustrate the ways in which the Mosquito Coast represents a single, albeit highly diverse, society with a regionally specific social structure that has been shaped historically by unique political and economic forces. Following a chronological framework that begins with the pre-Columbian period and ends in the aftermath of the Contra War, each chapter chronicles the construction of group identity (particularly as it relates to Blackness and Indianness) in the Mosquito Coast. The scholarship of the region relies on an analytical framework that invests socio-racial categories with a degree of fixity and cultural content that in my opinion obscures the pan-regional culture that I describe. I employ a Barthian approach to ethnic identity that heeds his call to analytically separate the boundaries of social groups from their presumed content (Barth 1969). The analysis developed here provides an alternative to other approaches that have tended to reify the socio-racial categories of the region.

I interrogate some of the main assumptions of the dominant perspective by providing an ethnographically grounded case study of the way in which ideologies of race work in Puerto Cabezas after the Revolution. Whereas other analysts have focused on so-called cultural and ethnic factors in explaining the conflict in the region and the rise of the Miskito Indian movement, the analysis developed in this book focuses on the interplay between the practice of racial self-identification and key regionally grounded political-economic shifts that occurred in the 1980s. Although this book lays a foundation for a more accurate general understanding of the nature of the recent crisis, the conclusions given here are grounded in ethnographic examples taken from a specific time and place: Puerto Cabezas in the 1990s, a city that had a unique revolutionary history.

This understanding, in turn, provides insight into the historical and modern conflicts that have arisen and which have been attributed to the racial heterogeneity of the region. The case that I make here relies on the assumption that an intensive ethnographic study of Puerto Cabezas that focuses on the racial ideologies and vocabularies of difference employed by ordinary Costeños and Spaniards can provide insight into the causes and meanings of political turmoil and social movements in the region. In the chapters that follow, I reveal the intersection of regional culture (one that exists in explicit contradistinction to the Pacific half of Nicaragua) with ideologies of racial, cultural, and linguistic difference in Puerto Cabezas.

Pacific Nicaraguans and others have conflated the region's geography (perceived as forested, underexploited, and impenetrable) with its people, who are regarded as wild, savage, and unrefined. These associations stand in direct opposition to Costeños's perception of themselves as cosmopolitan and worldly. I label the former the primitivist view of Costeño identity and the latter the cosmopolitan view of Costeño identity.[9] My use of cosmopolitan and primitivist views as sets of Weberian ideal types avoids the pitfall of linking particular ideological positions to identifiable groups. While the primitivist view is far more prevalent among Pacific Nicaraguans than it is among Costeños, Don Paco's case and others that I present in this book clearly demonstrate that this view is not confined to Atlantic Coast outsiders. To varying degrees Costeños themselves have internalized some of the premises of the primitivist view of their own nature. The competing cosmopolitan view provides an ideological counterbalance, however, against primitivist self-exoticization. In their ideal state of affairs Costeños do not envision themselves as Don Paco's noble Pacific Indian peasants that extract subsistence crops from an unforgiving soil; rather they hark back to a time in Mosquito Coast history where wage-labor jobs and imported goods were available in abundance. The Sandinista Revolution, with its well-publicized hostility to the United States and its policy of nationalization of industries, was a large step in the wrong direction away from achieving this ideal.

The flight of capital in the 1980s and the isolation caused by the Contra War only heightened the sense of environmental dissonance experienced by the inhabitants of the Atlantic Coast. Indeed, the opposition of Costeños to the revolutionary program in the first place should be understood not simply as a product of ethnic conflict (however defined) but also as the product of the perception that the revolutionary government would isolate the region and push it farther away from its people's cosmopolitan ideal. This, also, is a kind of cultural clash but not the sort posited in the literature on the region, which traced the conflict to so-called misunderstandings between Sandinistas and Miskitos.

MAKING FRIENDS AND MAKING ENEMIES

This book contributes to the anthropological understanding of cultural politics—an emerging theme in anthropological inquiry. Cultural anthropologists have recently begun to take a greater interest in what is often regarded as a relatively new phenomenon: the centrality of strategic appeals to culture, tradition, and identity in social life. Whereas in the past anthropologists enjoyed greater confidence in the separation of their own concepts and those of the people whom they studied, anthropologists in the present have had to confront the fact that in many cases their analytic categories have become native categories.[10] Anthropologists have increasingly placed the study of this entanglement at the center of their research projects as they specifically address what has come to be known as cultural politics, identity politics, and the cultural politics of difference.[11]

Scholars who have taken up these issues have often identified and struggled with two sources of tension that arise in conceptualizing and studying identity politics, one interpretive and the other ethical. The interpretive tension has given rise to an academic "polarity" (Hale 1999, 492) or "debate" between essentialism and constructivism (Hale 1997, 578; Wade 1999, 453), as well as a similar set of issues regarding questions of strategy and questions of identity (Escobar 1992, 82), and questions of expressive and instrumental culture (Foweracker 1995, 13).[12] Anti-essentialist anthropologists deploy the term *essentialism*, conceived as an approach that regards social groups (however defined) as bounded and internally homogenous entities, as a "dirty word" (Fischer 1999, 473) that stands in contrast to more processual and dynamic approaches to group identity and culture.[13] As a result of these positions, anthropologists have increasingly called into question the value of their most traditional concepts and perspectives, to the extent that some have advocated "writing against culture" (Abu-Lughod 1991).

The tensions provoked by this shift towards anti-essentialism and writing against culture have led social scientists directly to an ethical hornet's nest because they find themselves in the uncomfortable position of feeling obligated to render a critique of essentialism and its organic metaphors of culture (Abu-Lughod 1991, 144) in the very moment that many subordinate minority and indigenous movements are laying claims, at times using essentialist language, to culture and bounded group identity in the context of their political struggles (Friedman 1999, 1). This tension is particularly troubling for anthropologists of an activist bent who desire to serve as advocates to the communities in which they conduct fieldwork (Field 1999, 195). Gerald Sider identifies this problem as the activist's dilemma (Sider 1993, xxiii). The activist's dilemma becomes increasingly pressing in light of the fact that across the globe dominant groups increasingly adopt anti-essentialist theoretical armature from North American and European academe in order to launch post-modern salvos at subaltern movements.[14]

James Fernandez places the main voices who are "writing against culture" into two camps: making friends and making enemies (Fernandez 1994, 15).[15] The most striking difference between these camps, given that both foreground the conflict between epistemology and politics (Handler 1999, 492), lies in their respective posture vis-à-vis all or some of the groups and movements that they identify. These can be labeled: (1) the invention-of-tradition approach, and (2) the revitalization approach.

The invention-of-tradition approach takes the critical bait and moves forward with an anti-essentialist critique that brings attention to the penetration of misleading and potentially dangerous Euro-American elite notions of culture, race, tradition, and ethnicity (Handler 1999, 492). Within this approach, two kinds of analyses generally emerge, each focusing on one of the following issues: (1) the conscious, rhetorical or manipulative use of appeals to culture and group difference made by groups in their political wars of position within national or international contexts; and (2) the acceptance by subordinate groups of hegemonic ideologies of racial and ethnic difference that reinforce, often unwittingly, their subordinate position within the larger society, region, or world-system.[16] Both of these analyses, however—by emphasizing the potentially negative effects of the contagious spread of essentialist ideologies from the world's cores to its peripheries—find themselves debunking, in one way or another, the appeals to cultural distinctiveness and group difference in the context of social life of their subjects of study, hence potentially making enemies.[17]

On the other hand, the revitalization approach, while not denying the essentialized nature of identity politics, brings attention to the possibilities for the creation of anti-hegemonic identities that can serve subaltern groups in their resistance against more powerful actors.[18] The self-conscious appeal to cultural distinctiveness, according to this approach, represents a powerful tool that subordinate groups can manufacture and refine with the aid of anthropological theory, if not anthropologists themselves; hence anthropology is making friends.

Each of these approaches responds in a different way to a common uneasiness that many anthropologists quite justifiably experience regarding the implications of the conclusions of their research vis-à-vis the aspirations or organized political movements of all or some of their subjects.

In this book, I offer two responses, one theoretical and one methodological, to the problems outlined above. I follow Abu-Lughod's lead in her call for writing against culture and, in this case, the intimately related concept of ethnicity (Abu-Lughod 1991). Specifically, I take up her strategy for addressing the fallacy of false coherence based on organic metaphors of wholeness by adopting an analytic framework that relies on discourse and practice, as outlined by Bourdieu (1977), in a manner that favors strategies, interests, and improvisations over the more static and homogenizing cultural tropes of rules, models, and texts (Abu-Lughod 1991, 147). Bringing attention to the ways that discourses of essentialism and constructivism are often both deployed in practice by actors in the course of social life serves to address the theoretical problem of the relationship between culture and politics (Field 1999, 199). From a methodological point of view, this book provides an illustration of the advantages of conducting multiethnic field research, particularly in situations where culture and identity are highly politicized or ethnicized, such as the contemporary Atlantic Coast of Nicaragua (Diskin 1989, 24).[19]

ORGANIZATION OF THE BOOK

The chapters that follow proceed from a wider geographic scope to a narrower one as the narrative sharpens its focus, both in time and space, on Bilwi/Puerto Cabezas. Chapter 2 establishes the salience of the regional distinction between the Atlantic and Pacific coasts of what is now Nicaragua. In this chapter I compare and contrast the pre-Columbian and early colonial histories of the Mosquito Coast region and the Pacific Coast region. I focus on the impact of English and Spanish colonialism in the Mosquito Coast, particularly regarding slavery and mestizaje.

In chapters 3, 4, and 5 I link these themes with an ethnographic description of Puerto Cabezas. These chapters tell the story of the transformation of the small village of Bilwi at the turn of the century into a

US company town at mid-century, and finally into the capital of the North Atlantic Autonomous Region in the present.

In chapter 6 I critically review the literature on the Costeño-Sandinista confrontation of the 1980s and demonstrate the role and influence of social scientists and their theoretical approaches in the events of the time.

The ethnographic chapters (3, 4, and 5) consist of oral histories and participant observation among the modern inhabitants of the city of Puerto Cabezas. With the exception of chapter 6, all of the evidence that I use to make my case comes from historical and ethnographic information firmly grounded in my field site.

Although the narrative unfolds chronologically, each chapter has a distinct thematic emphasis. In chapter 2 I demonstrate the antiquity of the perception of inhabitants of the Mosquito Coast as uncivilized and primitive. Social scientists and historians have to some degree inherited this bias from the Spanish, who were frustrated by their inability to conquer the populations of the Atlantic Coast. This inability to conquer Atlantic Coast groups also resulted in a situation of socio-racial classificatory discord. The fact that the Spanish failed to colonize the region was reflected in their frustrated and contested attempts to classify and label the social groups of the region. I argue that a similar and historically related process actually preceded European colonization of the Americas, occurring between the stratified pre-Columbian chiefdoms of the Pacific Coast and the smaller and more mobile groups of the Atlantic Coast.

In chapter 3 I discuss in detail the ambivalence with which historians and social scientists have viewed the racial composition of the region, specifically with reference to the status of Costeños as Indians or Blacks. A form of racial determinism exists in the scholarship on the region such that miscegenation has been regarded as a primary agent of social change. In this chapter I offer an alternative explanation of the process of miscegenation in the colonial history of the Mosquito Coast. In modern Nicaragua the Mosquito Coast is commonly regarded as being populated by Indians and Africans, and the Pacific by Amerindian-European Mestizos. My interpretation focuses on the primacy of changes in the categorical systems of socio-racial difference versus the common-sense notion that the difference between the two regions can be taken at face value as the product of different levels of African and Indian miscegenation. Addressing the paradox of the disappearance of an African term in the Pacific system of racial classification (as well as the lack of recognition of an African role in the history of Pacific Nicaragua) reveals interesting conclusions about the nature of racial ideologies in Nicaragua.

In chapter 3 I address two related issues: (1) the attitudes of Pacific Nicaraguans with regard to the Atlantic Coast as it pertains to the ideological work involved in promoting Nicaraguan Mestizo nationalism in the Mosquito Coast during the first half of the twentieth century; and (2) the struggle over land that was precipitated by the transformation of Bilwi into a US company town. I describe the ways in which both Pacific Nicaraguans and North Americans invoked stereotypical notions of Indians as nomads and savages in order to discredit land claims made by the inhabitants of Bilwi. I employ an essentially biographical method to analyze the racial, cultural, and gender ideologies of two Pacific Nicaraguans, Frutos Ruiz y Ruiz and Augusto Cesar Sandino, both of whom played an important role in the development of Puerto Cabezas during the 1920s and 1930s. I simultaneously outline the impact of US company labor policies on the process of socio-racial identification in the burgeoning port city.

Chapter 4 deals with the period in the history of Bilwi that is known as company time. I assess the social and cultural impact of the boom-and-bust cycles of North American extractive industries in the region. I recognize that the presence of the US companies, particularly the so-called class/ethnic hierarchy that they promoted, served to institutionalize racial boundaries. The presence of these companies undoubtedly exercised a centrifugal effect on the socio-racial structure of the region. However, I argue that the presence of these companies also had a centripetal effect, as a single regionally specific consumer culture was created. I argue that during this time, Porteños (Port People) became even more dependent on wage labor and North American manufactured goods. They in turn internalized their dependence on wage labor and foreign goods as a positive collective trait that distinguished them from Spanish Nicaraguans. Change in the political economy of the region also provided the material basis for increased Porteño socio-racial identification as Black people.

In chapter 5 I focus on another tumultuous series of events that profoundly impacted Puerto Cabezas—the Sandinista revolution. Continuing with the theme of the interpenetration of racial ideologies and political economy, I highlight the process in which Puerto Cabezas came to be regarded as an Indian city as a result of the drastic economic changes in the region. I also analyze the role of mythically encapsulated beliefs in the use and contestation of racial categories in Puerto Cabezas. I provide ethnographic examples of the cognitive effects on Porteños of the rapid decapitalization of the region. I argue that Costeño opposition to the Sandinista revolution must be viewed within the preexisting context of regionally based status distinctions that crosscut socio-racial categories. My interpretation stands in opposition to much of the work by social scientists and journalists who contended that the Costeño-Sandinista crisis was caused by a cultural clash. I complicate and refute this standard position by providing clear ethnographic examples of how cultural and racial ideologies intersect with regional and class-based distinctions in the social life of Puerto Cabezas.

In Chapter 6 I specifically address the issue of the Contra War and the Costeño-Sandinista confrontation of the 1980s. I review in detail the social science literature on the conflict. I argue that this literature manifested a deep polarization along cold-war lines. I distinguish two theoretical camps that corresponded closely to the pro-Sandinista or anti-Sandinista sympathies of the theorists involved. The first theoretical camp, which I label deconstructionist, was championed by pro-Sandinistas who established as their main interpretive problem the explanation of Costeño false consciousness. Their task was to explain the paradox of the Costeño insistence on viewing their reality through a false ethnic lens that obscured the true class-based root of their troubles. On the other hand, anti-Sandinistas employed an essentialist framework that relied on stereotypical notions of an ahistorical and unchanging Indian identity. I demonstrate some of the theoretical and conceptual limitations of this polarized literature. I argue that despite their differences, both perspectives were united in their common tendency to reify ethnic boundaries.

In the course of the Costeño-Sandinista conflict of the 1980s (as well as the disputes between the national government and the people of the Mosquito Coast that continue today over natural resource management), social scientists and social science concepts were employed by all parties involved. This fact is particularly compelling reason to place our interventions and our approaches as anthropologists under scrutiny in our writings.

THE FIELD SITE

Puerto Cabezas rose to regional importance in the early twentieth century when it became the regional headquarters for the Standard Fruit Company and a series of US lumber companies. These companies constructed railroads and a large pier, transforming the small village into the most important port north of Bluefields on Nicaragua's Atlantic Coast. The size and importance of the city has waxed and waned in tune with the boom-and-bust cycles in coastal industries such as banana, rubber, lumber, and mining.

The population of the Atlantic Coast in general, however, has increased at a very rapid pace since the 1950s, when both spontaneous and governmentally planned migration from the Pacific region caused the eastward spread of what the government in Managua viewed as the agricultural frontier. From 1963 to 1973 the population of the Department of Zelaya, which constituted what is now the Northern and Southern Autonomous Regions (known locally as *la RAAN* and *la RAAS*), almost doubled, growing from 87,823 to 157,484 (Ministerio de Economía 1963, 1973). By 1985 the population of the Atlantic Coast region had doubled again, reaching 325,454 (Instituto Nacional de Estadisticas y Censos 1985). Census projections by the Nicaraguan government estimate that the 2005 population of the Atlantic Coast region was 630,000. The population increase was compounded in Puerto Cabezas in the 1980s by the Contra War, which caused the evacuation of almost the entire eastern border region between Nicaragua and Honduras. Many Costeño refugees, displaced from their homes along the Rio Coco, relocated to Puerto Cabezas. The population of the city, according to some estimates, quadrupled after 1980 (Norwood 1987, 210), reaching 25,000 inhabitants by 1985.

Census projections for 2005 estimate that Puerto Cabezas now has about 34,000 inhabitants. According to Norwood the ethnic composition of the city in 1985 was as follows: Miskitu, 50 percent; Mestizo, 30 percent; and Creole, 10 percent. The remaining 10 percent was divided between Sumus, foreigners, and Chinese-Nicaraguans (Norwood 1987, 211). Although the Nicaraguan census does not include data on race and ethnicity, it appears that this general distribution has persisted over the last twenty years.

A remarkable amount of bi- and tri-lingualism exists in the region. In a linguistic survey conducted by Norwood in Puerto Cabezas in 1985, she found that 70 percent of Miskito identified themselves as either bi- or tri-lingual, a figure surpassed by the Creoles, 95 percent of whom spoke, in addition to English, either Spanish, Miskitu, or both. Zero percent of recently immigrated Mestizos spoke another language, while only a quarter of Costeño Mestizos were multilingual (Norwood 1987, 217).

Although residential racial segregation in Puerto Cabezas is not stark, there do exist neighborhoods that are generally perceived to have an ethnic character, such as the Creole neighborhood of El Muelle, the Miskitu neighborhood of El Cocal, and the Spaniard neighborhood of La Revolución. Rapidly constructed neighborhoods, built by Coco River refugees, sprung up in the late 1980s. The infrastructure of the city has not been able to keep pace with this growth, leaving many houses without running water or electricity. Mired in extreme poverty despite the abundant human and natural resources of the region, Porteños continue to wait anxiously for their fortunes to change.

CHAPTER 2

Nicaragua's Two Coasts

IN THE PRE-COLUMBIAN PERIOD human populations in what is now the country of Nicaragua occupied three distinct ecological zones: (1) the Pacific Lowlands, (2) the Central Highlands, and (3) the Caribbean Coastal Plain (Newson 1987, 42, 88). The Pacific Lowlands, made fertile by the volcanic deposits left by the chain of thirty volcanoes that split the lowlands from north to south, contained a climate that was ideal for maize agriculture. It received plentiful rainfall, although the long dry season between November and May necessitated the use of irrigation (ibid., 43). Although in the present these lands are heavily deforested, evergreen and deciduous forests formerly flourished in the Pacific Lowlands.[1]

The Central Highlands contain peaks that rise as high as 2,000 meters, making the climate more temperate. The highlands, composed of a number of east-west *cordilleras* divided by valleys that drained to the Caribbean coast, received limited and inconsistent rainfall, and had relatively poor soils and an uneven topography. These conditions discouraged large-scale agriculture. In contrast to other highland areas of Mesoamerica at the time of the Conquest (such as Guatemala and central Mexico), the Nicaraguan highlands did not sustain very large human populations. Newson estimates that the pre-Conquest population density of the highlands was only one-fourth that of the Pacific lowlands.[2]

The Caribbean Coastal Plain, an extensive lowland strip that at its widest point stretches for 150 kilometers, contained (in the 1500s) the largest tropical rain forest in Central America. In this region, one of the wettest in the Americas and which experiences only brief (and not very dry) dry seasons, the boundary between land and water is often quite porous (Nietschmann 1973, 64). Chronically flooded, the region has a large number of large, slow rivers that, before flowing into brackish lagoons, swamps and deltas, commonly spill over into vast floodplains.

Beyond the coast, the shallow marine shelf (also the largest formation of its kind in Central America) extends as far as 100 kilometers into the western Caribbean, providing ideal feeding conditions (in the form of underwater marine pastures known as turtle banks) for marine life— particularly sea turtles (Nietschmann 1973, 92). Along the marine shelf lie a veritable swarm of thousands of small banks, cays, and reefs (a geographical feature that was immediately taken note of by the seafaring English, who called them the Mosquito keys).

A great diversity of flora and fauna abound in the region, but, as is common to most tropical rain forests, the underlying soils are leached by heavy rainfalls and are of very poor quality (P. Sanchez 1976; Newson 1987, 47).[3] With the exception of riverbanks, which are made fertile by yearly deposits of silt, the region's soils are more apt for swidden agriculture than extensive agriculture.

Primarily as a result of these marked geographical differences, the inhabitants of these different regions practiced different productive strategies. Natives of the Pacific Lowlands engaged in extensive maize agriculture that was supplemented by hunting, fishing, and gathering. This agriculture sustained upward of one million people in a relatively small area (Newson 1987, 88). Cacao was used as a medium of exchange in the busy markets (*tianguez*) of the region in which a wide variety of manufactured goods were traded, including cotton textiles, rope, pottery, basketry, and gold and silver ornaments, as well as tools and weapons of stone, wood, and obsidian (Moscoso 1991, 80; Newson 1987, 49–56). Pacific societies manifested a significant degree of social stratification in which *caciques* sat at the top of a hierarchical system of nobles, commoners, and slaves.[4] A powerful and educated clergy practiced an elaborate ritual calendar (which included human sacrifice and self-mutilation—practices associated with their Central Mexican ancestors and neighbors) at large manmade temples.

In contrast to the Pacific regions, the Caribbean Coastal Plain was peopled by native groups that used less-elaborate technology, had a lesser degree of social stratification, cultivated different major crops, and lived in settlements that were often seasonal and were absent of elaborate permanent structures. Inhabitants of the Caribbean Coastal Plain mixed hunting and gathering with shifting cultivation of plantain and roots crops of South American origin, such as manioc, a crop that was favored over maize. The groups that resided closer to the coast took advantage of coastal protein resources such as manatee, fish, and turtle (Newson 1987, 65–78). Archaeologist Richard Magnus, one of the few researchers to take up the challenge of conducting excavations and surveys in this region where the heat, humidity, and rain are hostile to archaeological research, argues that Caribbean Indians relied more on riverine swidden agriculture and hunting and gathering than on fishing and coastal agriculture.[5]

In contrast to the colonial period, which witnessed the proliferation of coastal villages in response to intensified market demands for forest and coastal products, natives in the immediate pre-Columbian period constructed permanent settlements primarily in inland areas, building temporary settlements near the coast (Stone 1964, 214; Magnus 1978). Permanent markets seem to have been absent from the region, as well as money (Newson 1987, 77).

Caribbean natives did produce pottery, stone tools, and cotton goods, although they used clothes made of bark. Interestingly, many native groups, particularly those on the coast, abandoned and lost these skills during the colonial period as they became more dependent upon Caribbean networks of trade.[6] This is ironic because Pacific and High-land groups, which during the colonial period came to be known as non-Indian *Ladinos*, Mestizos, and campesinos, retained and elaborated many of the skilled crafts that had been associated with Indian communities. Their Caribbean counterparts, in contrast, continued to be known as Indians in many contexts but left their crafts behind in favor of manufactured goods acquired through an expanding system of global trade.

Ethnonyms and Toponyms

The association of the peoples of the Mosquito Coast with primitivism on the part of dominant groups predated the Spanish conquest of the Americas. In lower Central America, dominant groups lived on the Pacific and claimed central Mexican descent. These groups in almost all cases represented large, relatively sedentary populations that engaged in intensive maize agriculture. In contrast to the South American-derived

Chibchan languages spoken by central and eastern Nicaraguan Indians, the predominant languages of the Pacific came from two separate central Mexican language families: Uto-Aztecan and Otomanguean (Stone 1964, 210).

In the six centuries prior to 1492, the Nicaraguan Pacific region had received a series of large-scale migrations from central Mexico and Chiapas, resulting in the displacement or incorporation of previously autochthonous groups, some of which receded to the east (Guerrero and Guerrero 1982, 15).[7] The establishment of Aztec trading colonies represented the most recent revival of central Mexican influence in lower Central America—a resurgence that was primarily, but not completely, cut short by the Spanish conquest. In light of Nicaragua's history of contact with the central Mexican Nahua languages, in conjunction with the fact that the Spanish conquerors used many Nahua-speaking troops (followed by Nahuatl-speaking Spanish missionaries) to overpower the peoples of both central Mexico and Central America, it is not surprising to find that the Spanish incorporated central Mexican and central Mexican-derived biases into their colonial practice. This is particularly true with regard to naming practices.[8]

Based on both archeological evidence, as well as the testimonies collected by the earliest Spanish chroniclers in Central America, it is commonly held that the first wave of northern immigrants arrived in Pacific Nicaragua from Soconusco (Chiapas) around the ninth century AD, establishing themselves in western Nicaragua and the Nicoya Peninsula. They spoke a variety of related Otomanguean languages that, although possessing a number of names, were generally referred to as Mangue by the Spanish. The Spanish generally referred to groups that spoke these languages as Chorotega, although some of these groups were mutually hostile and were divided into competing factions (Newson 1987, 28).

The first wave of Uto-Aztecan migration occurred slightly after the Otomanguean migration. The first Nahau-speaking people arrived in the ninth and tenth centuries, and settled in what is now El Salvador and northwestern Nicaragua (Fowler 1985). The second wave, whose descendants eventually came to be known by the Spanish as the *Nicarao*, arrived in the twelfth century and settled on the western shore of Lake Nicaragua (Arellano 1993, 12). They, like all other Nahua-speaking peoples in Central American, were at times referred to as Pipil (meaning rulers in Nahuatl) (Wolf 1959, 40). Mexican Nahuatl speakers who accompanied the Spanish on their expeditions into Central America held the Nahuat languages of Nicaragua in contempt, labeling them *Mexicana Corrupta* or *Pipil Corrupta*.[9] Hence, Francisco Vázquez, a Spanish chronicler, referred to the Pipil language ". . . as we would say the language of children or that spoken by those of little intelligence" (quoted in Newson 1987, 30).

Just as Nahuatl-speaking Mexicans who accompanied the Spanish conquistadores denigrated the Nahuat dialects of Nicaragua spoken by the Nicarao as base and inferior, so did these Nahuat-speaking groups denigrate the language and culture of non-Nahua groups. Given that Nahua-speaking groups (both Mexican and Nicarao) had been dominant groups in their respective areas, the names and concepts that they used to apply to other groups often were adopted by the Spanish.

The Spanish early colonial modus operandi, which they successfully implemented in both central Mexico and Pacific Nicaragua, was to subjugate the most populous, dominant, and hierarchically organized native societies. As a result, the Spanish often adopted the ethnonyms and toponyms that the dominant native groups used to refer to subordinate groups. These names often reflected a lack of understanding and even contempt on the part of the dominant groups. In the case of central Mexico, the homeland of Nahuatl-speaking Mexicans, Eric Wolf concisely described this process:

To groups who could not speak Nahua, the Nahua applied contemptuous epithets that have remained to serve as their official designations to this day—epithets such as *chontal* ("foreigner"), *popoluca* or *popoloca* ("unintelligible"), *totonac* ("rustic"). Thus we find today linguistically quite unrelated groups like Chontal (in Tabasco and Oaxaca), Popoluca (in Puebla, Veracruz, and Guatemala), Totonac (in Veracruz, but also in sixteenth-century Spanish reports from Jalisco and Oaxaca), to the confusion of the investigator. Nahua names have also become the standard designations of other populations, such as the Mixtec (from *mixtlán*, "cloud land"), the Zapotec (after the zapote tree, *Achras Zapota*), and the Otomí (apparently from Nahuatl *totomitl*, "man who wings birds with arrows"). The Mixtec call themselves *ñusabi*; the Zapotec, *di'z^*, with a suffix designating the territory they inhabit; the Otomí, *nhyú*. (Wolf 1959, 41)

In the case of Nicaragua, the Nicarao used the blanket term *Chontal* (foreigner) to refer to those groups that did not speak a related language and lived to the east in the area now known as the Central Highlands and the Mosquito Coast.[10] Just as the Mixtec, Zapotec, and Otomi had a variety of names to refer to themselves, undoubtedly so did the indigenous inhabitants of these regions have their own vocabularies of self-reference. However, the Spanish did not generally recognize these terms during the early colonial period.

Not only did Nahua-speaking Pacific groups use value-laden terms in their labeling of their eastern Nicaraguan indigenous neighbors, but they also seem to have looked down at these groups as inferior. This posture was noticed by the Spanish, who in turn adopted both the referential terms used as well as a similar attitude with regard to eastern Nicaraguan native groups. Ironically, these were precisely the Indians whom the Spanish found themselves unable or unwilling to subdue, notwithstanding their alleged inferiority (Newson 1987, 37). Antonio Vázquez de Espinosa, a sixteenth-century Spanish chronicler, noted that Pacific coastal Indians manifested this perspective towards the Indians of the eastern provinces when he wrote, "The Indians of those provinces are particularly rustic to the degree that when others [Indians] want to insult someone, they call that person a Chontal—which is a way of calling someone an idiot" (Incer 1990, 250). The Spanish chronicler Fernandez de Oviedo, writing in 1528, described the "chondales" as "villainous people who live in the mountains or in the foothills" (Guerrero and Guerrero 1982, 18). Another Spanish historian, Father Franciso López de Gómara, described the Chontal language as "*grocero y serrano*" (coarse and boorish) (18). In addition to Chontal, the Spanish also adopted the Nahua terms *Popoluca* (unintelligible or stuttering), *Xicaque* (wild), *Lenca*, and *Caribe* as generic terms to refer to the natives that plagued the eastern and northern fringes of their Nahua-speaking strongholds (Incer 1990, 258).[11]

On his fourth voyage to the New World in 1502, many years before the Spanish invaded and occupied the Pacific Coast, Columbus visited what is now the Mosquito Coast of Nicaragua and Honduras. The name that he gave to the region, *Costa de Orejas* (Coast of Ears—from the ear elongation practiced by the region's inhabitants), did not enter into widespread use (Conzemius 1932, 29; Potthast 1988, 15). Rather, the Spanish borrowed two terms used by the Aztecs to refer to this region: Taguzgalpa (place of gold) and Tologalpa (place of tule). Although Taguzgalpa was often used to refer to both of these unconquered "provinces" (to use the ambitious term of the Spanish), it specifically referred to the area delineated by the Coco River, which emptied at Cape Gracias a Dios, and the Aguán river east of the modern Honduran city of Trujillo (Incer 1990, 255). Tologalpa referred to the area between the Coco River and the San Juan River that, not coincidentally, corresponds with the modern limits of the Nicaraguan Atlantic Coast.

According to Vázquez de Espinosa, the Aztecs manifested a sustained interest in Taguzgalpa, ". . . where many mexican indians live . . . who owing to the richness of the place were sent every year by Montezuma to collect tribute in the form of gold and other precious items" (Incer 1990, 248). The Aztecs referred to the Indians of Taguzgalpa (the tribute-paying regions actually seem to have been located primarily in what is now southeastern Honduras) as Jicaques. Later the Spanish adopted this term to refer to the "unfaithful Indians" (*indios infieles*) of Taguzgalpa and used the term *Chontal* to refer to the equally unfaithful Indians of Tologalpa, although the distinction, inconsistently applied, was most definitely one of a geographical rather than sociological nature (ibid., 265). Twentieth-century ethnology continues to use the terms *Jicaque* and *Lenca* to distinguish Indians of eastern Honduras from their Nicaraguan counterparts across the border (see Kirchoff 1948, 219).

Although the Aztecs began to draw Taguzgalpa into the far reaches of their empire, they did not exercise colonial control over the indigenous groups of the region. However, they left tribute-collecting and trading colonies in Taguzgalpa. Although the Spanish area of control slowly intruded eastward into the Pacific slope of the Central Highlands, the sixteenth-century Spanish attempts to conquer Taguzgalpa, which took the form of three separate armed expeditions, all failed as so-called Jicaques and Caribes attacked and destroyed the Spanish garrisons and mining camps established in remote Atlantic Coast areas (Incer 1990, 252).

In the seventeenth century the Spanish then turned to the Franciscan order to subjugate the indomitable Indians of the region. Nahuatl was often the language of early Christian proselytization in early colonial Mesoamerica, and therefore the Franciscan friars hoped to first Christianize and settle the Nahuatl-speaking groups in *reducciones* (permanent settlements used by Europeans to settle and convert natives as well as harness their labor). The Franciscans, however, were frustrated by the tremendous social diversity they encountered in the region—a diversity that stood in contrast to the more familiar sedentary and hierarchically organized societies of central Mexico and the Nicaraguan Pacific. None of these groups spoke Nahuatl, they lacked large permanent settlements, and, most importantly, they were often hostile to the Spanish.

At the beginning of the eighteenth century Francisco Vázquez wrote about the century-long Franciscan attempts to pacify the region's inhabitants:

> The names of the known nations, many of which are mutually hostile from one family ["*agnación*"] or tribe to another, are these: *lencas, tahuas, alhatuinas, xicaques, mexicanos, payas, jaras, taupanes, taos, fantasmas, gualas, alaucas, aguncualcas, yguyales, cujes, bocayes, tomayes, bucataguacas, quimacas, panamakas, itziles, guayaes, motucas, barucas, apzinas, nanaicas* and many others; and it is known among these as well as others there are many whites and blonds, others more or less black according to the mixtures of nations and foreign peoples [referring to pirates and merchants] that come to this land to mate and trade trinkets and machetes for provisions and very good gold nuggets that are taken from the rivers. (Incer 1990, 256)

The segmentary nature of Atlantic Coast social groupings, combined with the remoteness of the region and the hostility of its inhabitants, made the Franciscans' task extremely difficult. Unlike supposedly more advanced areas where Europeans used the institutional authority of high-level indigenous leaders, the Franciscans found no accurate way to identify Indian groups, let alone their leaders. "Without law nor king they roam around in herds like wild beasts," lamented Francisco Vázquez (ibid., 258).

Although the Franciscans achieved considerable success in setting up *reducciones* among the Nahuatl-speaking Mexicans in Taguzgalpa, these settlements were subject to constant attack by other groups (Stone 1964, 214). When they did succeed in attracting Taguzgalpan people to their settlements, the Indians frequently abandoned the settlement or violently mutinied, killing a series of Franciscan missionaries (Incer 1990, 259–266). As further proof of the barbarousness of the region's occupants, the Franciscans were unable to locate permanent native settlements, concluding, to their dismay, that they practiced a tropical forest version of nomadism.[12] Vázquez wrote that the Indians of Taguzgalpa were ungovernable because "their lands are naturally impenetrable and the Indians have becomes untamed, living in free villages [*behetrías*], camping today in one place and then tomorrow in another, without holding lands as their own, and at any moment fleeing and retreating to the most difficult of bush and god-forsaken [*incultos*] mountain plains" (Incer 1990, 258).

At the beginning of the eighteenth century, after more than a century of failure, the Spanish abandoned their attempts to control Taguzgalpa.[13] However, they did manage to expand the area of Spanish control further eastward into the Central Highlands, leaving only the Atlantic slope of the Highlands and the Atlantic Coastal plain in the hands of the infidel (Incer 1990, 253). In Spanish colonial documents, unconquered eastern groups were, in addition to the above-mentioned pseudo-tribal names, often referred to as "*indios de guerra*" (literally, Indians of war) and "*indios infieles*" (literally, unfaithful Indians), as opposed to the subjugated "*indios cristianos*" (Christian Indians) of the Pacific Coast (Romero Vargas 1995, 221). Throughout Latin America the Spanish, once they recognized that Americans had souls and were capable of understanding and embracing Christianity, distinguished Christian Indians, who deserved a greater level of consideration, from non-Christian Indians, who as enemies did not deserve the so-called legal protections provided by the Spanish Crown. During the seventeenth century, Atlantic Coast Indians situated themselves within an expanding world market, establishing regular trading ties with English merchants and colonists such as those that occupied the failed Providence Island colony (Parsons 1956, 11).

The names that the Spanish used to describe Atlantic Coast groups gradually became more specific after a century and a half of frustrated contact. The general and geographically vague names like *indios de guerra* and *indios infieles* were replaced over time. The slightly less generic terms *Chontal, Jicaque, Lenca,* and *Caribe* came to be more consistently applied to specific large regions. *Lenca* and *Jicaque* were used to describe groups north of the Coco River, and *Chontal* and *Caribe* for groups south of the Coco River.[14] At the most specific level, a large number of ethnonyms (names of human groups) came into limited use that were often applied to natives who inhabited specific sections of the major Atlantic-flowing rivers of the region; hence native groups tended to be identified with specific river valleys (Incer 1990, 255). For example, colonial sources mention the following "nations" among the inhabitants of Taguzgalpa (in what is now the eastern slope of the Nicaraguan Segovias): the Bocayes of the Bocay River; the Tomayes of the Tuma River; the Bucataguacas (or Taguacas) of the Butuk/Patuka River; the Taupanes of the Waspuk River; the Nanaicas and Guayaes of the Pantasma River; and the Tahuas or Taguacas of the upper Coco River, as well as the Jaras, Quimacas, Iguyales, Cujes, and Alaucas of the Olancho River valley (Incer 1990, 257). These are a few of the wide variety of names that appear in the Spanish colonial documents that refer to Taguzgalpan Indians.

This practice of identifying and naming indigenous groups according to river valleys stood in contrast to the Pacific, where groups were most frequently identified and named according to the name of a particular cacique (chief). This difference in naming practices resulted from two related factors: (1) the lack of Spanish colonial success on the Atlantic Coast, and (2) the differences in social organization between Pacific and Atlantic societies that were related to different ecological conditions in each region.

Borrowing from pre-Columbian institutional arrangements, the Spanish organized Pacific Indian society into a system of hierarchically named groupings. At the lowest level was the *galpón* (a Spanish word that tellingly means communal slave dwelling), which consisted of an extended group of agnatic kin. A number of *galpones* constituted a *plaza,* which was led by a *cacique* or *teyte*. A *pueblo indio*, in turn, consisted of a conglomeration of *plazas*. Using this institutional structure, the Spanish were able to quite rationally extract labor and tribute from the *pueblos indios* (Romero Vargas 1993a, 15). The entire system depended on the existence of clearly defined communal ties on the part of Indians. Nicaraguan historian Germán Romero Vargas explained:

> Communal life was the main feature of Indian society in Nicaragua under Spanish rule. The *"pueblo indio"* was its concrete manifestation.

> Every Indian was a "*natural*" of a *pueblo*. If an Indian from another place were to establish himself in that *pueblo* he would be known as a "*laborío*" . . . Being a "*natural*" was like the proof of citizenship of an Indian. It was on the basis of being a "*natural*" of a particular place that one had a series of rights and obligations in one, and only one, *pueblo*. By not being a "*natural*" an Indian escaped those rights and obligations. (Romero Vargas 1993a, 11)

In the Pacific region, the Spanish colonial administration carefully documented and promoted the group identifications of Nicaraguan natives in order to maximize and rationalize the exploitation of these Indians. In contrast, European colonial governments (Spanish and English) did not institutionalize Indian group identity in the Atlantic region in the early colonial period. That is to say, their inability to subjugate Atlantic Coast Indian groups contributed to their inability to invent or discover ethnonyms for them that corresponded to the contours of their social world. Whereas in the Pacific the process of extracting resources (in the form of labor and tribute) from indigenous people necessitated the existence and perpetuation of named communal groupings, the Atlantic Coast successfully resisted the Spanish imposition of this process.[15] Thus in the Atlantic, identification as part of a native group carried with it different meanings and consequences than such identification had for the Indians of the Pacific.

The irony of this history lies in the fact many of the peoples of the Atlantic that were labeled, in one way or another, as wild, rustic, and uncivilized (by both the Spanish and Pacific Indians) were able to successfully resist the cultural, social, and biological devastation brought on by the Spanish. The so-called civilized and Christian societies of the Pacific were shackled throughout the colonial period by oppressive tribute taxation and outright enslavement, not to mention European diseases. According to Newson's estimates, which she admits are conservative, the aboriginal population of Nicaragua declined a staggering 93 percent in the first fifty years of European contact, from 546,000 to 44,000. The corresponding figure for the same period in the Atlantic zone is 33 percent, dropping to 145,000 from a pre-contact population of 217,000 (Newson 1987, 336). Although Atlantic populations did suffer from European diseases and enslavement, apart from the coastal settlement at Black River in today's Honduras, Europeans did not directly control any portion of the Mosquito Coast in the colonial period.

One strategy for escaping the negative consequences of being an Indian in Pacific Nicaragua was simply not to be an Indian any more.[16] By breaking ties with indigenous polities and in turn being recognized as *Mestizo, Ladino,* or campesino, Pacific Indians stood to improve their status within colonial and republican society, societies that in many ways lived parasitically off organized indigenous communities.[17] The early Spanish colonial institutions (including the *encomienda* and later *repartimiento*) assigned the labor or tribute of specific native groups to Spanish overlords, who most frequently extracted this labor and tribute through the use of indigenous leaders, *los principales* (Romero Vargas 1992, 25). This practice depended upon the existence of a legitimately constituted indigenous hierarchy and a corporatively organized indigenous population. With the onset of the Republican period and the subsequent growth of a liberal export-oriented economy, the Indian communal lands, which the laws of the Spanish colony had self-servingly protected, came into the covetous gaze of national elites. Thus the last advantage of Indian status (communal lands) was largely eliminated in the Pacific, driving the nail into the coffin of Nicaragua's Pacific Indian communities.[18]

Mestizaje is popularly regarded primarily as a biological phenomenon in which Indians and Europeans, driven by the lack of white women in the Americas, produced *Mestizo* offspring. In contrast to this common-sense notion, however, the process of racial mixing must also be understood as an institutional phenomenon in which natives broke corporate affiliations and slowly mingled into a Mestizo mainstream that lacked Indian corporate obligations.[19] Viewed in this light, biological mixing was not a precondition for the shift from Indian identification to non-Indian that happened in Pacific Nicaragua. It is important to recall that the Spanish population (Spanish-born *penisulares* and American-born *criollos* alike) never represented more than 5% of the population of the colony (Romero Vargas 1993b, 153). For this and other reasons it is important to view mestizaje as a sociological and institutional phenomena as well as a biological one.

In the Atlantic Coast during the colonial period, the population remained almost entirely free from colonial institutions such as the encomienda and other forms of tribute. Costeño communities both maintained and developed old and new strategies of corporate unity, strategies that were different from those encountered by the Spanish in Pacific Nicaragua. In contrast to the Pacific region, there were few institutional pressures to sever ties with native communal groups and enter into the non-Indian peasant class, or *campesinado*. Although the colonial record, as well as twentieth-century ethnography, is full of references to the intermixing of Atlantic Coast Indians with Europeans and Africans, the Latin American prototypical (Indian-European) process of mestizaje simply did not occur in Atlantic Nicaragua (Taguzgalpa and Tologalpa). The Atlantic Coast did not witness the formation of a class of putatively racially mixed people that lacked the social status and the institutional rights and obligations of inclusion as either Indian or European. The communal organization of Atlantic society into explicitly non-European (neither White nor Mestizo) groupings in fact accelerated. According to the common-sense view of mestizaje, which takes racial mixing at face value as a biological process, this fact would seem a paradox, the paradox being that equal or comparable levels of European, Indian, and African intermixing would lead to a Mestizo population in one area and a predominantly Indian population in another. However, this is exactly what happened in Nicaragua, and in order to understand and interpret how this happened, we must discard perspectives that in anthropologist Raymond Smith's words, "biologize social relations" (Smith 1992, 263).

Most of the tribal terms mentioned above (tomayes, quimacas, etc.) had disappeared by the nineteenth century. There was a major restructuring of Mosquito Coast society in which a new system of group classification began to emerge, which had two principle ethnonyms: (1) Creole, a term used after the eighteenth century that identified English-speakers of putative African descent; and (2) Miskito, a term used to identify Miskitu-speakers of putative Indian and mixed (Sambo) descent. Both terms are absent from use in the early colonial period. Conspicuously absent from the colonial and modern system of group classification was a Mestizo or Ladino category such as that used in the Pacific, where the great majority of Nicaraguans are classified today as Mestizo.

THE SHIPWRECK THEORY
OF MISKITO ORIGINS

The appearance of the Miskito as a presumably distinct socio-racial group has been attributed to two features of Mosquito Coast history: (1) the influx of African and Afro-Caribbean slaves and escaped slaves, and (2) trading ties established in the seventeenth century and continued until the end of the nineteenth century between the British and coastal Indians. Each factor has been commonly perceived, in the historical and ethnographic literature, to have resulted in the emergence of the Miskito, Sumu, Rama, and Creole groups—an emergence that has been portrayed as a process of cultural differentiation in which each of these groups developed its own particular culture and race. In other words, the appearance of a new set of ethnonyms is perceived to have been pre-cipitated by the separation of a corresponding number of culture-bearing groups whose boundaries are constituted by racial and cultural features particular to each group. This is a misleading assumption that does not do justice to the complexity of social relations in the Mosquito Coast.

The first of two standard causes cited for the emergence of the Miskito Indians as a distinguishable group was the influx of African slaves and escapees to the region. The shipwreck of a slave ship in the area of the Mosquito Keys in the 1640s is presumed to have begun a long-term migratory trend in which escaped slaves of African descent trickled into the Mosquito Coast. This trend ultimately resulted in the rise of the Miskito as a new *"raza mixta"* (mixed race) (Gamez 1939, 57) or "hybrid" (Conzemius 1932, 17) Indian group. Hereafter I refer to this explanation as the shipwreck theory of Miskito origins.

The shipwreck theory appears in one form or another in almost all academic and journalistic accounts of Miskito origins and history.[20] According to this theory, the region was populated by related but highly localized Indian groups (which later would come to be known under the collective term *Sumu*). The intermarriage of Africans with a Sumu group that lived around the mouth of the Coco River at Cape Gracias a Dios is presumed to have led to the rise of a dominant group that eventually expanded throughout the Mosquito Coast, either destroying or incor-porating Sumu groups as it expanded.[21] The shipwreck theory of Miskito "genesis" assumes that race, particularly African race or "blood," becomes a self-evident feature of human bodies that inevitably precipitates a transformation in social and racial categorization. This assumption, relying on a model of biological determinism that does not give sufficient attention to the social construction of race, cannot be sustained in this case.[22]

In the historical record (in this case primarily the published accounts of northern European traders, pirates, and colonists),[23] the perception that the inhabitants of the Mosquito Coast were the product of African and Indian miscegenation appears more or less simultaneously as the use of some variation of the term *Mosquito* to denominate a nation or tribe.[24] Before the mid-sixteenth century, *Mosquito* was used exclusively as a toponym (place name) that, depending on the source, referred to the Coco River, the island-like delta at the mouth of this river (the cape Gracias a Dios), and the densely packed group of small islands and keys that dot the shallow sea shelf beyond the cape Gracias a Dios. These islands today are known as the Mosquito Keys or *Cayos Miskitos* (Houwald 1990, 203; Incer 1990, 292; Romero Vargas 1995, 125). Over the centuries both Europeans and Americans have offered countless interpretations as to the origin of the use of the term *Miskito* and its variants in Central America, some of which assume that the term originated as an ethnonym and some of which assume that the term originated as a toponym. According to the most recent historical research by Nicaraguan and other scholars, it appears most likely that the term was first applied to the Mosquito Keys (Incer 1990, 292), which because of their density and small size reminded the seafaring Europeans of a swarm of mosquitoes. Later this term was applied to inhabitants of the adjacent mainland (Potthast 1988, 66; Romero Vargas 1995, 125; Offen 2002).

In the earliest English accounts of the region (1630–1650) the inhabitants were referred to generically as Indians or as "Cape Indians"—the term "Cape" deriving from Columbus' geographical term Cabo Gracias a Dios (Romero Vargas 1995, 125). The English did not adopt the term *Guaba*, which the Franciscans (whose last attempt to pacify the region resulted in the execution of three Spanish missionaries by the feared "Albatuinas" of the inland portion of the Coco River in 1623) had in the early 1600s applied to the coastal Indians of the region between the Cape and the Caratasca Lagoon to the North (Incer 1990, 271). English Puritan colonists who had settled on Providence Island in

1629 were the first Europeans to extensively interact on peaceful terms with the indigenous people of the region. Under specific instructions to ingratiate themselves with the Indians of the adjacent coast, they set up trading posts on the Cape and the Mosquito Keys in order to acquire provisions and items of trade for their precarious island colony (Naylor 1989, 30).[25] The Spanish destroyed the Providence Island colony in 1640, sending English refugees and their Negro slaves to the shores of the Spanish Main, primarily to the area that is today Belize but also to the Bay Islands, the Cape Gracias a Dios and Mosquito Keys region, and the Bluefields Bay region (Naylor 1989, 30–34; Parsons 1956, 10). Although historians and so-called ethnohistorians of the Mosquito Coast and the eastern Anglo-Caribbean, such as Dennis and Olien (1984), Naylor (1989), Olien (1983) and Parsons (1956), have portrayed this early (1630–1670) interaction as having occurred between the English and the Miskito Indians, Romero Vargas has convincingly demonstrated that Europeans referred to the inhabitants of the region as Zambos, Mulattoes, and Indians before they used Mosquito as a tribal term (Romero Vargas 1995, 125; also see Incer 1990, 360).

In later accounts (1670s) the terms *Zambo* (Spanish for the offspring of a Black and an Indian), *Indian, Mulatto,* and *Negro* came to be used in both English and Spanish sources to describe the coastal dwellers around the Cape.[26] Although these sources inconsistently applied these four terms to inhabitants of the Cape Gracias a Dios region, they uniformly explained the African presence as having resulted from the shipwreck of a slave ship (Helms 1977, 158).[27] In the 1670s Europeans referred to the inhabitants of the region as Zambos, Mulattoes, Negroes, or Indians from Mosquito (or "the Mosquitos") (Incer 1990, 360; Romero Vargas 1995, 125). The Spanish continued to refer to the aggressive groups that plagued the eastern border of Nicaragua as both *Carives* and *Zambos del Mosquito* until well into the eighteenth century (Incer 1990, 378–380); tellingly, the Spanish colonial officials also referred to the inhabitants of the region as *el enemigo zambo* (the zambo enemy) (ibid., 375).

The first European reference to the Mosquito Indians as a "small nation" (Exquemelin 1685, 93) came from English, Dutch, and French, pirates who visited the area in the 1660s and 1670s.[28] They noted the well-established social, commercial, and military ties between European pirates and the inhabitants of the Cape Gracias a Dios area (Dampier

1698; Lussan 1689; M.W. 1728).[29] All of the seventeenth-century non-Spanish sources regarded the Cape Gracias a Dios area of the Central American shoreline (or Spanish Main as it was known by the covetous English) to be typified by its friendly and resourceful natives—a feature that attracted northern European newcomers to the Caribbean. After a century and a half of Spanish monopoly, they started preying upon these rich colonies from their bases in Jamaica and Tortuga Island. For example, Alexandre Exquemelin, a Dutch pirate based in Jamaica, regularly stopped at the Cape with the intention of safely acquiring provisions. He wrote: "We direction our course towards the Cape of *Gracias a Dios*, where we had fixed our last hopes of finding Provisions. For thither do usually resort many Pirats [sic], who entertain a friendly Correspondence and Trade with the *Indians* of those parts" (Exquemelin 1685, 91).

He added:

Through the frequent Converse and Familiarity these *Indians* have with the Pirats, they sometimes use to go to Sea with them, and remain among them for whole years, without returning home. From whence it cometh, that many of them can speak *English*, and *French*, and some of the Pirats their *Indian* Language. They are very dextrous at darting with the Javelin whereby they are very useful to the Pirats, towards the victualling their Ships, by the fishery of Tortoises, and *Manita's* [manatees]. . . . For of these *Indians*, is alone sufficient to victual a Vessel of an 100 persons. We had among our Crew, two Pirats, who could speak very well the *Indian* Language. By the Help of these men, I was so curious as to enquire into their Customs, Lives and Policy. (ibid., 92–93)

In the above quotations, it is apparent that as of the 1670s, northern European pirates and the Indians of the Cape Gracias a Dios region dealt with each other extensively, extensively enough to speak one another's languages, accompany one another on long voyages, and learn about one another's customs. One of the "Policies" that most encouraged these Europeans with regard to their native allies was their unwillingness to "entertain any Friendship, or Correspondence, with other neighbouring Islands, much less with the *Spaniards*" (Exquemelin 1685, 93).

Exquemelin's pirate contemporary William Dampier echoed this state-ment:"It is very rare to find Privateers destitute of one ore more of them, when the Commander, or most of the men are *English*; but they do not love the *French*, and the *Spaniards* they hate mortally" (Dampier 1698, 8).

The seemingly benign nature of the relationship between the English and the Cape Gracias a Dios Indians had less to do with, as the English claimed, the affinity of Mosquito Coast peoples for the English and more to do with the precarious legal and military position in which the English found themselves in the western Caribbean mainland. Indeed, throughout the 275 years of English activity in the region (start-ing with the foundation of the short-lived Puritan Providence Island Company in 1629 and ending with the Harrison-Altamirano Treaty between England and Nicaragua in 1905), the precariousness and volatility of the English presence greatly mitigated the negative impact of their presence on certain segments of Mosquito Coast society.

These early sources depicted the Mosquito Indians as a small, sea-oriented, highly localized, and loosely organized group with a popula-tion from about 200 (Dampier 1698, 7) to 2,000 (Exquemelin 1685, 93). M.W., an English trader and pirate who visited the Cape in 1699, described the Indians he encountered in the following manner:[30] "They live peaceably together in several families, yet accounting all *Indians* of one tongue, to be the same people and friends, and are in quality all equal, neither king nor captains of families bearing any more command that the meanest, unless it be at such times when they make any expe-ditions against the *Alboawinneys*; at that time they submit to the conduct, and obey the orders of their kings and captains" (Olien 1983, 199).

Driven by seventy years of growing opportunities for trade with the English, the inhabitants of the Cape had extended the sweep of their raiding activities to as far south as the Matina cacao plantation district of Costa Rica, where, according to M.W., they "carry away many of their Indians [Costa Rican Indians], of which they kill the men, but the women, and boys they reserve to trade with to the Jamaica-men, who take off their hands all their cocoa-nuts, moneloes, turtle-shell, amber-greese, plate, slaves, and what else they get by such rapines, which with them is a fair war" (Helms 1983, 183).[31] It appears that this process resulted in the emergence of higher levels of social stratification in which certain "captains" assumed leadership positions with influence above and beyond local kin groups, which in modern Miskitu are known as *taya* (bi-lateral kin groups) and *kiamp* (uni-lateral kin groups; the word itself probably derived from the English "camp"). In her ethnography of Asang, a twentieth-century Rio Coco Miskito village, Helms identified fifty of these groups, which she described as "a loose kindred" that includes "all living relatives to a distance of third cousin from ego" within the riverine village of approximately 700 (Helms 1971, 72). Although these terms are completely absent from the historical literature, most of the historical sources, such as M.W. above, mention the importance of multiple kin groups within Mosquito Coast settlements, Zambo and Mosquito alike.

With regard to the relationship between the Blacks and Indians of the area, historical sources provided consistently contradictory accounts. Exquemelin claimed that the Mosquito Indians (referring to the Indians of the Cape whom he perceived to be typical of the "Island Caribes") cohabited the "Island" with "Negros," some of whom were held as slaves (Exquemelin 1685, 93, 98).[32] According to Exquemelin the "Negros" lived in separate settlements where they lived "according to the Customs of their own *Countrey*" (ibid., 100). Other sources, such as the English pirate M.W. and early eighteenth-century Spanish officials Luis Antonio Muñoz and Santaella Melgarejo, claimed that the Black slaves promptly blended into the Indian groups of the Cape (Conzemius 1932, 17; Naylor 1989, 230). Still other sources argued that the Negroes and Indians entered into bloody warfare, with the Negroes eventually vanquishing the Indians, taking Indian women as mates. Take, for example, the following testimony of Fray Benito Garret y Arloví, Bishop of Nicaragua, who in 1711 wrote:

> In the year 1641 a ship carrying Blacks [*negros*] was wrecked on the coast of the North sea . . . they took shelter in the bush of those mountains which was occupied by Carib Indians [*indios caribes*] who, threatened by their new guests, made war against them and for many years held the upper hand. With time the Blacks defeated the Caribs who withdrew to mountains towards the Segovias and Chontales . . . with the women of the defeated the winners multiplied and, because the first people there had died, today their descendants are called zambos because they are the children of Black

men and Indian women. This story was told to me by a Black man called Juan Ramón who lives in this city [Granada], and whose advanced age makes plausible his recollection of the events that he narrates. (Incer 1990, 294)

Variations of this story have continued to be recounted, both inside and outside of the Mosquito Coast, to the present day and, not surprisingly, the specific details of these stories tend to reveal more about the prejudices and interests of the sources than they do about the fate of the survivors of the legendary seventeenth-century shipwreck.

For example, consider the variation in the versions of the story found in diplomatic correspondence between the United States and Great Britain. In 1842 US Diplomat William Murphy reported to Secretary of State Daniel Webster that, according to his understanding, the "Indian-Negro mixture" found in the Mosquito Coast had resulted from the extermination of native men (and subsequent union with native women) committed by shipwrecked Negro slaves. In the late eighteenth century the British superintendent to the Mosquito Shore provided an opposite version in which the African men were killed by Mosquito Indians, who then procreated with African women (Naylor 1989, 231). In light of the efforts by US diplomats to discredit British claims on the mainland of Central America by asserting the Negro (and therefore illegitimate) origins of the "Mosquito Kingdom," the American account corresponds with the goals of US foreign policy at the time. By emphasizing the Indian racial makeup of the Mosquito Shore, the British account supported British claims to the legitimacy of the inclusion of the country of Mosquito as a protectorate.

Just as the interpretations that various actors make regarding the details of the shipwreck reveal something about their interests and biases, the various theories regarding the origin of the term *Miskito* are similarly revealing about their authors and supporters. The common explanation among today's Miskito is that the term derives from the name of a mythical leader, Miskut, who is said to have brought the Miskito from Honduras to a place around Bismona Lagoon. This version has become the official theory of the modern Miskito Indian movement (see Nietschmann 1989, 16, and 1993, 29). According to Stedman Fagoth, contemporary Miskito politician, former military leader, and historian, this group of migrants came to be known as "Miskut Uplika Nani" (Miskut's People), and eventually this name was shortened to Miskito by the Sumo, who could not pronounce the entire phrase well (Fagoth 1986, 12).

At the turn of the century, Moravian linguist George Heath collected an origin myth from a Miskito informant who claimed that Miskito was derived from the Miskitu phrase "Dis-kitwras-nani" ("they who cannot be dislodged") (Heath 1913, 49). Heath himself speculated that the term came from the Spanish phrase "*indios mixtos*" (ibid., 51). He wrote: "Through the importation of slaves by former British settlers (who afterward removed to Belize), and through more recent immigration of negroes of more or less pure African blood, chiefly from Jamaica, the Miskuto people have come to present Sambo characteristics in nearly all of their villages. May it not be that the much-discussed name "Miskuto" has originated in the phrase "Indios Mixtos," used perhaps at first of the Sambos?" (ibid., 51).

His theory lends support to the racial determinism of the time. Along these lines, J. Dyneley Prince, an *American Anthropologist* editor of Heath's 1913 article, used a racial metaphor to describe the "mongrel nature of the present Miskuto idiom" (ibid., 62). Another early twentieth-century German Moravian linguist, Walter Lehmann, speculated that the term was the product of the region's South American cultural roots, deriving from a Columbian Chibchan language in which "Muyska" or "Muisca" means "men" (Lehmann 1920; also see Valle 1944, 102, and Guerrero and Guerrero 1982, 98; see Smutko 1985, 73, for another variation of this theory).

Mary Helms favored Charles Gibson's theory that "the term may be derived from the idea of 'musket' since the population in question was distinguished from its neighbors literally as a musket-bearing group" (Helms 1971, 16). This was thoroughly in line with Helms's emphasis on the socio-economic roots of Miskito origin as a "purchase society." Following with this theme of the economic and occupational roots of ethnic identity, linguist John Holm linked the term to the Miskitu verb *miskaia* (to fish) (Holm 1978, 306). Presumably the Miskito came to be identified as a tribe as a result of their coastal adaptation.

Nietschmann's less polemical pre-Sandinista Revolution work supported this position (Nietschmann 1973, 26). In accordance with his staunch primordialist position with regard to the Miskito (which he developed even before the Miskito-Sandinista crisis), he insisted, in contrast to the "colonial tribe" camp, that the Miskito constituted a distinct tribe, albeit with a different name, on the basis of their unique "coastal orientation" before European contact (ibid., 26).

Since at least the nineteenth century, European visitors to the Coast have speculated that the term derives from the abundance of mosquitoes (the insect) in the region (Guerrero and Guerrero 1982, 98). Throughout the colonial period and continuing to the present, the terms *Mosco* and *Mosca* (fly in Spanish) are frequently used, often in a derogatory fashion, to refer to the Miskito. Clearly these last usages represent after-the-fact rationalizations that incorporate negative images of the Miskito. In all of this speculation as to the origin of the term *Miskito*, each of the theories reflects the varying perspectives and agendas of those involved.

Although the seventeenth-century sources are not unanimous with regard to the group labels of the Cape Gracias a Dios people, they are unanimous in regarding these people as having a distinctive relationship with Europeans. Regardless of whether these sources referred to the inhabitants of the coast as Zambos, Mulattoes, or Indians, they observed that all of the inhabitants of the area were available, willing, and useful trading and raiding partners. Herein lies a key to understanding the transformation and consolidation of Mosquito Coast society.

ZAMBOS, MOSQUITOS, ZAMBOS MOSQUITOS: SLAVERY AND MIXED RACE

In the eighteenth century, sources began to describe the Mosquito and Zambo as subgroups or "branches" (Naylor 1989, 41) of an expanding and increasingly hierarchically organized Mosquito Indian population. At times the groups that were considered to be "pure Indians" were referred to as *Tawira* (straight-haired in Miskitu) or simply as Mosquitos, while the groups that were portrayed as mixed with Africans were referred to as Sambos (in English) or Zambos Mosquitos (Offen 2002). Whereas in the seventeenth century the application of the term *Mosquito*, as both a toponym and ethnonym, was confined to a very circumscribed referent, in the eighteenth century the term started to be applied to larger and more dispersed groups. Also as a toponym it came to be applied to a much larger area. In the seventeenth century the term was used to describe a small population that cooperated with the English, but in the eighteenth century it was used to describe what were perceived to be, at some level, a broader population that was divided into geographically centered subgroups, which were united by a common language.

The region was witnessing a transformation, not only in the system of tribal terminology, but much more significantly in economic orientation—a transformation that directly affected the process of group formation and social stratification (Romero Vargas 1995, 157). Mosquito Coast society in the pre-Columbian and early colonial period was characterized by a relatively dispersed system (in comparison to the Pacific) of socio-political organization. Although widespread groups did possess cultural and linguistic affinities with one another, they were not organized into region-wide institutional structures. In the eighteenth century, however, this situation changed as a coastal "trading and raiding" population began to increase in size, strength, and political integration (Olien 1988a). These social and economic transformations have been commonly viewed as having directly resulted from a change in the racial composition of the region's Indians.

In the eighteenth century, as the inhabitants of the Cape Gracias a Dios region began to expand, internal and external power struggles emerged within splinter groups that, according to colonial sources, were composed of about ten families (Incer 1990, 371). In order to consolidate their position within their own communities and cement their ties with English merchants and pirates, native leaders sought recognition of self-bestowed English titles such as admiral, governor, captain, general, and king. Initially this process lacked the systematicness and hierarchy that these titles imply. In the early 1700s, for example, Spanish documents refer to many different "Kings" (Olien 1983, 204). But as the century progressed, a set of regional leaders emerged, each of whom held a title that was officially recognized by the British authorities in Jamaica. These authorities in Jamaica frequently issued "commissions" as well as diplomatic gifts that helped to legitimate the authority of the titleholder (Romero Vargas 1995, 164). The English, encouraged by Mosquito aggression against Spanish territory, claimed that all of the Mosquito leaders considered themselves subjects of the British king and loathed Spaniards. Among themselves, however, they ridiculed as savage and gullible the aspiring Mosquito Coast leaders whose authority they selectively bolstered—at times even going to the lengths of "educating" them in England and Jamaica.

Notwithstanding the historical antipathy between Spaniards and Costeños that has so often been cited in the modern literature as lying at the root of the modern Sandinista-Costeño conflict, the fact that at different times Miskito leaders solicited Spanish support (from the colonial governments of Costa Rica and New Granada) in order to enhance their positions speaks to the tactical and contingent nature of the Mosquito alliance with the British. In her book on Anglo-Spanish politics in the Mosquito Coast, Historian Barbara Potthast devoted a chapter to this little-known history in which Mosquito Coast leaders attempted to solidify Spanish support (Potthast 1988, 253–303; also see Olien 1983, 213; Helms 1986, 512; Romero Vargas 1995, 188; Offen 1999). Miskito leaders consciously manipulated European sources of power and prestige in local and regional political negotiations (Olien 1983, 204; Offen 1999).

In Mosquito Coast society, power came to be marked by British symbols and goods. In the words of linguist John Holm, "The Miskito began to think of themselves as partly European (as indeed they were becoming, both culturally and genetically) and thus less vulnerable than 'wild' Indians to destruction at the hands of the Spaniards" (Holm 1978, 38). The Mosquito kings displayed their ties to the British through a silver crown and scepter given by the governor of Jamaica. Later, Mosquito titleholders were known to dress in British naval uniforms (Dennis and Olien 1984, 727). An Indian and African-influenced Creole English, which Holm described as "one of the oldest varieties of English spoken outside of England," was used along with Miskitu as the two lingua francas in the region in the eighteenth century (Holm 1978, 95). Local and regional leaders also legitimated their authority on the basis of their mastery of English, the prestige language of the Coast. These and other symbols played a central role in Mosquito political structure, where "at least as early as 1687, the Miskito believed that in order for an individual to legitimate his claim as king, he must first be recognized as the group's leader by the English" (Olien 1983, 200).

The Miskito king never ruled over a "state-type political structure" (Dennis and Olien 1984, 718).[33] The king, governor, admiral, and general represented the highest level of their authority in their respective regions, and at different times the latter three wielded more power than the king. In 1740, for example, the general ruled from Cape Cameron to Cape Gracias a Dios in what is known as the Honduran Mosquitia; the king ruled from Cape Gracias a Dios to Sandy Bay; and the governor ruled from Sandy Bay to Pearl Lagoon (Olien 1983, 208; Potthast 1988, 174). According to Robert Hodgson, first British superintendent of the Mosquito Shore, "Three chiefs ruled over separate Mosquito provinces, or 'guards'" (Olien 1983, 209). On many occasions these leaders made treaties with foreign interests and issued land grants to foreign investors (Romero Vargas 1995, 163–169).

At no point did the English establish a large-scale plantation economy (such as those created in Jamaica, British Honduras, and other parts of the Caribbean) on the Mosquito Coast. From 1740 to 1786 Mosquito Coast society started to move in that direction, but in 1787 Britain signed a treaty with Spain in which it agreed to abandon the Mosquito Shore. This treaty precipitated the flight of the English residents and their slaves, who had been used primarily in the logging industry, to the logging areas of Belize. African slaves and freemen represented three-fourths of the 2,214 evacuees (Bolland 1977, 40). Even in the height of African slavery in the Mosquito Coast (1740–1786), African slave numbers were low and export-oriented agricultural plantations were few (Gabbert 1992, 46; Parsons 1956, 12). In the Mosquito Coast, as opposed to Spanish Central America where Indian chattel slavery had long been abolished, African slavery actually seems not to have been significantly more prevalent than Indian slavery.[34] Romero Vargas estimated that before the end of eighteenth century, more than 20,000 Indian slaves had been captured by the Mosquito Indians and sold to buyers, primarily in Jamaica but also Belize and the Mosquito Coast (Romero Vargas 1995, 290).[35]

Although African slavery existed in comparable levels in both Pacific Nicaragua and the Mosquito Coast, the Spanish institutions of encomienda, repartimiento, and Indian tribute and taxation created a form of Indian semi-slavery in the Pacific that was quite different from the Indian and African slavery in the Mosquito Coast. These Spanish institutions relied on the communal organization of Indian groups. In contrast, African and Indian slavery practiced on the Mosquito Coast was predicated upon wrenching the slave from aboriginal communal affiliations.

The regionally specific nature of slavery in the Mosquito Coast profoundly affected the construction of race in the Mosquito Coast. To be defined as in some way African in the Mosquito Coast did not carry the same social and legal ramifications as it did in the slave-holding strongholds of both English and Spanish America. Throughout Latin America, the Spanish placed a host of restrictions on the movement, dress, marriage, political aspirations, and self-defense of different categories of African Americans (whether Negro, free "*Pardo*," or Zambo) (Helms 1977, 163). In the Atlantic Coast of Nicaragua such institutional disincentives to Black identification played a much less important role. Indeed the capture of the Indian slaves for sale continued, although at a much reduced pace, until the second half of the nineteenth century— well after African slaves received their formal emancipation in the British West Indies (1838) (Bolland 1977, 4; Naylor 1989, 93).[36] Although Mosquito leaders had been known to hold some African slaves during the eighteenth century, the supply of African slaves was never replenished after the British evacuation of the Coast in 1787 (Olien 1988b, 44). A few of the White settlers who pledged allegiance to the Spanish Crown, rather than relocating to British Honduras, continued to hold a limited number of slaves. However, by 1800 African slavery in the region, no longer economically viable, was all but over (Olien 1988a).[37]

For this reason the distinction between Sambo and "pure Indian," although an important distinction within Mosquito Coast society, was quite irrelevant with regard to the matter of slavery. As Karl Offen notes, "The Miskitu elite thought of themselves as 'a free and unconquered people' and the only comparative people who also fit this description were elites of other powerful nations" (Offen 1999, 276). Miskito Indians of the eighteenth century knew that they were free men and women regardless of their physical appearance or whether they belonged to a community that was defined as Sambo or Indian. In light of their successful raiding of Spanish settlements and their extraordinary successes in defining the terms in their interactions with the British, their freedom was indeed never in question.

In the Pacific region the system of racial categorization was simultaneously taking a very different path in which an African or mixed-African racial category disappeared entirely (Romero Vargas 1993a; 1995). This categorical shift, and the subsequent historiographical erasure, has been so complete that today in Nicaraguan popular imagination it is not recognized that there ever was a significant African presence in the Pacific region. It is common knowledge in Nicaragua, despite evidence to the contrary, that African slavery characterized the Atlantic Coast, not the Pacific. Vargas identified this process of erasure in the following manner:

> We should emphasize the importance that the African element of colonial society acquired in the Nicaraguan province particularly in the nineteenth century. Paradoxically, this society tried to hide and disguise this presence—terrorized by a complex of legal transgression. At this time the myth that *mestizaje* occurred only between the Spanish and the Indians was created. This myth survives in modern Nicaraguan society. In contrast to what happens in the Atlantic Coast, people [from the Pacific] conceal the African elements of Nicaraguan social formation. (Romero Vargas 1993b)

As Romero Vargas's archival investigations have revealed, the Spanish colonial elite in the Pacific region not only imported very significant numbers of African slaves, but also they imported far more African slaves than their colonial counterparts on the Atlantic Coast. In the mid-sixteenth century, after fifty years of human devastation wrought by the Indian slave trade, Africans became the main source of forced labor in the Spanish Colonies from Mexico to Peru.[38] African slaves continued to be imported into the province of Nicaragua throughout the colonial period, but by the early eighteenth century they represented a very small amount of the population. Their descendants, however, who the colonial society sought to officially identify as Mullatoes and Zambos, represented as much as half of the population of the colony (Romero Vargas 1993b, 163). Ironically, these free Mulattoes and Zambos primarily worked in the colonial militias, defending the Pacific region against Mosquito Zambo raids. In the major colonial cities this figure was even higher. For example, in 1790 Granada the population (12,400) possessed the following official racial profile: 400 Spanish, 1,500 Mestizos, 8,000 Mulattoes and Zambos, 400 Negros, 100 slaves, and 2,000 Indians (ibid., 159). After independence, however, the percentage of the population considered African (Zambo, Mulatto, or Negro), both in official statistics and popular usage, drastically declined such that by the end of the nineteenth century the African had disappeared in name from the Pacific Nicaraguan population. They had been categorically shifted into the Mestizo majority. That is to say, the official as well as unofficial systems of racial categorization in the Pacific region became transformed such that individuals were much less frequently categorized as Zambo, Mulatto, and Negro.

In 1740 the English, newly at war with the Spanish, began to place the Mosquito Shore more firmly into their colonial grip.[39] The Governor of Jamaica appointed an English "superintendent" to oversee and formalize British interests in the region as well as to direct English and Mosquito incursions against Spanish settlements (Romero Vargas 1993b, 170).[40] During the period from 1740 to 1787, after which the British withdrew from the region, the leadership hierarchy within the Mosquito Shore became increasingly rationalized. According to Robert Hodgson, the first British superintendent of the Mosquito Shore, the chain of command was as follows: (1) at the top, the three major leaders—the king, governor, and general; (2) historically established captains and leaders of tribes and smaller districts; (3) recently elevated, either by the Mosquito or British authorities, captains and others "with similar influence"; (4) quartermasters, which was the lowest title of distinction; (5) foot soldiers; and (6) individuals of "little importance" (Romero Vargas 1995, 162).

European sources characterize the internally stratified "guards"—districts within the territory of each king, governor, or general that were led by a local leader—as racially distinct because they were presumed to contain differing relative levels of Indian vs. Black "blood." By the late eighteenth century and continuing into the nineteenth century, historical sources consistently claimed that the Northern guards contained Samboes that possessed a greater amount of African "blood," while the Southern guards were peopled by "pure Indians" (Olien 1983, 209). Bryan Edwards, late eighteenth-century British historian of the West Indies, described his perception of the racial makeup of the region in the following manner: "The general's people are Samboes, and stretch from Black River to near Cape Gracias-a-Dios. The king's chief residence is about twelve leagues south of the cape, his people are also Samboes, and his immediate precinct reaches to the cape, and runs far up the country. The governor's precinct joins to the king's, and extends between twenty and thirty leagues to the southward, till it meets the admiral's. The people under these chieftains are pure Indians" (Olien 1983, 209).

Edwards explained that these separate "tribes" could be differentiated as distinct "both by nature and by policy: by nature, from the general distinction of pure Indians and Samboes; by policy, as living and acting under several chieftains" (Helms 1977, 159). Edwards's contemporary and fellow historian Edward Long stated that the "Mosquitos" (a term that he regarded a "general name") were composed of several "tribes" composed of either "Samboes" or "Pure Indians" (Long 1972 [1774], 316).

Not only did the eighteenth-century sources, as well as the nineteenth-century sources, describe the political divisions as corresponding with racial differences ("nature"), but, more significantly, the sources infused their characterizations of these sub-tribes with the racial prejudices and stereotypes of their day. English sources typically attributed what they perceived to be the most negative features of the Mosquito Indians to their African ancestry, and they consistently characterized the Sambo wings of the Mosquito as being subject to those character traits (laziness and treachery) that they most used to describe the Negroes of their own slave societies.

Take, for example, Edward Long's description of the Samboes of Mosquito: "Among them is a mixed race, called *Samboes*, supposed to derive their origin from a Guiney ship; which traditions says, was wrecked on the coast above a century ago; certain it is, that their hair, complexion, features, and make, clearly denote an African ancestry; from whom they have also inherited some of the true characteristics of the African mind; for they are generally false, designing, treacherous, knavish, impudent, and revengeful" (Long 1972 [1774], 316).

Contrast this statement to Edwards's portrayal of the pure Indians whom he differentiated from the "treacherous" Samboes: "The pure Indians are so called, because they are free from any mixture of negro blood; and their general conduct gives a very favourable idea of Indian nature. They are seldom guilty of positive evil, and often rise to positive good, when positive good does not require much exertion of mind. Their modesty, docility, good faith, disposition to friendship and gratitude, ought to engage equally our regard and protection" (Helms 1977, 159). Here Edwards portrays the Mosquito Indians as being culturally degraded on the basis of their racial admixture with Africans in a fashion that is typical of the eighteenth-century and nineteenth-century accounts of the Mosquito Coast.

Nineteenth-century and twentieth-century accounts of the Mosquito Coast continue to emphasize the degrading effects of the African admixture in the region. Take for example the following quotation from early twentieth-century economic historian Samuel Crowther:

> The Mosquito Coast is a strip of land stretching some two hundred miles along the shore of Nicaragua from Cape Gracias a Dios to Bluefields Lagoon and once upon a time was the home of the Mosquito Indians. In the latter part of the seventeenth century a slave ship was wrecked on the coast. The Africans intermarried with the Indians, were joined by Jamaica negroes and escaped slaves and these together with a few renegade whites combines to form a polyglot race of utter worthlessness. It was a nation only in the sense that its people were quite unlike the people of any other nation. (Crowther 1929, 113)

In an academic article, geographer Wolfgang von Hagen wrote in 1940: "In fact, the social retrogression described by Earl Hanson as occurring in the Orinoco basin is beginning in the Mosquitia of Honduras. There is further complication for the reason that, as times grow worse in the Caribbean, more Jamaican Negroes come to the Coast, intermarry with the Miskito, and add to the Negroid inheritances of the tribe: the more or less pure-blooded Indians who live to the south of Caratasca will be absorbed" (von Hagen 1940, 259). In these accounts the Indian part of the Miskito Indian admixture is seen as that which is valuable and worth preserving, while the Negro element is seen to be corrupting.

The attempt to discredit the Mosquito government on the grounds that their populations of Miskito Indians were actually "Negroes" was consistent with the US foreign policy goal of discrediting the English-allied government of the country of Mosquito. Not surprisingly in light of racial ideologies in the United States at the time, the US government and its agents fervently linked the perceived backwardness of the country of Mosquito to the African influence of its people. Anthropologist Michael Olien exposed the lengths taken by a US diplomat and ethnologist, E. G. Squier, in the mid 1800s to discredit the government of Mosquito on explicitly racial grounds (Olien 1985).

Traces of this negative portrayal of Africaness have seeped into the modern historiography of the region, and more importantly, Pacific Nicaraguan views about Costeños. Take, for example, the following quotation from contemporary Nicaraguan Historian Jaime Incer, whose book, *Nicaragua: Viajes, Rutas y Encuentros—1502–1838*, represents one of the few histories of Nicaragua to simultaneously treat the Atlantic and Pacific coast:

When the 17th century pirates described the Misquitos they undoubtedly were referring to the pure indians. As generations passed and the African features began to increasingly manifest themselves phenotypically, the term Misquito did not just cover solely Indians but also their Zambo descendants which had been raised as Misquitos by Misquita mothers. The colonial documents of the 18th century and the beginnings of the 19th century frequently mention the "Zambos-Mosquitos" as if they were a single nation.

The Misquitos emerge as a distinct people coincidentally with the infusion of African blood and although they conserve many of the ancient customs that they shared with the Sumus they came to dominate and enslave them thanks to the firearms that they acquired from their English allies. Those friendly and scattered natives that the pirates found living primitively and precariously in Cape Gracias a Dios were, in the following centuries, converted into an aggressive and expansionist nation which neighboring tribes as well as the Spanish had to suffer. Their leaders, the Mosco Kings, exchanged *mishla* (native alcohol) for Jamaican rum and in their alcoholic deliriums terrorized the coasts of Honduras, Nicaragua, Costa Rica and Panama in complicity with the English. (Incer 1990, 295)

This quotation reveals both a strong Hispanicist bias manifested by Pacific Nicaraguans against Costeños, as well as the proclivity to equate Indians with "noble savages" and Africans with brutality and unbridled aggression. Consider the following quotation from contemporary

historian Flor Solórzano: "It is obvious that during the 17th century survivors of the shipwreck mixed with the aboriginal population of the
place [Cape Gracias a Dios]. In this remarkable miscegenation, the product of an accident, the black race contributed physical durability and
warrior traditions while the miskito contributed cunning and natural
abilities which together was unleashed on the region in the form of the
fearful race known as the 'zambos-mosquitos'" (Solórzano 1992, 38).

Although less openly contemptuous of the mixed Mosquitos, Solórzano operates under the assumption that each so-called race contributed
a distinct quality to the resulting hybrid population. Once more, she
reproduces commonly held beliefs, historically rooted in New World
slavery, that associate Africans with brute physical strength and Indians
with harmony with nature.

This approach towards the role of Africans vis-à-vis Indians in Mosquito Coast history, however, also resonates in North American scholarship. US historian Robert Naylor, for example, employs a form of
racial determinism in his explanation of the rise of ascendancy of the
Miskito Indians. For example, he wrote:

> The Sambos had come a long way from their origins at Cape
> Gracias a Dios some seventy-five years earlier, when the survivors of
> a wrecked slave ship had taken up life among the Mosquito Indians.
> Their descendants had increased in number and expanded territori-
> ally. They were generally darker in color than the Indians, although
> they came in all shades; they were also a little taller than their Indian
> counterparts, and were noted for their frizzy hair and African
> features. They had tended to become even more bellicose, arrogant
> and adventurous that the pure Mosquito Indians, and before long
> they had emerged as the dominant element at the cape. (Naylor
> 1989, 41)

US Anthropologist Charles Hale recapitulated this view in 1987
when he wrote:

> *Africanization* of the Indian population at Cabo Gracias occurred
> during the same period that the tribal name *Miskitu* (with various
> spellings) first appears in historical documents, and that these coastal
> Indians developed a reputation as outstanding warriors and traders.

Having managed to escape the arduous conditions of slavery, these Africans must have been worldly-wise and aggressive. Intermarriage produced Miskitu offspring, but would also have transformed the ethnic identity, strengthening their orientation towards assertive relations with outsiders. (Hale 1987a, 37)

Much of the scholarship on the Mosquito Coast has reproduced an unsubstantiated correlation between Africanness and aggressiveness. More fundamentally, statements such as these can too easily be read as committing the fallacy of viewing race and miscegenation as being at the root of the social transformation of the region, thereby conflating social processes with biological processes. The emergence of a Costeño pattern of "assertive relations with outsiders" can be explained in terms of political and ecological factors without recourse to racial determinism. In the seventeenth century, inhabitants of the Cabo Gracias a Dios region of the Mosquito Coast, regardless of their biological origins, adopted a common set of political and economic strategies that entailed cooperation with the English and hostility to Spanish and Indians from the interior.

THE CASE OF THE CREOLES: IDENTITY POLITICS IN THE MOSQUITO NATION

Mosquito Coast anthropologist Michael Olien, whose work on Afro-Caribbean populations of lower Central America precedes his historical work on the Mosquito Kingdom, has written extensively on the origins of the Creole category (1987, 1988b, 1988c). According to Olien, inhabitants of the Mosquito Coast, all of whom were racially "mixed" to a varying degree, decided in the nineteenth century to gravitate toward one of two poles: the Mosquito-Zambo or the Creole.

The Mosquito-Zambos "were beginning to emphasize their Indian characteristics at this time and to de-emphasize their previous categorization as a zambo [Afro-Indian] population" (Olien 1988b, 45). The descendants of ex-slaves who "followed Miskito cultural traditions . . . continued to be known as Miskito." He added, however, that "another mixed group" that was "emulating English customs" came to be known as the Creoles (ibid., 44). The term *Creole* (borrowed from Jamaicans who were beginning to come to the Central American coast in search of wage labor) was used in the Mosquito Coast to distinguish Blacks who had been born in the region from Miskitos. In Latin America and the Caribbean as a whole during the colonial period, the term *Creole* distinguished native-born people of all races from European-born people.

With the evacuation of the English from the Atlantic coast at the end of the eighteenth century, the term became, according to Olien, an ideal "signifier" to differentiate the native-born descendants of slaves from the "foreign"-born Jamaicans. Olien therefore argued that the term "had essentially become a linguistic category in search of an ethnic group" (ibid., 45). In this sense, the existence of the "signifier" Creole brought about the existence of the "signified," the Creole group. Olien described this as a dialectical process in which changes in the political dynamics on the coast precipitated this symbolic change.

Olien implied that what distinguished Creoles from Miskitos was a set of entirely different customs, one oriented toward being Indian and the other toward being English. Olien glossed over the fact that identification with English symbols, be they language, commodities, or "customs," had long been associated with prestige among all groups on the Mosquito Coast. The Miskito king had since the seventeenth century used British symbols such as military uniforms, swords, and other British naval regalia as tools with which to legitimate their power to their subjects.[41] Since the administrative structure of the Kingdom was not rigidly formalized, many other regional Miskito leaders acted within the same symbolic universe, adopting British titles such as admiral, general, and commander. These regional leaders often had free reign within their region and often negotiated with foreign governments and investors autonomously. Hence, Helms has suggested that the British represented an "important new political resource" that was brought to bear on internal power struggles (Helms 1986, 510).

I argue that the Creole "ethnogenesis" did not result from Creoles choosing to adopt English customs instead of Indian customs. Rather, I contend that groups that later would be called Creoles increased in prominence as they were able to form stronger alliances with the British who began to return to the Coast in the 1820s. The importance of the Creoles in regional power structures increased in the next years, especially after 1848 when the gold rush in California brought the Mosquito Coast into global focus. Britain, the United States, France, and even

Spain had long hoped to build a canal that would connect the Atlantic and the Pacific. The port of Greytown, at the mouth of the San Juan River on the southern edge of the Mosquito Coast, was considered the ideal entrance point for a passage across the isthmus. Britain, therefore, moved the seat of the Miskito Kingdom south from Sandy Bay to Bluefields, which was much closer to Greytown. Later, the Mosquito government was moved to Greytown itself, far from the centers of Costeño population—particularly Miskitu-speaking Costeños whose concentration was greater in the northern Mosquito Coast. This tip in the scale of regional importance toward the south favored the inhabitants of Bluefields and Pearl Lagoon, where *Creoles* had recently become the dominant term of racial identification.

At this time the United States, following the Monroe Doctrine, attempted to dislodge Britain from the coast of Central America. As part of this effort, the United States engaged in an active propaganda campaign to discredit the Mosquito government. US diplomat and ethnologist E. G. Squier was a key player in the effort. He ridiculed the Mosquito king as a drunken "Negro" puppet of British imperialist interests. Central American governments, in turn, echoed these and similar assaults on the Mosquito king. This hostility towards the Mosquito government increased the pressure on the Mosquito government to present itself as a legitimately constituted Indian government. For this reason the Mosquito government began to officially note the racial make up of its members, in effect institutionalizing racial categories such as Indian and Creole. For example, the election protocol of 1865 systematically categorized the race of the electors as either "Creoles," "Indians," or "Half-Indians." This classification was introduced in the official protocol because "every document of the Reserve was under pressure to display a specifically Indian legitimacy" (Oertzen, Rossbach, and Wunderich 1990, 67). The practice of socio-racial identification in the region cannot simply be viewed as a matter of the assertion by individuals or groups of customs or culture, however defined, without placing adequate emphasis on the political (and indeed geopolitical) contexts in which these assertions were made.

Olien's approach to Creole ethnogenesis tends to regarded mutually exclusive cultural difference as the substance of regional ethnic diversity. However, it is worth noting that the Miskito Indian elite, some of whom were educated in Jamaica or Great Britain, regarded their knowledge of English, as well as their sustained relationships with the British and Germans, as civilizing influences that distinguished them from the "wild" Indians of the interior. They resisted incorporation into the Nicaraguan state on the grounds that their government was more progressive and civilized (to use their terminology) than that of Nicaragua. They self-consciously adopted British laws and customs, and regarded themselves as loyal subjects of the British Crown. To regard the substance of regional diversity as consisting of separate cultures is to misunderstand the status variables operating in the Mosquito Coast. The specific system of socio-racial identification in the Coast must be understood in part as the product of the conflict between the increased status afforded by English identification and the political advantages of Indian identification. The way different groups juggled these variables in response to the changing political situation in the Coast influenced the nature of the identification of its residents as Creoles or Miskito Indians.

In the nineteenth century, the matter of racial identification of the inhabitants of the Mosquito Coast consistently entered into geopolitical struggles between Britain, the United States, and Nicaragua over the status of the region (Bolland 1992). In 1860 the British, heavily pressured by the United States, decided to politically and militarily reduce their activity in the area. The trade in mahogany had declined, and London had become very dependent on American cotton. Already at war with Russia, Britain could not afford a war with the United States (Olien 1987, 281). In 1860 Britain signed the Treaty of Managua with the government of Nicaragua, in which Britain agreed to withdraw its Protectorate from the Mosquito territory. The Mosquito Reservation, as it later came to be known, was thus created. The respective governments of Britain and the United States signed the Treaty of Managua without the input of the residents of the Coast. The treaty stated: "The Mosquito Indians . . . shall enjoy the right of governing, according to their own customs, and according to any regulations which may from time to time be adopted by them, not inconsistent with the sovereign rights of the Republic of Nicaragua" (Olien 1987, 316).

The treaty provided the Indians the option to choose, if they so desired, "absolute incorporation into the Republic of Nicaragua." The Miskito king was hereafter to become the Mosquito "Chief," and became a salaried employee of the Nicaraguan government, earning $5,000 per year. Greytown, now Britain's major interest in the area, was declared a free port where no taxes could be levied on international trading vessels. Britain hoped to withdraw active presence in the region without losing its advantageous economic arrangements. The British counted on being able to continue to freely exploit the natural resources of the area under the new Mosquito government. The previous Mosquito governments, as we have seen, were by "custom" receptive to British economic interests.

In 1861 Hereditary Chief George Augustus Frederick called "a Public Convention of the Headman of the Mosquitos, and of the mixed population" in which a government was formed and a constitution drafted (Olien 1987, 318–326). Of the fifty-one delegates that arrived, the majority, thirty-nine, came from the southern parts of the Mosquito Coast: Bluefields, Rama Key, Corn Island and Pearl Lagoon. The delegates that came from these places undoubtedly represented the "mixed population."

Since the early 1800s Jamaicans of African descent had come to the Mosquito Coast, settling primarily in the southern communities of Bluefields, Pearl Lagoon, and Corn Island. These areas had been the primary site of English residence and therefore had been populated by the descendants of slaves brought by the English. These people came to refer to themselves and be referred to as Creoles. Before 1880 the Creole population was estimated to be around 2,000, far fewer than the Indian population of 10,000 to 15,000. Half of these Indians were known to the Miskito as Sumu, a general term they used to describe inland Indian groups (Vilas 1989, 32; Laird 1972, 21).

A "General Council" of forty-four men was formed, consisting of all of the southern delegates, excluding seven of the eleven delegates who were presumably identified as Miskito Indians. George Augustus Frederick was officially elected chief and president of the General Council, and Henry Patterson was elected vice president and John H. Hooker, secretary. Patterson was the Pearl Lagoon-born son of a Scottish trader and Miskito mother who, according to Oertzen, spoke Miskitu, "although, culturally, he undoubtedly was a Creole" (Oertzen, Rossbach, and Wunderich 1990, 68). Note Oertzen's apparent equation of racial difference with cultural difference.

Apart from the chief, the majority of rural village leaders (who were generally regarded at the time as Indians) were marginalized from taking part in the administration of what was nominally an Indian government. In the south, English-speaking leaders, who increasingly came to be identified as Creoles despite their extensive cultural and kin ties to the Miskito (as Patterson's case above illustrates), took the reigns of the Mosquito government. They represented a local upper class who maintained their status by monopolizing trade with the British and North American companies in the area. However, it is crucial not to mistake this situation (as many historians and anthropologists have done) for a situation in which a culturally distinct racial group exercises power over a subordinate racial group. Rather, a regional shift in power was occurring—a regional shift that undoubtedly had racialized implications.

According to the logic of the relevant treaties, the Miskito nation was to be an Indian nation, which functioned according to its "own customs" and "regulations." Inhabitants of the region created a government based on a model of the modern liberal state, derived explicitly from the British. The regulations that they enacted were distinctly British. This fact, given the highly Anglicized nature of the region, does not represent a contradiction. In 1874 Hereditary Chief William Henry Clarence, in an address to the "Chiefs and Headmen and Representatives of Mosquito," stated: "In turning to domestic affairs, my residence in Jamaica, and my acquaintance with its institutions, and trade, and people, show me much that is necessary among us, and I am sure the best means to consolidate and execute the laws, to educate and protect the people, to encourage and control honourable trade, to secure and increase the revenue, require speedy attention. . . . I wish to see Mosquito respected by other States, and recognized amongst the nations" (Oertzen, Rossbach, and Wunderich 1990, 338).

Some of the first acts of the Mosquito government were to declare the ports and rivers as open for duty-free commerce, levy a personal income tax, and enact legislation regulating the use of public lands. A public land office was created that was empowered to "let and lease the public lands, and to regulate the sale and disposition of its natural productions." Another law was enacted that forbid obtaining "from any Mosquito Indian, within the Reservation Tassa [rubber], or other property, by misrepresentation, false weight or measure, or by fraud or violence" (Oertzen, Rossbach, and Wunderich 1990, 332).

In a significant reversal by the late nineteenth century, both insiders in the Mosquito government, as well as English, North American, and Nicaraguan outsiders, no longer portrayed the Miskito Indians as a fierce and dominant people. Rather, village-oriented Miskito Indians were often portrayed as passive, vulnerable, and economically insecure in contrast to Creole and Miskito city dwellers. Anthropologist Nancie Gonzalez, who conducted fieldwork among the *Garifuna* of Honduras, noted that "the Miskito image changed from fierce warrior and entre-preneurial raider and trader during the seventeenth and eighteenth centuries to that of backward and harmless savage in the nineteenth cen-tury" (Gonzalez 1988, 32). For example, Chief William Henry Clarence, in a late nineteenth-century speech, expressed his outrage at the treat-ment of Indians by foreigners:

> I have to call your attention to the oppressions under which the poor Indians suffer from those who trade amongst them. I am of their blood, and feel it my duty in every way to vindicate the wrongs committed amongst them. Regulations should be made to free them at once from the slavery under which they labour. I can-not understand, that men who profess to be civilized should so far forget themselves as to dare to flog and otherwise ill-treat those poor inoffensive people. Gentlemen of the Council, I expect that you will assist me to protect the interests of the welfare of the people. (Oertzen, Rossbach, and Wunderich 1990, 167)

Apart from the law mentioned above, the government passed other laws aimed at decreasing the exploitation of Indians and "natives" (the term used to describe all residents of the Reservation). Natives often accrued large debts to foreign merchants. In 1883 the government abol-ished the debtor's prison and cancelled debts not paid by March 1884. It put debtors on the payroll at fifty cents a day, half of which went toward the service of their debt. A maximum interest rate was fixed, and household goods were declared free from confiscation. All of this was condemned by foreigners as a "fiasco" (Vilas 1989, 32).

Although the majority of Miskito Indians did not participate in the highest levels of government, this is not to say that the government was run only by Creoles for Creoles. The Mosquito government integrated all villages into the government through their village headmen. The Mosquito government constituted village headmen as local governmental authorities who served as arbiters for local disputes. Under the civil and penal laws of the Reservation, they became rural judges (Vilas 1989, 32).

Nicaragua viewed the existence of Mosquito as an affront to national sovereignty and planned to annex its territory. Nicaragua refused to comply with the stipulation of the Treaty of Managua wherein they were obligated to pay the king a stipend. This was bitterly resented by the Mosquito government. In 1877 Chief William, in a letter to the Earl of Derby, outlined four reasons why "The Mosquito Indians are not willing to enter into closer connection with Nicaragua":

> 1. The Reserve has maintained during the above-mentioned period a peaceful Government, whilst in Nicaragua there are continued revolution, wars . . . 2. There are established on the coast of the Reserve seven Mission stations, with schools, where the people are educated, and instructed to become good members of society, but nothing has been done by the Government of Nicaragua to improve the places or instruct the Mosquito people given over by the Treaty. 3. The religion, customs, manners, and laws of Nicaragua are in no way compatible. 4. The malicious conducts and disposition of transient Nicaraguan subjects in the Reserve. (Oertzen, Rossbach, and Wunderich 1990, 349)[42]

These reasons are particularly interesting when viewed in contrast to those of the modern Miskito nationalist leaders, who have emphasized their aboriginal rights and culture in their political struggles against the modern Nicaraguan state, which I will explore in chapter 6.

For Chief William the Nicaraguan nation was not a progressive nation; therefore, to become part of this nation would represent a step backward. Indeed, the Mosquito government approximated European governments of its time more than the Nicaraguan government. For example, the Mosquito government printed a national currency before Nicaragua had a national currency (Vilas 1989, 31). The chief's statement as to the incompatibility of cultures is particularly interesting. For him, this incompatibility was not the product of an opposition between Indian culture and Nicaraguan and Spanish culture. Rather, it stemmed from the incompatibility between English and Spanish culture: the religion of the Mosquito nation was Protestant not Catholic, and its customs, manners, and law were based on those of the English.

In 1894, using a border dispute with Honduras as a pretext, General Rigoberto Cabezas and a contingent of armed men occupied Bluefields, taking charge of the government buildings. They declared the sovereignty of the Nicaraguan state and unfurled the Nicaraguan flag. The Nicaraguan government began to levy import and export duties and to grant concessions for the exploitation of natural resources (US Department of State 1894, 85). Spanish was declared the national language, to be used in government and education (Vilas 1989, 40). Within days, warships from Great Britain and the United States were sent to the region to "protect the lives and property" of their respective citizens.

American corporate enterprises, which by then controlled 90 percent of the capital invested in the area (Hale 1987a, 42), protested the move by Nicaragua (Dozier 1985, 141–162). Beginning with the rubber boom in the 1860s, American capital had become very active in the Mosquito Coast region. Gold was extracted from mines in the interior, but by far the most important product was bananas. In 1893 Bluefields was the world's leading banana exporter (Olien 1983, 235). American companies had good relations with the Mosquito government and saw no advantage to the establishment of a new government. The British vice-consul explained the motives of this attitude well: "The whole foreign population has come to Bluefields simply and solely on the chance of making money rapidly, and they care nothing for Mosquitos or Nicaraguans as long as their trade in not interfered with" (Oertzen, Rossbach, and Wunderich 1990, 402). In light of this prevailing US sentiment, Nicaragua acted cautiously and deliberately in order not to incur the wrath of the American or British investors, who could in turn call upon their governments to protect them. The Zelaya government, which at this time was encouraging modernization through the investment of foreign capital, had no desire to scare away foreign business interests.

The outraged inhabitants of the Coast categorically refused to accept Nicaraguan domination, and the Mosquito government made appeals to both the British and American governments to come to their aid. In a petition to the queen, the reigning chief Robert Henry Clarence pleaded: "We will be in the hands of a Government and people who have not the slightest interest, sympathy, or good feeling for the inhabitants of the Mosquito Reservation; and as our manners, customs, religion, laws and language are not in accord, there can never be unity. . . . We most respectfully beg to lay before you Majesty . . . to take back your protection of the Mosquito nation and people, so that we may become a people of your Majesty's Empire" (Oertzen, Rossbach, and Wunderich 1990, 369).

This petition was signed by 1,800 natives, Indians and Creoles alike. Britain and the United States, however, refused to support the re-installation of the Mosquito government. In fact, on various occasions British and US forces were deployed to keep the peace between the Nicaraguan forces and rebellious Creole and Indian factions. In July of 1894 a rebellion succeeded in driving the occupying Nicaraguan army from Bluefields for three weeks. The rebels reinstated Chief Robert Henry Clarence and raised the Mosquito flag (ibid., 380). When the Nicaraguan forces returned, the chief and many "natives" fled aboard a British naval ship. The chief lived the rest of his life in exile in Jamaica.

The clamor of American and British merchants and local diplomats for intervention in favor of the Mosquito government was unheeded by their respective governments for a variety of reasons. The first and most important reason for the United States was that Nicaragua was a possible site for a canal (Dozier 1985, 154). The existence of a weak British-friendly Indian government could only complicate matters. By supporting Nicaragua they also achieved their long-held goal of ending all British influence in the area. Britain did not act on the "trace of responsibility for the personal safety of a feeble remnant of an inferior and deteriorating race who were once under her protection" (ibid., 154). Instead, it allowed the United States to dictate policy in the region, only ensuring the safety and transport, should they desire, of Jamaicans and Mosquitians. The inability to acquire support from foreign powers doomed the Mosquitian insurgency.

The Nicaraguan government subsequently convened a meeting with Costeño delegates. The agreement signed by Costeño delegates was aimed chiefly at clarifying the status of the ex-Mosquito Reservation and placed the region strictly under the sovereignty of Nicaragua. Nicaragua would henceforth exercise absolute political and administrative control over the Mosquito Coast. Although the armed resistance to the Nicaraguan annexation subsided, the protests from natives about the violation of the Treaty of Managua continued for many years to come. They protested Nicaraguan presence on the grounds that "our political rights have been destroyed," "schools have been closed, because it was impossible to teach only the Spanish language," and taxation on imports had increased greatly (ibid., 433–435). The Nicaraguan government, while not declaring void Mosquito government land grants, insisted on verifying all titles to land. Land whose ownership was not verified by the original title would revert to the Nicaraguan state.

Despite the changing valences of Indian and Creole self-identification, Costeños asserted political rights in an international context as members of a single nation that had aspirations to independent status vis-à-vis the Nicaraguan state. In the scholarship on this period, the categorical distinction between the Miskito and Creole has been emphasized unduly to the exclusion of other kinds of social differentiation that operated at the time. Charles Hale, for example, citing the fact self-proclaimed Creoles occupied the higher levels of the Mosquito Reservation, concluded that "Mosquitian nationalism, like the Mosquito government itself, was a Creole-dominated political construct" (Hale 1987a, 46). Creoles, according to Hale, affixed Miskito signatures to their post-reincorporation protests only in order to disguise the contradiction that the Mosquito government was legally supposed to be run by Indians. Hence, he hypothesized that the main reason that Mosquitian nationalism never prospered in the early twentieth century was because "Creoles must have found it distasteful for the legitimacy of their political claim to be dependent on ancestral links with members of a socially subordinate ethnic group" (ibid., 45).

Contrary to the implications of this formulation, the inhabitants of the Mosquito Coast cooperated in their attempts to protest the political dissolution of the Mosquito Reserve well into the twentieth century. In 1926, for example, representatives of the "Miskito Indian Patriotic League" sent a letter to the secretary of state of the United States (Oertzen, Rossbach, and Wunderich 1990, 454–456). The delegates, identified as both Creoles and Miskitos, protested the illegal presence of

the Nicaraguan government that had "forcibly misappropriated and mis-
used over Thirty million dollars of our Revenues and have also debarred
and denied us of every political and local right, thereby inflicting undue
universal punishment which has pauperized and crippled our race"
(ibid., 455). Their claim to nationhood was phrased in terms of their
race and of their "civilization" (what we now sometimes call "culture"),
both of which they presented as being incompatible with the Pacific
Nicaragua government. The signers of the document identified themselves as "Indians" and "natives of amalgamated Indian ancestry," and
claimed their "civilization" to be mostly "Anglo-Saxon" (ibid., 454):

> Having always been in constant intercourse with the nations of
> Anglo-Saxon civilization training and religion and being of a differ-
> ent race we cannot under existing conditions assimilate or amalga-
> mate with the people of Latin civilization. . . . We beg that for the
> future economic prosperity and universal welfare of our race that
> the consideration solicited be duly granted to this Petition, and the
> United States Government will in the name of Christian civilization,
> Progress and Humanity, hearken to the pleading voice of a helpless
> race, for relief from untold suffering and misery. (ibid., 455–456)

This alliance of Creoles and Miskitos, claiming unity of race and
civilization, should not be looked upon as anomalous. Costeños had
long known that if they were to enjoy any amount of control over their
affairs, it would be achieved politically only through the means of the
Mosquito government. As we have seen, Mosquito was both a racial and
tribal, and a geographical term. Regardless of whether they identified
themselves (or were identified by others) as Creoles or Miskitos,
Costeños throughout their history had participated with one another
and with the English in opposition to Spanish-speaking Spaniards and
Nicaraguans. They often worked side by side as wage laborers and practiced similar professions, such as fishing and turtling. They also inter-
married extensively and participated increasingly in the Moravian
missionary church, particularly after the "Great Awakening" of the
1880s.[43] The differentiation between Creole and Miskito, although
undeniably important at some level, was not the product of mutually
exclusive racial or cultural systems. Or, to put this in the appropriate

Barthian terms, the boundaries between these ethnic groups was not constituted by distinct cultural content (Barth 1969).

NICARAGUAN INDIAN POLICY: CULTURE AND COMMUNAL LAND

The official status of Mosquito remained cloudy until Great Britain and Nicaragua signed the Harrison-Altamirano treaty of 1905, abrogating the Treaty of Managua. The treaty obliged Nicaragua to make various concessions to Great Britain in favor of the inhabitants of the region because the Mosquito Indians were "at one time under the protection of Great Britain." Although the two-page text of the Harrison-Altamirano Treaty, a document intended to resolve the status of the former Mosquito Reserve, primarily used the term Mosquito Indians to refer to the region's inhabitants, it explicitly identified Mosquito Indians and Creoles as the inhabitants of the area whose legal status needed to be resolved.[44] In other words, as far as the Harrison-Altamirano treaty was concerned, the distinction between Creole and Miskito was not significant.

The treaty granted both Creoles and Miskitos (indeed as well as "the other inhabitants of the former Reserve") a special set of rights and obligations which would smooth their transition into full Nicaraguan citizenship (Oertzen, Rossbach, and Wunderich 1990, 437). As far as the recognition of these special rights within Nicaraguan law was concerned, the salient distinction was between inhabitants of the former Reserve (whose status needed to be clarified) and Pacific Nicaraguans to whom the Harrison-Altamirano Treaty did not apply. For example, take the following quotation from the text of the treaty: "The [Nicaraguan] Government will submit to the National Assembly a law exempting, for fifty years from the date of the ratification of this Treaty, all the Mosquito Indians and the Creoles born before the year 1894, from military service, and from all direct taxation of their persons, property, possessions, animals, and means of subsistence" (ibid., 436). The treaty did not grant any special rights and obligations to the Mosquito Indians that it did not also grant to Creoles. In this sense, Nicaraguan Indian policy applied to all natives of the Atlantic Coast—all Costeños.

In the transition from limited Nicaraguan sovereignty over the region to full Nicaraguan sovereignty, the question of land ownership and titles represented the most controversial issue. The terms of the Harrison-Altamirano Treaty provided that the Nicaraguan government should "allow the Indians to live in their villages . . . following their own customs, in so far as they are not opposed to the laws of the country and to public morality" (ibid.). The treaty also stipulated that "public pasture lands will be reserved for the use of the inhabitants in the neighborhood of each Indian village" (ibid.). Again, it is important to note that despite the fact that the wording of the treaty referred to the residents of the region using the blanket term Mosquito Indians, it clearly intended to cover both Indians and Creoles.

According to the terms of the treaty, Indians and Creoles were given two years to legalize under Nicaraguan law their claim to all the property that they had acquired before 1894 according to the laws of Mosquito (pre-1860) and the Mosquito Reserve (1860–1894). If they could not present such a legal title, they would be granted eight *manzanas* (roughly 2 acres) of land per family, the location of which would be chosen by the government. With regard to the lands that in the last ten years had been stripped from Creoles and Indians and given to foreigners and Pacific Nicaraguans, the government agreed to "indemnify them by the grant of suitable public lands of approximate value as near as possible to their present residence" (ibid.).

Over the next twenty years the situation of land titles was a matter of constant confusion and conflict. The Nicaraguan government, having achieved its goal of governing the extraction of resources from the Mosquito Coast, raised taxes and intensified concessions to foreign companies. Although the Atlantic coast contained only about 10 percent of the country's population, it contributed 40 percent of the duties collected by the government (Dozier 1985, 161). The government, however, neglected to spend these revenues on maintenance of government offices and infrastructure, which allowed foreign companies to act as the de facto government. Lumber and banana companies built railroads strictly for resource extraction with no intention of creating a sustainable system of regional transportation, and built other forms of temporary infrastructure aimed at cost-efficient plunder. Foreign companies were granted monopolies on resources and transportation, thus eliminating competition and putting independent planters at the mercy of the company (ibid., 158).[45]

CHAPTER 3

From Bilwi to Puerto Cabezas

MESTIZO NATIONALISM IN THE AGE OF AGRO-INDUSTRY

It is greatly to be hoped that the scholars of Nicaragua, who have rightly preserved in some form the native Indian names of the Western part of the country, will adopt the native names of Eastern Nicaragua also, undisguised and undisfigured, as part of the national heritage; and beyond all doubt, the unreserved recognition of these names would help to cement the unity of the nation. Where native Indian names exist, they should never be superseded by either Spanish or English nomenclature. Let us have done with Rio Grande and Great River both alike, and say only Awaltara, or better still Awoltara; let us abolish alike Bragman's Bluff and Puerto Cabezas and say only Bilwi. Let us revive the old name of Auya for Little Sandy Bay; of Akiwita for Wounta Haulover, and Iniwas or Iniwaska for Wawa Saw Mill, where for 2 decades the old sawmill has ceased to exist.

—George Heath

IN THE ABOVE QUOTATION, North American linguist George Heath calls on Nicaraguan scholars to perform the ideological work of promoting the use of Mosquito Coast indigeneity, in this case the use of Indian place names, for the purpose of cementing Nicaraguan nationalism on a coast-to-coast basis (Heath 1927, 88). Throughout Latin America, national governments have historically promoted the use of indigenous toponyms as a way of inscribing a vision of national identity that would incorporate both Indian and Spanish imagery in the construction of Euro-American Mestizo nationalism. In the case of eastern Nicaragua the matter was made more complicated and contentious by virtue of the fact that the region's natives, and its toponyms, were deeply influenced by their interaction with the English-speaking Caribbean world. This made their indigeneity suspect for the purposes of the creation of Nicaraguan Mestizo nationalism. Such was the case for tiny Bilwi, which, despite Heath's urging, continues to be known officially as Puerto Cabezas.

At the turn of the century, Bilwi, as Puerto Cabezas is called in Miskitu, represented one of a long string of small fishing villages that extended up and down the Mosquito Coast. Starting in 1921 a consortium of New Orleans companies, one of which would soon become the Standard Fruit Company, rapidly began to establish a multimillion-dollar banana and lumber operation complete with a lumber mill, a pier, port facilities, and a railroad. Soon the village of Bilwi, renamed Puerto Cabezas by the Nicaraguan government, experienced a stage of momentous growth and transformation that was not foreshadowed by its bucolic past. Over the next ten years it was briefly made the provisional capital of Nicaragua. It was militarily occupied by the US Marines—twice. It even saw the opening of a British consular office, a US consular office, and the regional headquarters of a missionary church. In the meantime the Bragman's Bluff Lumber Company became the largest employer in all of Nicaragua, and the town grew in size from a population of under 100 (mostly native Costeños) to over 5,000 (including North Americans, West Indians, Pacific Nicaraguans, and Costeños from other parts of the Mosquito Coast) (Karnes 1978, 115).[1]

The tumultuous events of the interwar years of the twentieth century in Puerto Cabezas brought into focus, primarily for two reasons, the profound political implications of the Blackness and Indianess of Costeños as perceived by Pacific Nicaraguans, who for the first time were establishing the direct control of the region by the Nicaraguan state. The first reason was that the lumber and banana companies brought in many Black workers from the West Indies and the US South, who were perceived by the agents of the Nicaraguan state as a foreign and alien threat to the Nicaraguan nation-building process, which was predicated on Mestizo nationalism. The influx of Black workers, many of whom possessed skills that put them at a rank above Nicaraguan and

Costeño workers, served to reinforce and transform the Creole category. The second reason was that the operations of North American companies required control over large tracts of land. This increased demand in a region where land pressure was minimal and land tenure arrangements were poorly formalized inevitably led to land disputes between and among communities that held title to the land as Indians.

In this chapter I analyze the contexts in which appeals to cultural and racial difference were made by inhabitants of Puerto Cabezas in their efforts to retain control over the city in the face of the massive assault by US companies and the Nicaraguan state. I also analyze the views of Pacific Nicaraguans and North Americans with regard to the race and culture of Costeños that ultimately conditioned their responses to the conflicts in the region.

As a result of the historical separation between eastern and western Nicaragua, Costeños entered into the twentieth century possessing particular attitudes and loyalties towards Spain, England, Nicaragua, and the United States; the Spanish language and the English language; and Spanish and Nicaraguan culture, and Anglo-American culture. In general, Costeños associated progress and civilization with English and North American customs and institutions, and regarded Central American nations as unstable, antagonistic, and in many ways inferior. Contrarily, Pacific Nicaraguans regarded the inhabitants and institutions of the Atlantic Coast as backward culturally, economically, and racially. This ideological rivalry represents a key element of the context in which the controversies that arose from the penetration of powerful North American and Nicaraguan actors in the city must be understood.

In the first section of this chapter, I chronicle the struggle over land that occurred between the Nicaraguan government, the Standard Fruit Company, and the communities of Karatá and Bilwi. The leaders of Bilwi faced a peculiar dilemma as they asserted their rights as Indians to negotiate with foreign companies on the matter of land use and ownership to a Nicaraguan government that was ideologically hostile to such demands. Costeños as cosmopolitans were ideologically predisposed to welcome the connection to the Anglo-Caribbean world that the companies represented, but in order to deal with these companies most effectively, they needed to do so, to some degree, as Indians. For the Nicaraguan state, the all-powerful role of the US companies was an affront to Nicaraguan nationalism that needed to be opposed by a strong, sovereign, and unified Nicaraguan state—not Miskito Indians. The most extreme manifestation of Nicaraguan nationalist opposition to the US companies was renegade Liberal leader Augusto Sandino's attack on company installations and personnel in 1931.

In this chapter I pay particular attention to the issue of Pacific Nicaraguan perceptions towards Costeños and the Mosquito Coast. Given that at the turn of the century, Pacific Nicaraguans were for the first time exercising governmental authority in the Atlantic Coast, creating a power differential between Costeños and Pacific Nicaraguan authorities, the perceptions regarding each other held by Costeños and Pacific Nicaraguans became particularly charged. I construct a critical reading of the Nicaraguan national project in the Mosquito Coast by analyzing the statements and decisions of an important Nicaraguan official who played a crucial role in the establishment of Nicaraguan governmental authority in the new port city of Puerto Cabezas. Continuing with this issue of Pacific Nicaraguan ideology vis-à-vis the Atlantic Coast, I focus on another major player in the history of Puerto Cabezas: the Nicaraguan revolutionary leader Augusto Cesar Sandino, who despite his revolutionary credentials manifested a distinctly colonialist approach to the Mosquito Coast's Costeños.

Bragman's Bluff:
A Nicely Situated Place

In Managua on January 28, 1921, Leroy T. Miles, a US citizen representing the Salmen Brick and Lumber Company and the Vacarro Bros. Inc. of New Orleans, signed an agreement with the Nicaraguan government that would dramatically change the course of history in the distant Mosquito Coast settlement of Bilwi. At the turn of the twentieth century, Bilwi, a coastal village ten miles north of the Wawa River and sixty miles south of the mouth of the Coco River, was even on regional standards an unimportant village. It did not play a significant role as a port in the coastal export-oriented economy, which at the turn of the century was based primarily on lumber. In the northern sector, lumber and other natural resources were extracted by way of the three major rivers (Prinzapolka, Wawa, and Coco), each of which had ports on or around their mouths. Cape Gracias a Dios, at the mouth of the Coco

River, had long been the major port of the northern Mosquito Coast, while other villages sprang up along these rivers to meet the needs of the extractive industries.[2]

Although the relatively poor soils around Bilwi historically had prevented it from sustaining a larger indigenous population, Bilwi's strategic position on the ridge of the only significant promontory on the northern Mosquito Coast had long attracted English traders to the place, which they named "Bragman's Bluff" (De Kalb 1893, 249).[3] The earliest mention of permanent habitation of the place appeared in the account of M.W., an English pirate who visited the Mosquito Coast at the end of the seventeenth century. M.W. claimed that Thomas Arkes and John Thomas, two English buccaneers who were refugees from a historic English raiding party that sacked Nueva Segovia in 1674, lived a "pagan" life there among forty "savage" Indians, some of whom served them as slaves and prostitutes (Romero Vargas 1995, 274; Naylor 1989, 40).

Before the British evacuation of 1787, Bragman's Bluff represented one of the eight permanent English settlements in the region, along with Black River, Cape Gracias a Dios, Sandy Bay, Walpa Sixa, Great River, Pearl Lagoon, and Bluefields. Out of a total of fewer than five hundred permanent English settlers in the entire region, only Sandy Bay had fewer English residents than Bragman's Bluff, which had six (Potthast 1988, 231). Although the English settlement at Bragman's Bluff undoubtedly attracted native people of the region (some of whom stayed involuntarily as one of seventy Black and Indian slaves), the largest Costeño populations inhabited other villages, the closest and most important of which, Twappi, was located three miles to the north and was the home of the Mosquito governor.

After the British evacuation of the region, Bragman's Bluff appears to have been continuously occupied until the present. In the nineteenth century, historical sources began to identify an Indian village at the site called "Bilwi."[4] As previously noted, in the nineteenth century the racial identification of Costeños began to bifurcate towards either end of a Black-Indian ideological spectrum. Southern villages, with their "capital" at Bluefields, increasingly came to be identified as Creole. Northern villages, which in the past had often been identified with mixed Black/Indian peoples known, among other things, as Zambos

Mosquitos, came to be regarded generally as Indian. Such was the case for Bilwi, a northern village.[5]

In 1849 the British vice-consul mentioned Bilwi as one of the stops that he, along with the reigning Mosquito king, George Augustus Frederick, made on their rounds of the Mosquito Kingdom (Oertzen, Rossbach, and Wunderich 1990, 127). Two German Moravian missionaries on a reconnaissance trip in May of 1859 wrote: "At 11 O'clock we arrived at Billwi, a nicely situated place of only about 9 houses, and disembarked. We then paid a short visit to the inhabitants and by 3 O'clock we had thrown the anchor close to the village of Twappi" (ibid., 145). Bilwi appeared in missionary and other reports later in the century, but it was always regarded as a middle-sized or small-sized Indian village (ibid., 172, 176, 239). Writing in 1896, British Vice-Consul Herbert Harrison placed Bilwi in a regional perspective: "The Wawa River flows into the north of the Karata Lagoon, and there are many villages and settlements in this district, including Yulu, with upwards of 500 Indians, Klilna, Twappi, Krukira, with over 100 Indians each, and the smaller settlements of Shoubia, Bilwi and Auyla Pini" (ibid., 425).

Despite its small size, representatives from Bilwi did appear at the major late-nineteenth-century meetings between the government of Nicaragua and the Atlantic Coast villages that were at this time being affected by the gradual establishment of Nicaraguan sovereignty in the region. This Nicaraguan encroachment intensified in 1860 with the creation of the "Mosquito Reserve" and was punctuated by the 1894 invasion of the region by Nicaraguan troops. This invasion put an end to the English-supported independence of the Mosquito Coast vis-à-vis the Nicaraguan state and the preceding Spanish colonial government. After 1894 leaders from Bilwi consistently asserted their rights to obtain legal titles to communal lands and signed various petitions protesting their exploitation at the hands of the Nicaraguan government.

During the nineteenth century, as the institutions of the Mosquito government became increasingly regularized, it commonly staged "Public Conventions of the Headmen of the Mosquitos." Native "headmen" traveled from all over the coast to Bluefields to represent their communities and give legitimacy and the appearance of popular support to the decisions of the Mosquito government. At the death of "Hereditary Chief" George William Albert Hendy in 1888, the Mosquito Municipal

Authority called such a convention to elect a successor.[6] Headmen from twenty-two Costeño communities attended, including a representative from "Bilway" named "Allick" (Oertzen, Rossbach, and Wunderich 1990, 354).[7] In 1891 Bilwi sent Andrew and Alexander as representatives to the election of Robert Henry Clarence, the last Mosquito chief (ibid., 357). At the controversial 1894 Mosquito Convention, in which the government of Nicaragua officially annexed the country of Mosquito, Andrew Wita was present as "Alcalde and Delegate," and Pabas and Pax also attended as "Delegates" (ibid., 393).[8]

After the so-called Reincorporation of 1894, leaders from Bilwi consistently asserted their right to obtain legal titles to communal lands and signed various petitions protesting their exploitation at the hands of the Nicaraguan government. Before 1894 individual Costeño villages had never been compelled to obtain legal title to lands, but the encroachment of the Nicaraguan government spurred them to attempt to formalize their control over the lands that they had historically occupied and used. Britain, whose interests happened to coincide with those of the people of Mosquito, exerted its influence on the behalf of Costeños, both Indians and Creoles, who were struggling to insure that the Nicaraguan government would respect their land rights.

The 1905 Harrison-Altamirano Treaty between Great Britain and Nicaragua guaranteed the right of Indians and Creoles of the former country of Mosquito to acquire and possess title to private and communal lands. Each family would have the right to obtain eight acres of land, and each Indian "community" would acquire titles to "public pasture lands." The stipulations of this treaty with regard to land were not formally put into practice until 1915. In that year the Nicaraguan government created a special "*Comisión Tituladora*" (Land Titles Commission) to measure Costeño communal lands (Jenkins Molieri 1986, 288). Many Costeño communities succeeded in receiving land titles through this commission, although many others did not. They cited corruption and negligence on the part of Nicaraguan officials and the prohibitive expenses involved in surveying land. Costeño leaders repeatedly expressed their grievances to both the British and US governments (US Department of State Records 817.52/16, 17).

While many individual Miskito communities all over the Mosquitia scrambled to survey and register lands, some of northern Miskito Indian communities banded together to make a single land claim. The Wawa River District communities of Kambla, Twappi, Krukira, Yulu Tingni, Bum Sirpi, Auyapihni, Sisín, Kuakuil, Sangni Laya, and Bilwi (which together for the purposes of land titles were called the "*Diez Comunidades*," or Ten Communities) petitioned the Land Titles Commission for 10,000 acres of agricultural land and 10,000 acres of pasture land. The agricultural land was to be located along both banks of the Wawa River from Tabalaya to Walpatara and Snakie to Arrawas.

In 1916 the Land Titles Commissions granted the Ten Communities titles to all 10,000 acres of pasture land claimed, while giving titles to only 1,080 acres of agricultural land (US Department of State Records 817.52/35). In the years from 1915 to 1923 the Nicaraguan government made three attempts to survey and title the remaining land. Initially a French surveyor living in Bluefields undertook the task, but due to lack of funds from the government, he did not continue. A North American engineer also received the assignment with the same results. Finally, in the early 1920s, a Nicaraguan civil engineer, George Sequeira, attempted to complete the survey. By this time, however, the land in question, which the Nicaraguan government valued little, came under the covetous gaze of a party much more powerful than the Ten Communities villages. This party was Leroy T. Miles and his New Orleans backers, who, according to the US consul in Bluefields, "interposed and Sequeira returned without doing anything" (US Department of State Records 817.52/17; see also 817.52/35).

The contract that Miles signed with the Nicaraguan government in 1921 authorized broad tax exemptions and granted a concession of 20,000 hectares of "national lands" at $2 per hectare. While the enterprise initially focused on lumbering, the investors also hoped that banana production could parallel lumber extraction and take advantage of the same infrastructure, such as railroads and port facilities. Indeed, the Bragman's Bluff Lumber Company, the name given to the company, was founded with New Orleans capital from both a lumber company (Salmen Brick and Lumber Company) and a fruit company (Vacarro Bros. Inc.). Vacarro Bros. Inc. would later (1926) become the Standard Fruit Company of New Orleans (Karnes 1978, 106–142).[9]

Due to this dual interest, Miles and his associates desired lands both on the banks of the Wawa River, where the fertile land is ideal for banana plantations, and the pine savannas of the interior. The contract between Miles and the Nicaraguan government stated: "By virtue of the Powers contained in the Agriculture law the Government will order suspended any denouncement of land which may have been made or may be made in the region that the contractor [Miles] desires which is that region situated north of the Wawa River, five to twenty miles from the coast and surrounded by National lands except on the east, where there are lands belonging to the Miskitos" (US Department of State Records 817.6172/1). Thus the Nicaraguan government granted Miles almost unlimited discretion in selecting lands, some of which the government and Miles knew were used, inhabited, and in the process of being legally claimed by various Miskito communities. It is not surprising to discover that this situation soon began to generate friction between the company and the Ten Communities.

Given that the special rights to land that Costeño communities enjoyed had resulted from a treaty between Great Britain and Nicaragua, Costeño leaders quite logically appealed to the British government for their defense. In a letter signed in Twappi and dated August 20, 1923, the "syndices" of six out of the "ten communities" (a representative from Bilwi did not sign the letter) wrote to the British vice-consul in Bluefields:[10]

> Under the Harrison Altamirano Treaty, we the Indians of Twappi, Sis Sin, Kukera, Aupenie, Boom, Licos, were granted certain lands from Tublaya to Walpatara and from Snaki to Arrowas. Gomez and Lyman came up and measured these lands and we were given titles which was supposed to cover these lands.
>
> We understand the Mr. Miles is taking these same lands that were given to us and we would ask your good offices in protecting our rights. At the time, also the Government was supposed to measure these lands at their expense, though now they want us to pay for the same measurement, or the checking up of the original measurement.
>
> We are poor people and have not enough means to pay this additional expense and also to fight Mr. Miles from taking up our lands, and hope that you in your official capacity will be able to give us the protection of these lands that were given to us in the treaty signed by the English and Nic. Government.

We thank you for the efforts, we know you will take in our
behalf. (US Department of State Records 817.52/35)

The British government eventually took action on their behalf, rec-
ommending to both the United States and Nicaragua that a special
international tribunal be formed to insure that the international agree-
ments regarding the Miskito Indians and Creoles would be respected.
The United States consul and the Nicaraguan government agreed to sit
on such a tribunal (ibid.).

The leaders of the Ten Communities, cognizant of their legal
predicament, defended their land claims within a national and international political and legal order. They hired a lawyer, Charles Casanova,
to argue their case in Bluefields.[11] Casanova, who in his own words represented "several indians and indian communities of this coast," wrote
the following to the British consul in Bluefields in a letter dated August
17, 1923:

> I am almost sure that if at least these indian communities were gov-
> erned by their own chiefs who understand their dialect and who are
> one with them in religion and custom, a provision which is amply
> made in the Treaty, we should have a more law abiding people, and
> above all, the shameful case of bloodshed and other outrages that
> from time to time occur on the Wanks River especially, would be
> avoided. It is simply a repetition of history to exact that the transi-
> tion of people from one people to another who are different in
> every respect, should be done gradually and not at rapid strides as is
> our case, because the result is a degenerated and criminal hord [sic]
> of lawless citizens on this Coast. Trusting that these few hints will
> not pass unheeded by His Britannic Majesty's Consul Resident, who
> is the only one capable of saving the Indians and coloured people of
> this Coast from utter ruin. (US Department of State Records
> 817.52/16)

This passage is typical of turn-of-the-century appeals that
Mosquitians made to the British and the United States in which they
emphasized how incorporation into Nicaragua would represent a step
backward from more to less civilized (Pineda 1991). Mosquitians continued to condemn the "transition" from English hands to Nicaraguans

hands as a transition from order and progress to "lawlessness" and ruin. For the inhabitants of Bilwi and other communities in the northern Mosquito Coast, the fact that the Nicaraguan government granted large concessions of land to foreign companies, showing little regard for native land claims, provided a glaring example of this lawlessness.

In June of 1924 the multi-lateral commission formed to arbitrate the dispute recommended that "the Government of Nicaragua grant the request of the Indians of Crukira, Twappy, Bilway and other villages within the jurisdiction of the Wawa River" (US Department of State Records 817.52/35). The US consulate had previously warned Miles and his associates that the land they desired should not conflict with the land claimed by the Indians (US Department of State Records 817.52/17).

Miles, in a letter addressed to the US chargé d'affaires on September 1, 1923, denied any wrongdoing on several grounds. First, he claimed that the Indians of the Wawa district "had made no protest to the denouncement when I made it and which was advertised and posted, and notice thereof was given by the Comandante of the district according to law, nor did they make any protest to the surveyor when he went to make the survey." Second, he speculated that the Indians already possessed a great deal more land than what the treaty intended them to have. Third, he objected that "there are thousands of hectares to which they already have title that have never been cultivated or used for any purpose." These arguments, with their defensive and conjectural tone, were secondary in comparison to the irrefutable logic of his final argument in the final paragraph:

> I am writing this letter for the purpose of laying before you the true situation. I have built a wharf at Bragman Bluff 1188 ft. long with sixteen ft. of water at low tide and nineteen ft. at high tide, a saw mill with a capacity of forty thousand feet daily, a planing mill operated by electricity, and I am now constructing something like fifty miles of railroad. I have so far spent nearly four hundred thousand dollars and will spend that much more within the next four months. Respectfully, Leroy T. Miles. (US Department of State Records 817.52/17)

It is not surprising to find that the ultimate authority in this dispute was not the US, British, or Nicaraguan governments, and much less the

Ten Communities. Rather, it was the ever-expanding dollar. As Miles's Bragman's Bluff Lumber Company continued to grow and transform the landscape of the northern Mosquitia from forgotten backwater to major export zone, the prospect for Nicaraguan recognition of Costeño lands greatly diminished. The lands were converted by the power of the dollar into political fait accompli, reified and effectively alienated in Pacific Coast eyes from the claims of their inhabitants.

The foreign policy of the US government in the Caribbean in the early part of the twentieth century was characterized as "dollar diplomacy," in which the expansion of US companies into the region was actively defended and propagated by the State Department and the military. This undoubtedly was true for Nicaragua—a country that was occupied by the Marines on a regular basis from 1907 to 1933. Nevertheless, the US government and US companies did not always act as a single actor with a clearly defined project. The mild State Department support of Costeño land claims, claims that conflicted with those of the Bragman's Bluff Lumber Company, provided an example of this disparity of interest between the US government and US companies. In fact, the State Department in 1928 objected to the terms of the renewed contract between Nicaragua and Bragman's Bluff Lumber Company on the grounds that the tax exemptions and land concessions were too broad and could lead to unrest. The State Department, however, never followed through on its threat to withdraw its support and protection of the company (US Department of State Records 817.52/4, 5, 6). On the contrary it would in the next decade repeatedly intervene militarily in Puerto Cabezas "to protect American lives and property."

Undaunted by the land controversy, and the protests and admonitions it generated, Bragman's Bluff Lumber Company rapidly grew. In 1923 the company, which since 1921 had been exporting lumber, began to harvest and export bananas and built many miles of railroad (US Department of State Records 817.6172/5). It controlled 33,000 hectares of land and would soon control 50,000 more hectares. The employment opportunities in the company also attracted laborers from throughout Nicaragua. The company contracted White skilled laborers from the United States and Italy, while Black skilled and "unskilled" laborers arrived from the United States and the West Indies.[12] West Indians primarily arrived directly or indirectly by way of the canal zone (Karnes

1978, 113). Race-related disturbances immediately arose as Nicaraguans protested the use of foreign labor.

Within a few years of its creation, Bragman's Bluff Lumber Company became the largest employer and investor in all of Nicaragua. William Heard, the US consul in Bluefields, summarized the extent of the company's growth in March of 1924:

> The developments so far at Bragman Bluff consists of a railway wharf 1200 feet long, the erection of a sawmill capable of sawing 25 M. feet of lumber daily and a planing mill with two planers which when equipped with electric motors will plane 45 M. feet of lumber daily. The company has erected two large hotels, each having 20 rooms, for the use of their employees. They have also built a large two story office building, a commissary, a material store house, residences for a doctor and assistant manager, about ten buildings for laborers as well as other small buildings. A steel water tank with a capacity of 50,000 gallons has recently been completed, and work is now progressing on a well which is to furnish 500 gallons of water per minute. About ten days ago this well had been drilled 300 feet. . . . In addition to the saw mill above described, there are three portable mills located along the line of the railway and in the heaviest timbered tracts. Each of these mills is capable of sawing 10 M feet daily. It has been estimated that the timber land at present under lease contains 17,000,000 feet of excellent pine. (US Department of State Records 817.6172/6)

Much of this so-called timberland, of course, was used and inhabited by Costeños, who argued that their claim to these lands devolved from their status as Indian villages protected under the Harrison-Altamirano Treaty of 1905. The subsequent US consul in Bluefields, A. J. McConnico, who was less sympathetic to Miskito land claims than his predecessor, supported the lumber company's position, referring to the Wawa District villagers as "Indian squatters" (US Department of State Records 817.504/22). Thus, the once unconquerable inhabitants of Mosquito, the native kings of the colonial Central American Coast and the scourge of the Spanish Empire, found themselves pitted against an enemy that they could not defeat—an enemy that regarded them as "squatters" on lands that they had for generations occupied.

In light of the explosion of investment and agro-industrial development in the region, the Nicaraguan government chose to reevaluate its
policy of legally recognizing Indian community lands. On an ideological level this policy had, since its inception, clashed with the widespread
conviction in Nicaragua, and indeed throughout the Americas, that the
Indian populations were socially and culturally backward and therefore
represented an obstacle to the progress of the modern nation state.
Throughout the colonial period in Latin America, the Spanish colonial
government recognized (and often actively organized) communal land
and labor arrangements as a strategy to harness and control Indian populations. Spanish colonial governments quite consciously provided legal
and administrative structures (known in Mexico, for example, as *la
república de los indios*) that fostered the formation of corporate Indian
communities that possessed a special, albeit decidedly disadvantageous,
relationship with the Spanish authorities.

With the onset of independent republican governments and the
growth of an export-oriented national economy based on wage labor
and private property, the modernizing liberal elite often came to view
these colonial arrangements as obsolete and detrimental to national
growth. Latin American governments therefore attempted to dismantle
Indian communities in order to release their land and labor into growing national and international markets. In the Pacific region at the turn
of the century, Nicaraguan Liberals and the burgeoning coffee-growing
elite had finally won the long battle against the Indian communities and
their Conservative party patrons to dispossess the last highland Indian
groups that still retained communal landholdings (Gould 1993a, 428).
Within this context the Nicaraguan government attempted to discredit
Indian land claims in the Atlantic Coast because it perceived these as an
obstacle both to economic progress and the development of Nicaraguan
nationalism.

SPANISH IDEOLOGIES OF RACE, LANGUAGE, CULTURE, AND PROGRESS

In 1925 the national government sent a commission to resolve the
land and labor disputes in the region. The chief of the commission, Doctor Frutos Ruiz y Ruiz, arrived in August and heard the complaints of
the *síndicos* of Bilwi, Krukira, and Sisín. Ruiz's general attitude toward

the Atlantic Coast and its inhabitants, as manifested in his report to the national government (Ruiz y Ruiz 1927), is particularly instructive in understanding his ultimate decision in the conflict. His writings lucidly portray the deeply rooted primitivism manifested by Pacific Nicaraguans with regard to the Atlantic Coast and its Costeño inhabitants.

In contrast to the Costeños, who regarded their historical connection with the Anglo-Caribbean as positive and "civilizing," and took pride in their ability to remain outside of the sphere of Spanish (and later Nicaraguan) control, Ruiz considered that the backwardness and poverty of the region resulted directly from, insofar as history was concerned, the English interference in the colonial project of the Spanish.[13] He wrote nostalgically:

> One still regards with distaste the small Costeño villages, where there is nothing more than signs of death. The english protection and the moravian propaganda have not left the smallest trace of culture in the Mosquito Coast. This is why that when one passes the "Fortress", the old spanish fort that defended the hispanic-nicaraguan civilization against piracy which had its hideaway in the bay of Bluefields, one's spirit jumps to life and exultant one cries in admiration of this glorious monument, a legacy from Spain to the nicaraguan colony.[14] (ibid., 154)

Ruiz regarded the Atlantic Coast as an underpopulated region where "piracy impeded the development of Spanish culture" (ibid., 182).[15] The absence of this Spanish culture, according to Ruiz, represented a threat to Nicaraguan unity and an obstacle to the progress of the region. Ruiz therefore called for the national government to "attract settlers to these deserted lands where the spirit of nicaraguan patriotism barely clings to life" (ibid., 181). He explicitly conceived of the incorporation of the region into national life as a colonial project. He wrote: "Assuming that we do not want barbarity to triumph, we should agree that hispanic-nicaraguan civilization should provide an example and fulfill the legacy of the Spanish Empire, colonizing the Coast, invading the Coast, populating the Coast with hispanic-nicaraguan blood, language, customs and culture" (ibid., 115).

For Ruiz, not only did the Atlantic Coast with its English culture and indigenous languages suffer from the absence of the appropriate

Spanish language and culture, but it also lacked suitable levels of "Hispanic-Nicaraguan" blood. For Ruiz, the importance of such blood resided not only in its capacity to lighten the skin of Costeños, but also in its ability to uplift the level of "civilization" in the region.[16]

It is interesting to note that while Ruiz decried the presence of English "customs" and "culture," he did not retroactively extol the contribution of the white English "blood" that presumably accompanied this dispersal of English customs. His appeal to the whitening influence of Hispanic-Nicaraguan blood is particularly interesting in light of the fact that from a purely demographic standpoint the biological impact of the Spaniards in the Pacific Coast was not significantly greater than that of the English in the Atlantic Coast; in other words, the Spanish migration to Pacific Nicaragua was not proportionally much greater than the English migration to the Mosquito Coast.

At the end of the colonial period the racial system of Pacific Nicaragua, although recognizing small white (*blanco*) and Indian minorities, was dominated by the category of the Mestizo, a White-Indian mixed category. On the other hand, the Atlantic Coast system recognized Indians and Creoles (both explicitly non-white terms) but did not possess a category that was defined as even partially white. Once more, in the absence of Englishmen in the Mosquito Coast (and a declining presence in the English colonies such as Belize and Jamaica), Afro-Caribbean peoples had become the bearers, in the minds of Pacific Nicaraguans and indeed West Indians themselves, of English culture. This created an ideological environment in which Nicaraguan nationalization of the area was favorable because "English culture" traveled with "Black blood" but "Spanish culture" traveled with Mestizo blood, which after all was, by definition, part white.

Ruiz and his superiors in the Nicaraguan government were deeply troubled by two features of Mosquito Coast society: (1) the influx of Black workers from the West Indies and the United States, and (2) the preexisting abundance of Indians. The fact that a US company was transforming Bilwi into a major export zone and a regular stop along Caribbean trade routes made the completion of this civilizing project urgent. Ruiz and Nicaraguans like him viewed the presence of Blacks and Indians on the Atlantic Coast as a blemish on the national racial landscape and an obstacle to national progress, in much the same way that they viewed the role of the dark-skinned Spanish monoglot campesinos and Mestizos that formed the great majority of the Nicaraguan population in the Pacific. Pacific Nicaragua at the time was, and continues to be, a skin-color-conscious society in which light skin and European features are favored over dark skin and indigenous features. The fact that the Pacific Indians had supposedly abandoned their indigenous languages and customs and allowed themselves to be incorporated into a Hispanic national culture represented a great step forward from the perspective of the Nicaraguan State.[17]

According to the national project of the Nicaraguan state, progress was to be achieved through the attainment of greater civilization. This civilizing project, however, was conceived of in racial terms: to become more civilized was to become more like the whites, who inherited their civilization from the Spanish. Therefore the incorporation of other races into the polity represented a step backwards. Ruiz wrote:

> The real Coast, the Mosquitia today is only interesting as an ethnological curiosity; the different races of pure indians should be studied before their impending disappearance. These indians have not made the slightest contribution to civilization, and given that there are so few of them, only a few thousand, they are utterly without value. The few blacks, which seem greater in number because it is an under populated country, do not even provide this curiosity because they don't even have their own language and they are only valued as beasts of burden for foreign companies, which prefer them over the rest of nicaraguans. (Ruiz y Ruiz 1927, v)

Here Ruiz added the concept of "value" to the equation between blood and level of civilization. Ruiz's distinction between Indians and Blacks with regard to their respective possession of culture revealed a great deal regarding his underlying assumptions about the relationship between race and culture. Namely, Indians have culture, albeit primitive, and Blacks (in the Americas) do not; rather, they are the imperfect bearers of English tradition.

In the colonial period a similar assumption on the part of the Spanish and Nicaraguan governments provided incentive for Zambo residents of the Mosquito Coast, as well as their British patrons, to define themselves as Indians rather than Blacks in order to legitimize their right to local rule. Ruiz granted that Indians had a culture (an "ethnological curiosity"); however, he refused to bestow the same dubious recognition on Blacks. From Ruiz's perspective, neither of the two races contributed to the national civilization, but Blacks were considered to have less to offer because they could not claim to have their own culture. This fact made them quintessential outsiders, in contrast to the Nicaraguan Indian insiders—albeit primitive ones. For this reason Blacks did not have a legitimate claim to a share of the Nicaraguan polity. Blacks, who from the perspective of Pacific Nicaraguans were regarded as English-speaking migrant sojourners from the English Caribbean, were considered too English (albeit in a degraded way) and therefore, unlike the Miskito, could not be considered primitive culture-bearing subjects.

In the context of Ruiz's formulation, consider the fact that although today Pacific Nicaraguans show a great demand for learning English, they do not often regard the Creole English spoken by Costeños as a resource for them in that endeavor. Foreigners such North Americans and British are sought-after English teachers, but in my experience, hiring Costeños as English teachers is not common. English is not viewed as a national resource. In other words, they do not commonly view Creole English as part of the cultural and linguistic patrimony of the Nicaraguan nation. This is because the English spoken by Costeños is considered to be at best only of regional value.

From the perspective of Ruiz and his Nicaraguan contemporaries, Blacks, even more than Indians, threatened the Nicaraguan nationalist project because they were perceived as a potentially limitless source of immigrants rather than a finite population living within national borders, and because they were favored as workers by the foreign companies investing in the Caribbean coast of Central America. The Nicaraguan government favored foreign investment because it promised to make the Coast economically productive, a task at the time unattainable for the Nicaraguan government. Yet the government feared the Caribbeanization of the region that accompanied this economic development.

This Caribbeanization was perceived as an invasion of African-Americans and the English language. The city of Colon in Panama, the Caribbean gateway to the Panama Canal, provided for Ruiz the most horrifying example of this phenomenon. The Atlantic Coast of Nicaragua was in grave danger of becoming another Colon, which he described as a "museum of races, without patriotism, without tradition, without common ideals, a confusion of languages, of colors, of bloods, of vice." He wrote: "Nicaraguans should prepare themselves so that the coast doesn't become a second Panama Canal. There must not be cities like Colon where patriotism is abolished and where reigns only confusion of languages, dissolution of customs and agglomeration of the most degraded races of the world" (Ruiz y Ruiz 1927, 116).

Ruiz here defined intra-Caribbean migration as inherently destructive to the social fabric of the countries in which it took place. For Ruiz the influx of Africans was not just a racial problem, but their presence also foretold a cultural and linguistic problem (and therefore a national problem) of disunity and cultural chaos. From this perspective, the Nicaraguan government found itself in a quandary in which economic growth and development would be won at the sacrifice of what they perceived to be an already-compromised racial and cultural homogeneity. Contrast this formulation to the value placed on cosmopolitanism displayed by Costeños.

Ruiz proposed that the government should oblige Bragman's Bluff Lumber Company to hire only *gentes del interior* (literally "people from the interior") to the exclusion of *negros* and *chinos* (Ruiz y Ruiz 1927, iv). In the Pacific region, where presumably Nicaraguan culture was irreversibly ingrained, immigrants could be assimilated to national life. For Ruiz, however, this was not the case in the Atlantic Coast. He wrote: "Nicaragua is a nation in formation without homogeneity of races and for this reason it isn't prepared to imprint its national seal on populations of such diversity in a region as under populated and un-nicaraguan as the atlantic littoral. Therefore immigrants should be carefully chosen to populate the Coast and un-assimilable races should be repudiated" (ibid., 7).

Lacking power and resources, the Nicaraguan government did not find itself in a position to dictate labor recruitment policies to the US company. It also lacked the resources to assimilate and Hispanicize immigrants, not to mention native Costeños. Education was perceived as a vital strategy in counteracting the divisive effect of unwanted immigration. Ruiz demanded that the Nicaraguan law requiring instruction in the Spanish language be enforced. Given that the US company funded the earliest schools in the city, however, this became difficult to carry out in practice.

In 1925 the Nicaraguan government created an official municipality in Bilwi that was given a Spanish name, Puerto Cabezas.[18] The dominance of the English language in the city disquieted Nicaraguan officials, often stirring up a great deal of nationalistic indignation. The perceived threat of the English language did not simply result from the perception that its dominance indicated foreign domination. This fact alone perhaps could have been stomached by Nicaraguan national leaders, who generally looked to the United States as a possible benefactor in the development and modernization of the country. English, however, was also the language of many Costeños as well as Black West Indian and Black US workers, the latter group being regarded by the Nicaraguan government as the least desirable candidates for citizenry. Ruiz expressed anti-English-language indignation after having visited the company hospital—the only hospital in the city: "The Commission visited the Hospital that the Company has in Puerto Cabezas. The first impression that your humble informant had was disagreeable—the doctor from the Hospital greeted me in english. What a surprise to learn that all the patients only spoke spanish—I wonder if their ailments spoke english? This anomaly must disappear. The doctors should know spanish and every sign in a foreign language should be considered a permanent insult to nicaraguan patriotism" (Ruiz y Ruiz 1927, 56).

English, although it was the language of the dominant country of the Americas, came to represent a national threat in the Atlantic Coast—a threat that was explicitly perceived in racial terms. The numbers of White American workers were low, their stays relatively brief, and their likelihood of settling in the region was also low. US agro-industrial penetration, the increased use of English, and the influx of Black West Indians and North Americans went hand in hand. This created a highly paradoxical and conflictive social and ideological context in which, on the one hand, the industrializing US presence represented a step away from Nicaraguan economic and societal backwardness (atraso), while on the other hand this presence inspired fear of cultural decline and racial degeneration.

The above analysis of Pacific Nicaraguan attitudes toward the Coast and its inhabitants helps us to understand the decisions that Ruiz would ultimately make with regard to the complaints of the Miskito communities. The principal complaint that the síndico of Bilwi, who at the time was Noah Columbus, made to the Ruiz commission was that Bragman's Bluff Lumber Company had illegally encroached on lands belonging to the Ten Communities. In addition, he complained that the company had erected a fence that separated the company buildings, including barracks and housing for employees, from the community of Bilwi. The company maintained a closed gate on the road between the company section of town and the dwellings of the "native" section of town.

This native section accommodated many small stores, restaurants, and, according to Ruiz, "nineteen cantinas." Craftsmen who performed periodic work for the company and its employees, such as shoe repairmen, bricklayers, carpenters, and even a doctor, also lived there (Ruiz y Ruiz 1927, 4). Ruiz described the "national" profile of Bilwi in the following manner: "With the development of the Bragman Bluff Company during the last 3 years the village of Bilue has been erected. Its inhabitants have come from a wide variety of places: there are 3 houses owned by english, 4 by germans, 3 by chinese, 5 by Jamaicans, 26 by Hispanicnicaraguans and 12 by mosquito indians.[19] The majority of the 350 total inhabitants are spanish—the term used in these parts to refer to Nicaraguans from the interior of the Republic" (ibid., 7). Ruiz added that about 1,000 workers lived within the company section. The company forbade inhabitants of Bilwi to erect constructions of any kind within those sections of Bilwi where it foresaw expansion. The police, whose salaries were paid by the company, enforced this policy.

The most serious grievance expressed by Columbus, the síndico of Bilwi, was that the company had illegally leased lands in and around Bilwi from the community of Karatá. Karatá claimed that the pasture lands to which it received title in 1918 included lands claimed and inhabited by the Miskito people of Bilwi. In 1924 the síndico of Karatá leased the entirety of its pasture lands to the US company for the price of six hundred córdobas annually. Bilwi presented a 1917 title granted to the Ten Communities that contradicted Karatá's claim. Thus two Miskito communities found themselves on opposite sides of a legal conflict regarding Indian land. Unfortunately for Bilwi, the US company had already provided a de facto solution to the conflict.

Residents of Bilwi, Miskito Indians and "Spanish" alike, had previously brought this conflict in land titles to the attention of the British Consul E. Owen Rees in the hope that he would arbitrate the dispute. Rees recommended to the Ruiz commission that the claim to the portion of Karatá's land that conflicted with Bilwi's claim be annulled. He concluded that Karatá's surveyor had incorrectly measured Karata's pasture lands, resulting in an absurd situation in which residents of Bilwi, whose land title predated that of Karatá, should be required to lease land from Karatá within the confines of their own community (Ruiz y Ruiz 1927, 13).

Ruiz rejected Rees's recommendations. Emboldened by the possibility of taking advantage of the conflict and confusion, he claimed all of the land in and around Bilwi, whose value increased daily, as national land: "Upon considering the arguments of all the parties in the conflict between the Bragman Bluff Company, the indians of Bilué, Caratá, and residents of Bilué it is clear that none is correct—neither those who constructed [houses], nor those who prohibited this construction. Only the state is the legitimate owner of the lands in question" (ibid., 12).

Ruiz asserted that Bilwi land claims could not be protected by the Harrison-Altamirano Treaty because at the time of the signing of this treaty (1905) and at the time of the granting of the Bilwi land title (1917), no Miskito village in fact existed. He further argued that Bilwi was not a Miskito village because the Miskito, as "nomadic" Indians, had not continuously occupied the site. He claimed that as a result of their nomadic nature, all of the Miskito Indians who lived in Puerto Cabezas during his visit, with the exception of Noah Columbus, had arrived within the last three years from other communities. What is particularly revealing about this approach taken by Ruiz was the way in which he discredited Costeño land claims by invoking primitivist conceptions of Indian culture.

According to Ruiz, the Miskito abandoned Bilwi in 1897 and scattered throughout the region, leaving Noah Columbus as the only inhabitant of Bilwi until 1922. For Ruiz, the fact that Bilwi did not contest the Karatá land title in 1918 supported his claim that the village had been essentially uninhabited during that period. In the following quotation, notice the way that Ruiz invoked the idea of primitive Indian culture to discredit Bilwi Indian land claims: "When the Bragman Bluff Company established itself there was nothing in this place, so it can be said that today Bilué indians do not exist. Therefore, to speak of the indians of Bilué, of their secular rights, of the land of their forefathers, of their sepulchers, of their homes, etc. etc. is pure imaginary fiction. They abandoned their lairs and their cemeteries and returned to their nomadic life, living only from hunting and fishing" (Ruiz y Ruiz 1927, 12).

For Ruiz, the land claims of the Bilwi Indians were necessarily linked to the degree to which they conformed to a stereotyped vision of being Indian. In this vision, steeped in exoticism, Indians were held to be part of the natural world rather than the man-made social and civilized world, and hence their claims to the land were of a cultural and spiritual, rather than legal, nature. Their alleged nomadic subsistence practice of hunting and fishing, which for Ruiz stood in contrast to "civilized" agriculture, weakened their claim to legal land ownership. For example, Ruiz explicitly placed the Miskito on par with the animal world by characterizing their past residences as "lairs." As part of the flora and fauna of the natural world, they had only a transitory connection to their places of residence and therefore should not enjoy any legal rights with regard to these. Once more, the Atlantic Coast land, like its indigenous inhabitants, was portrayed as wild, uncivilized, and without intrinsic value in its undeveloped state.

In this hostile context, in which development was pitted against Indian communal identity, the inhabitants of Bilwi found themselves in a peculiar bind. Not only did they have to assert their Miskito Indian identity in order to protect themselves, and where possible profit, from the encroachment of the US companies and the Nicaraguan government, they also were obliged to prove that they were Bilwi Indians. In the process of asserting land rights as Indians, however, they simultaneously invited the scorn of the Nicaraguan government, which viewed Miskito land claims as a threat to its project of Hispanic-Nicaraguan expansion. Given that the government regarded the Miskito as an uncivilized people, their attempt to achieve recognition of their land through civilized channels represented for the Nicaraguan government a contradiction that Ruiz resolved by questioning the motives of the litigants for claiming the land. Take, for example, the following quotation: "Only after a large agro-industrial Enterprise was created, and a new port was opened, and big business appeared in the old Bilwi could greed possibly have any reason to exist in such a inhospitable region. . . . In reality these lands did not have the slightest worth before the creation of Puerto Cabezas and for this reason the mosquito indians, neither those from Karatá nor those from the aforementioned communities, never bothered to claim them" (Ruiz y Ruiz 1927, 16).

This statement reveals the deeply ingrained exoticism with which the Miskito and the Mosquito Coast were perceived. The Nicaraguan government could consider the Miskito Indians capable of the very Euro-American emotion of greed only after these Indians were confronted by modern Western agro-industry. The land itself, in its wild state, could not possibly be the object of civilized avarice.

While in Puerto Cabezas, Ruiz discovered that many non-Indian residents of Bilwi agreed with and even advocated the positive resolution of many Miskito complaints and demands. He expressed great consternation and disbelief upon finding that a Spanish Nicaraguan or any non-Indian would ally himself with what he considered to be a retrograde and savage cause. To his dismay, however, the Indian cause appealed to people whom he considered non-Indians. Many Costeño inhabitants of Bilwi resented the exclusionary policies and extremely broad quasi-governmental powers of Bragman's Bluff Lumber Company. A successful resolution of the Miskito Indian dispute could have strengthened their position vis-à-vis the Nicaraguan government and the company.

Shop owners and tradesmen, who strongly opposed the company policy of paying wages in company script redeemable at the company commissary, stood to benefit most from a weakening of the company's powers. This sector, among others, was sympathetic to the Miskito cause. Ruiz lambasted this position as self-interested duplicity:

> One often hears talk of the abuses committed by foreign Companies against the mosquito indians and the newspapers turn around and spew this to the four winds. This in turn establishes an incontrovertible public image of an infinite number of martyred sons of the fatherland. However if one objectively examines the situation one will find that the entire situation can be reduced to the clamor of a tobacco trader or merchant whose least concern is the rights of the mosquito indians, with whom he does not share blood nor language. These men view everything through a bottle of liquor or a colombian cloth. (Ruiz y Ruiz 1927, 21)

Ruiz refused to accept the possibility that Costeños of all kinds (Indian and non-Indian alike) could, in certain circumstances, perceive and act upon a shared interest vis-à-vis the Nicaraguan government and the US company. This supra-ethnic regional unity was, for Ruiz and others, counterintuitive in light of the co-presence of disparate races, languages, and bloods that he and others believed engendered a muddled and volatile racial and linguistic context.

LABOR POLICIES AND RACIAL CONFLICT

Notwithstanding the potential for inter-group solidarity, the labor policies of the US companies created structural contradictions between different sectors of the society that to varying degrees frustrated the formation and exercise of Costeño solidarity. Nicaraguan laborers from the Pacific and the Atlantic found themselves excluded from higher-paying skilled and semiskilled jobs that the company filled with Black laborers from the West Indies and the United States. These workers, particularly the West Indians, who in many cases arrived primarily via the Canal Zone, had already mastered specialized lumber and banana industry tasks. Because the company brought them from outside the country, they often provided them housing in the form of barracks and bungalows. Nicaraguan nationals, who had to make their own transportation and housing arrangements, resented this policy (Ruiz y Ruiz 1927, 61). The flip side to this policy was that when their services were no longer wanted, the company shipped West Indian and US workers to other parts of the Caribbean. Company officials also favored English-speaking Costeños over monoglot Spanish-speaking or monoglot Miskitu-speaking Costeños for low-level administrative work. White North Americans occupied all the highest-paying administrative and technical jobs.

Those native Nicaraguans with little or no fluency in English, primarily campesinos from the interior but also some Costeños, experienced this preference for English-speaking workers in racial terms. That is to say, Pacific Nicaraguans perceived their low status in the workplace as being the result of the influx of Black workers from the Caribbean and the United States. Given the nature of this situation, it is not surprising to find that the first labor disturbances in Puerto Cabezas centered on racial differences among workers, rather than national or class differences between workers and management. This tension speaks to the importance of structural features of the local political economy in shaping race relations.

On August 30, 1925, resentment between Nicaraguan and foreign workers manifested itself in the form of riots and personal violence committed against West Indian and US Blacks. In the words of the commander of the USS Tulsa, which later arrived at the request of company officials, "trouble broke out between the native laborers and foreign negro workmen, composed of Americans and Jamaican negroes" (US Department of State Records 817.504/24). Nicaraguan employees of Bragman's Bluff Lumber Company threatened to kill Black workers. Three US Blacks and two Jamaicans were injured. Thirty-seven Nicaraguans were arrested and, according to H. D. Scott, company manager, forty to fifty "British colored subjects" left the city on account of the riots (US Department of State Records 817.504/23). Scott explained:

> For some time the native laborers here have been complaining about the introduction of negro laborers, and we have refrained from introducing any of these when the work could be done by people of the country. However it has been impossible to get people here who understand the business of making turpentine, also there are none who know how to make crossties. We have introduced some nineteen negroes for the turpentine business, and on the SS Algeria which arrived here on August 27th we introduced fourteen American negroes to make crossties. On the night these negroes arrived here there was a demonstration made against them by the local people, and this kept up and came to a head Sunday the 30th of August, at about 12 o'clock. (ibid.)

Nicaraguan discontentment toward company labor policies manifested itself in the form of acts of violence against individual Black laborers rather than in the form of protest directed to the North American leadership of the company. Whereas Nicaraguan workers did not find unbearable their subordination to white North American managers, their subordination to Black foreigners represented an intolerable inversion of a Pacific Nicaraguan ideological hierarchy of racial value, in which Blacks occupied the lowest position.

Two weeks prior to the disturbances mentioned above, the local labor union El Avance, anticipating the arrival of the Ruiz commission, addressed a letter to the Nicaraguan government in which it detailed the grievances of national workers against the US company. First on the list was a complaint that the company was trying to "colonize" the town of Bilwi. In response to this perceived colonization, workers felt obligated to "defend our race" (*defender nuestra raza*) against encroachment and to demand the protection of the Nicaraguan government as Nicaraguan citizens (Ruiz y Ruiz 1927, 60). The letter stated:

> We ask the Government to absolutely prohibit the entrance of blacks into the country because they cause the degeneration of our race and above all represent a detriment to our fellow workers. The Company in question is trying to colonize our town and undoubtedly is trying to do what it did in "la Ceiba" Honduras—introduce no less than 14,000 blacks. We think the amount that we have now in the country is sufficient. The government should in the name of justice imitate other governments which have repudiated that race in favor of the national race. (Ruiz y Ruiz 1927, 60)

Although the Spanish term *"raza"* is not necessarily equivalent to "race" as it is defined in the US context, here the Nicaraguan laborers clearly expressed their objection to the imported workers in racial terms. It is important to note that these workers, whose chief complaint was essentially the unfair preference for foreign workers in the labor market, did not protest the introduction of foreign white company employees, who enjoyed far greater advantages than foreign Blacks. At this conjuncture in the history of Puerto Cabezas, political economy and anti-Black racism fed off one another.

The position of Nicaraguan workers cannot be explained simply by the fact they were less likely to regard foreign white workers as competitors in the workplace. Undoubtedly, many Nicaraguans internalized an international labor hierarchy that assessed the value of North American labor as far greater than that of Nicaraguan labor. That is to say, many Nicaraguans did not consider themselves qualified for the kinds of jobs (management, engineering, clerical, etc.) that were occupied primarily by foreign Whites and therefore did not regard their exclusion from these positions as illegitimate. These same workers, however, deeply resented their exclusion from the sorts of tasks that Blacks were brought in to perform. The belief of Nicaraguan workers in their ability to perform the jobs performed by Blacks does not represent the only factor that helps to explain the resentment and violence by nationals against foreign Blacks. An ideological factor, a deeply ingrained hierarchy of relative human worth which valued light skin over dark skin, played a significant role in: (1) legitimizing Nicaraguan subordination to light-skinned North Americans, and (2) provoking discord between native Nicaraguans and imported Black laborers.

Although the main thrust of Nicaraguan opposition to the company was channeled into protest against the introduction of Black West Indians and North Americans, Nicaraguan workers also expressed other kinds of grievances. For example, they complained of high rents in the company-owned barracks and houses. They also objected to the high prices at the company commissary, which held workers as a captive market in Bilwi due to the practice of paying workers in company script and coupons. Workers bitterly joked that the money they earned only left the company office long enough "to take in some sun" (*coger sol*) before it returned to the company's coffers. Also nationalistic appeals were made against the ten-hour workday exacted by the company: "This Company has adopted a 10 hour work day. Let's not follow the lead of the civilized nations, rather let's follow the national customs—in all parts of this country the work day is nine hours" (Ruiz y Ruiz 1927, 61). This appeal conceded the exclusion of Nicaragua from consideration as a "civilized nation," yet it simultaneously opposed the unreasonably long workday, imposed by the civilized US company, on nationalistic grounds.

Similar ambivalence with regard to the legitimacy of North American dominance, both cultural and economic, manifested itself among all classes of Nicaraguans. For example, Commissioner Ruiz, although a supporter of the US companies and foreign investment in general, opposed certain company practices that he regarded as disrespectful of Nicaraguan patriotism. In addition to his aforementioned opposition to the dominance of the English language over Spanish in the city, Ruiz also condemned the fenced separation between the company-owned and operated section of the town and the so-called native section of Bilwi.[20] He wrote: "It should not be allowed that the village that gives homes to the workers of Puerto Cabezas, in numbers large enough to give it the appearance of a city, be separated from the population by any kind of fence. This dividing line is extremely humiliating, not only for the inconvenience it creates but more importantly for the significance that it carries. An honorable nation should not permit such divisions" (Ruiz y Ruiz 1927, 25). From Ruiz's perspective, the fenced division between US company and Nicaraguan town sections represented an unlicensed overstepping of foreign authority on Nicaraguan soil. The fence communicated a message that violated even his pro-US sensibilities. Ruiz objected not to the fact that the company should take extraordinary measures (beyond those taken by the Nicaraguan government) to protect its people and property. Rather, the company's effrontery in regarding this property and people as its own, in defiance of Nicaraguan authority and sovereignty, offended his sense of patriotism.

In general, Nicaraguans, particularly Costeños, welcomed the economic opportunities brought by US companies and accepted their subordination to the white North American bosses. Widespread racial ideologies that associated light skin with intelligence, industry, and leadership reinforced the acceptance of this subordination. Nicaraguans also no doubt recognized their subordinate position in a hemispheric order in which the United States exercised unchecked military and economic control. In opposition to these factors that served to naturalize and justify subordination, Nicaraguans simultaneously possessed and developed other ideologies that permitted dissent and opposed capitulation to North American supremacy.

The Nicaraguan civil war and the concurrent US Marine occupation (which lasted from 1926 to 1933) superseded this type of protest against company practices. The Atlantic Coast, and particularly the burgeoning new city of Puerto Cabezas, assumed the national spotlight on many occasions during this period. Both the US Marines and Pacific Nicaraguan revolutionaries used the Atlantic Coast and Puerto Cabezas as a staging ground from which to launch military expeditions. This political instability supplanted incipient social unrest within Puerto Cabezas. During this period, Puerto Cabezas witnessed by far the greatest expression of Nicaraguan opposition to North American military and economic occupation. This came in the form of a Pacific-born Liberal army officer, Augusto Cesar Sandino, who led a peasant army into an against-the-odds civil war against the National Guard and US Marines.

SANDINO AND THE MOSQUITO COAST:
RACE WAR AND REVOLUTIONARY
INDIGENISM

The war fought by the US Marines against the peasant army of Augusto Sandino from 1927 to 1933 represented the most extreme example of Nicaraguan resistance to United States military and economic domination. Sandino explicitly conceived of this war as a racial battle between Anglo-Saxon and what he called "Indo-Hispanic" cultures and peoples. He implored Nicaraguans to value national indigenous symbols that were not derived from Europe or the United States. He contributed to, and was a product of, a larger movement in Latin America that sought to define a Latin American character that was independent of Europe and Spain, going beyond the Creole nationalism of the nineteenth century. For Sandino, the Mosquito Coast region of Nicaragua suffered most acutely from the evils of US imperialism. This region, in which Sandino would conduct many of his operations and in which he would settle after the war, accommodated the largest US cultural, economic, and military presence.

Sandino and others also recognized that the Atlantic Coast contained the densest indigenous population and was the least populated and poorest region of the country. Sandino saw great economic potential in the rich and seemingly underutilized expanses of land of the Atlantic Coast. He also saw great symbolic potential for construction a homegrown version of Nicaraguan nationalism using the symbols of indigenous persistence that Costeños manifested. Furthermore, he believed that the intense exploitation and proletarianization of Costeños at the hands of foreign industries contributed to their potential as anticapitalist revolutionaries. In this section, I explore Sandino's prominent role in the history of the Mosquito Coast and Puerto Cabezas. Despite his glorification of native Nicaraguan peoples and cultures that stood in contrast to Ruiz's glorification of all things Spanish, ultimately Sandino shared many of the prejudices of his contemporaries with regard to the Atlantic Coast.

The main theater of operations for Sandino's armies was the Segovian Mountains and the northern Atlantic Coast, as well as adjacent districts along the Honduran border. These regions were the least populated and most impoverished (by conventional standards) regions of the country. Not coincidentally, they both were the areas with the highest level of export-oriented production, all of which was controlled by the United States. Sandino looted mines in both regions in order to raise money for his army, which was now being actively pursued by the Marines (Macaulay 1967, 73). In only the first year of military occupation, the Marine force in Nicaragua numbered over 5,000 and the US military spent over $3.5 million (Dozier 1985, 207). During 1927 and

1928, Sandinista and US troops met in several violent confrontations that caused significant casualties on both sides. The Marines were aided by the bombing and strafing runs of US warplanes. As Sandino's guerrilla tactics continued to have limited success, the undeclared war became increasingly unpopular in the United States.

In the presidential elections of 1928, a much-reduced Nicaraguan electorate elected Jose María Moncada, the Minister of War under whom Sandino served in the Constitutionalist War. When the Marines refused to fulfill their promise to withdraw from Nicaragua, Sandino resolved to continue the war against the United States, despite the fact that a Liberal was now in power. At this time the Marines started to form the infamous National Guard, which was supposedly intended to be a neutral force composed of Liberals and Conservatives. This National Guard and the family of dictators it propped up would not be overthrown until the 1979 Sandinista Revolution. Sandino and his armies, whose chief demand was the withdrawal of all US troops, continued to fight until 1933, when the Marines withdrew without having defeated the Sandinista troops.

Sandino explicitly conceived of his battle against the US Marines as a race war between what he called the Indo-Hispanic race and the Anglo-Saxon race. He repeatedly referred to the invading troops as "blond beasts," "blond beasts of the North," "blond pirates," and a "Nordic punitive army" (S. Ramirez 1988, 159; Conrad 1990, 140, 203–205). Sandino was an ardent advocate of Latin American unification, a unification that would be based on the links of a common "cosmic" Mestizo race. He wrote: "The spiritual vibration of the Indo-Hispanic race now depends on the Autonomist Army of Central America to save our racial dignity by throwing out of our territory, militarily, politically and economically, the withering Wall Street bankers" (S. Ramirez 1988, 536).

Sandino attempted to invert the self-deprecating Latin American attitude that accepted the notion that the sources of true high culture and civilization came from the United States and Europe. He characterized the United States as a land of barbarians who, despite all their claims to civilization and democracy, actually were reprehensible land-grabbing pirates with an imperialist fixation.

Sandino interpreted the US penetration into Nicaraguan territory through a gendered metaphor of rape and sexual penetration. Sandino

often referred to the Yankees as *"machos"* or *"macho* bandits" (Conrad
1990, 68, 92, 146). "Macho" is a Spanish term used to refer to the male
of an animal species, but in a Mexican context, with which Sandino was
familiar, macho can refer to "any agent or implement that overpowers or
invades another" (Hodges 1986, 114). The theme of rape in Sandino's
writing, of course, was not always simply metaphorical. He frequently
condemned the rape of Nicaraguan women by US troops: "With their
brutal acts the Yankees sow terror among the peaceful inhabitants. In
their punitive expedition [in Ocotal, July 1927] they violated 16
women, nine virgins among them, two of these unfortunate girls dying
as a result of the brutal outrage of the northern barbarians" (Conrad
1990, 89; also see S. Ramirez 1988, 203).

However, beyond the cases of actual rape, the image of the blond
Yankee invader raping the pure and defenseless Nicaraguan woman represented a trope through which Sandino understood Nicaragua's relationship with the United States. The following anecdote, written by
Sandino in Mexico in 1929, two years after the events described, is very
enlightening in this regard:

> Those regions [the Segovian Mountains] where our column oper-
> ated are very rich places, and our forces enjoyed an unusual sym-
> pathy, because all the inhabitants are revolutionaries and make
> common cause with us. There is one of those villages that is a true
> garden of humanity. The women there are uncommonly beautiful
> and generous. Our cavalry was made up of young men, furthermore
> for the most part romantic, and so that village was visited constantly
> by the several units that made up our column.
>
> Colonel Bosque, who distinguished himself as a brave man and as
> one of our cavalry's boldest horsemen, won the heart of one of our
> beautiful young Segovian girls. The girl was of the peasant class, but
> pretty and educated. The wedding was to take place at the end of
> the war.
>
> Our struggle constantly grew in intensity. . . . We left those
> regions to move on to others farther away. . . . The Yankee invaders
> of our territory and their allies, the Conservative sell-outs and the
> cowardly Moncadista Liberals attacked us furiously. That awful pres-
> sure from the enemies of the national sovereignty of Nicaragua

forced me to take refuge in the Segovian jungles, where we have upheld our country's honor and perhaps that of our race with strength and inflexibility. . . .

For more than a year I did not know the names of the unfortunate young girls who were violated by murderous Yankee invaders during their movements through those inoffensive and undefended towns, and so the impression I felt was a terrible one . . . when I came to know that that virgin bride of the late Colonel Bosque of my cavalry had been cruelly violated by miserable Yankee invaders and as a result of that savage and humiliating act the young girl was wasting away, pale, shocked, and the mother of a son with blue eyes and a ruddy skin, and nobody even knew who the father might be . . .

How terrible! Do my readers not see that that child is the fruit of indifference of the governments of our Latin America, before the sorrow of my beloved and many times blessed Nicaragua? (Conrad 1990, 279–281)

This passage is revelatory in a variety of ways. Here, as well as in other writings, Sandino, who was not from the mountainous Segovian regions and much less the Atlantic Coast, associated these isolated rural areas with an idealized male vision of purity and virginity. He portrayed the women of these regions, like the land that they inhabited, as being untouched and unspoiled. He boasted that many "Yankee pirates are buried in our virgin mountains" (ibid., 238, 386). For Sandino, the women of the Segovian Mountains, and the Atlantic Coast by extension, manifested a closeness to nature that, within his modified "*indigenista*" ideological framework, meant that they contained particular symbolic value as the vessel of authentic Nicaraguan blood—the essential "Indo" half of the Indo-Hispanic dyad. Through their isolation they personified an authentic Nicaraguan culture and race that Sandino was trying so hard to glorify in opposition to the "blond beasts."

Patriarchy and ideologies of femininity and masculinity played an integral role within this formulation. The Sandinista soldier represented the strong-willed and virulent man whose duty it was to protect the honor of the vulnerable women, thereby preserving his own honor. Only the Sandinistas could still claim to possess honor in Nicaragua because they refused to stand by and watch as the invaders raped their women. These were the women who should rightfully bear them the next generation of Indo-Hispanos. Indeed, Sandino disparaged Nicaraguan apologists of US occupation as "eunuchs." This metaphor perfectly suited Sandino's understanding of the Nicaraguan reality: the castrated Nicaraguan man sat in compliance as the invaders sexually exploited the women of the fatherland.

Sandino conceived of his war against the marines as a desperate attempt to prevent the emasculation of the Nicaraguan man by the North American man. They were locked in a struggle in which only the victor could retain his masculinity. Within a conceptual framework that associated femininity with submission and accommodation, the loser would therefore be relegated to the status of a woman. Sandino wrote:

> There is nothing that justifies their [the United States] meddling in our internal politics, nor do I believe that the greatness of the *"colossus"* is sufficient cause to employ that greatness to murder Nicaraguans. Because even if this should be their intention, it would in no way benefit them, because even if they annihilate us, they would find in our bloody remains only the treasure that envelops the hearts of Nicaraguan patriots. This would serve only to humiliate the "hen" [*"gallina"*] that is displayed on their coat of arms in the form of an eagle. (S. Ramirez 1988, 68)

Here Sandino attempted to invert the symbolism of domination by denying the masculinity of the American symbol, the eagle. Instead he equated it with a female chicken (gallina). Sandino sought to impose his own vision of the rightful pecking order in Nicaragua on the North American *"macho"* that arrogantly paraded about with impunity in what it presumed to be its' own "backyard."

Sandino's patriarchal thinking, however, differed from other forms of elite Latin American patriarchal thought in that the idealized and exoticized vision of the national woman was not a white woman, nor was she wealthy. Rather, she was embodied by the image of a dark-skinned peasant woman. This synechdochical relationship between woman and country emerges clearly in the following passage: "Our young country, this dark beauty of the tropics [*esa morena tropical*], should wear on her head the Phrygian cap of liberty bearing the magnificent slogan symbolized by our *red and black* flag. She should not be a victim raped [*violada*] by the Yankee adventurers who were invited here by the four horrid individuals who still claim to have been born in this land" (S. Ramirez 1988, 76).

In a country in which to this day light skin, and the European ancestry which it signals, is generally considered more attractive than dark skin (in both men and women), Sandino's valorization of the dark-skinned women and the Indian past represented a shift away from the dominant ideologies of racial worth and beauty. Despite his appeals to the worthiness of the Mestizo and the Indo-Hispanic race, Sandino manifested many contradictory attitudes and stances with regard to both halves of the Indo-Hispanic formulation.

Sandino regarded the Nicaraguan Indian as the most exploited and most vulnerable segment of society. As victims they deserved the help of some future Nicaraguan state to bring them out of their miserable situation. Sandino remembered the visit of a poor campesino adolescent to his camp: "Like so many children of our America, this child of pure Indian race, in whose eyes glowed the indomitable pride of our ancestors, was wearing something that looked like an undershirt . . . along with underpants, also in a tattered condition, hanging from his waist. Everything about the boy cried out in protest against the present civilization" (S. Ramirez 1988, 208).

For Sandino there was nothing particularly admirable or inspirational about the contemporary "Indian race." In their present pitiable condition they were to be uplifted and brought into the ranks of civilization. Although Sandino praised the Indian societies of the past as well as their subsequent contribution of "blood" in the formation of the Indo-Hispanic race, he regarded their present state as lamentable. In his writings he did not question the commonly held assumption that Indians were ignorant and therefore represented an obstacle to national progress. His attitude towards the "Indian problem" was similar in many respects to the patriarchal and condescending attitude he held towards women. The Indian must be protected because he represented what was distinctive about Nicaragua and Latin America, but these Indians lacked value in their own right and lacked the ability to protect their own interests. This represented basically a slight reworking of the "white man's burden" thesis. Sandino suggested that "what our Indians need is instruction and culture so that they can know themselves, respect themselves and love themselves" (S. Ramirez 1988, 485).

As a result of the war, Sandino came into intimate contact with the inhabitants of the Atlantic Coast, many of whom actively identified themselves as Indian. Whereas in the Pacific region of the 1920s, the last of the corporately organized Indian communities were being abolished and Pacific Nicaraguans rarely positively self-identified as Indians, in the Atlantic Coast, Costeño communities often consciously adopted the Indian or Creole label.[21] Sandino incorporated Costeños into his troops, some of them rising to the highest ranks of his army. He boasted in a "Manifesto" addressed to "The Oppressed Men of our Atlantic Littoral": "Our Army, which is composed of blacks, Indians, whites etc. etc. without racial nor class prejudice has determined to implant the principles of human fraternity in Nicaragua. And to do this it asks the Nicaraguan People for its unequivocal moral and material support of the Supreme Leadership [of the Sandinista Army]" (US Department of State Records, June 20, 1931. Consular Records from Puerto Cabezas).

Despite his willingness to court Costeño leaders, Sandino was generally unpopular among Costeños. Many of them resented his attacks against the US-owned mines and fruit companies (Brooks 1998). These companies represented their only source of wages and US and British products for which they had acquired a centuries-old taste. Costeños, who had been recently evangelized by the Moravian Church, also resented the killing of a German-North American priest by Sandinista forces, as well as their brutal executions of company workers (see Brooks 1998, Wünderich 1989, 67–85, and A. Adams 1995 for an ample discussion of this case). During my fieldwork in Puerto Cabezas, I spoke to a number of Costeños who were Sandino's contemporaries and who claim that Sandino was known in the Atlantic Coast as a "bandit" in the 1930s. In the present, Costeños generally continue to refer to Sandino as a bandit.

Although Sandino dreamed of improving the Atlantic Coast and integrating it into the national life, his plans betrayed an essentially colonialist mentality. Sandino viewed the extensive forests and savannas of the region as empty lands ("*tierras baldías*") that were ripe for settlement and development by the "New Nicaraguan Man" (Belausteguigoitia 1981 [1934], 183). Referring to the inhabitants of the Atlantic Coast,

Sandino stated: "They have been completely abandoned. There are about 100,000 of them without communication, without schools, without any kind of government. This is where I want to colonize—in order to raise them up and make them real men" (S. Ramirez 1988, 193). Sandino regarded the Atlantic Coast as the most fertile and potentially productive region of the country. If exploited correctly, the region could end Nicaraguan dependence on imported goods. As the war against the Marines began to wind down, Sandino focused all his energies on creating a utopian cooperative society on the Atlantic coast.

After the elections of 1932 the Marines finally retired from Nicaragua, leaving their nemesis alive and well. With the United States gone, Sandino, still distrusting the Liberals and especially the National Guard, began the difficult process of demilitarization. He proposed the creation of an enormous new district that would be named "Light and Truth." The new district, located in the Segovian Mountains and the Atlantic Coast, would be governed by Sandino's army. Under his direction this army would establish agricultural cooperatives: "I will take advantage of this time to organize agricultural cooperatives in these beautiful regions which for centuries have remained abandoned by men of Government . . . the abandoned lands . . . represent 36,000 square kilometers . . . people from the Central American proletariat and from any other part of the world should come to the region" (Wünderich 1989, 147). He added:

> We are going to go chop down the forests and make agricultural cooperatives where we all will be brothers. Those *campesinos* are great workers. We are going to make schools and construct cities. We will bring carpenters, mechanics, belt-makers, tailors etc. so that we will have everything. Everything will be in cooperatives. There is gold in abundance and with it we will buy whatever we need from other countries. . . . The wood here is magnificent for making houses and furniture. Now the *campesinos* don't have anything, but they soon will have everything . . . I already have a deal with a mexican company for the cultivation of banana in the Atlantic Coast and we will throw out United Fruit. We are also going to throw the Yankee companies out of the mines. We should keep fighting, this time peacefully, so that we can have a fatherland that is just for us Nicaraguans. (ibid., 148)

Sandino even proposed that this district could one day become the "Federal District" of a united Central America. It was fitting that Sandino should propose the most sparsely populated region in all of Central America as the site of the future Central American capital city. For Sandino the Atlantic Coast represented a fresh start, a geographic tabula rasa, in which the Indo-Hispanic race could fulfill its cosmic destiny. It represented an unspoiled virgin who was waiting to be impregnated by the "New Nicaraguan Man."

Which half of the Indo-Hispanic man would carry out this task? Clearly the Miskito, whose lands were offered to the Central American proletariat, were not intended to colonize the region. Although to Sandino's credit it should be mentioned he stated that after being educated "the sumus, mosquitos and zambos would have the opportunity to be managers and bankers of their cooperatives" (Wünderich 1989, 153). Rather, it was the Mestizo descendants of the Spanish colonizers, for whom Sandino did not hide his admiration, who would have to colonize the savage Atlantic Coast as their Spanish predecessors had colonized an untamed America. The "Manifesto to the Men of the Department of León," written by Sandino in 1931 before the US withdrawal from Nicaragua, sheds some light on the above question:

Do you know, people of Leon, what your name symbolizes? . . . The symbol of Spain is the lion, spiritual leader of the entire globe, the reason no other nation on earth before or after can imitate Spain's great deed, which is that of discovering the continent where we live, the promised land for all free men on earth. . . . The people, symbol of the spirit of the Nicaraguan people, are also being infected with servility and a spirit of betrayal toward the fatherland. For this reason, with more than adequate justification, the spirit of the Nicaraguan people has withdrawn from your department to the virgin Segovian forests, where all of you, men of the department of Leon, may be found, so that all good sons of Nicaragua, always standing together, may continue carrying our flag from peak to peak, the untarnished symbol of Nicaraguan Leon, of which you, the men of Leon, are the true guardians, before you old Spanish Leon, the spiritual symbol of this earth in the presence of the Father Creator of the Universe. (Conrad 1990, 386)

Sandino harbored deep sympathies for the "civilizing project" of colonial Spain. In a comment strikingly reminiscent of those of his enemy and countrymen Frutos Ruiz y Ruiz, Sandino recognized that Spain had given Latin America three unifying elements: "its language, its civilization and its blood" (Belausteguigotia 1981 [1934], 200). The Indian, like the continents he inhabited, contributed little more than a wild and exotic vessel in which Spanish blood and culture was to be poured. In this sense, Sandino, despite his revolutionary *"Indigenismo"* cultivated during his stay in Mexico, did not transcend the deeply-rooted ideological presuppositions of his time and place. On the one hand Sandino associated Spanish blood and language with the concept of civilization, and on the other hand he looked down on the peoples of the Atlantic Coast on the basis of their perceived exoticism and closeness to the natural world.

In 1933 Sandino was assassinated at the orders of Anastasio Somoza, the leader of the Nicaraguan National Guard that had been formed by the US Marines. Somoza's family and the National Guard, enjoying the unwavering complicity of the United States, dictatorially ruled Nicaraguan until 1979, when, to complete the full circle, the Somoza regime was toppled by Sandinista rebels. After his assassination in 1933, Sandino's dreams of anarcho-socialist paradise on the Atlantic Coast of Nicaragua died out along with the agricultural cooperative he had founded in Wiwilí. The day after his assassination, the National Guard, under the orders of Anastasio Somoza, surrounded this community of unarmed ex-Sandinista soldiers and proceeded to carry out an indiscriminate massacre in which as many as three hundred men and women lost their lives (Keller 1986, 66).

In sum, Sandino's attitudes and behaviors towards the Mosquito Coast reflected profound ambivalence and contradiction. With regard to his behavior, Sandino incorporated Costeños to an unprecedented degree into the leadership, as well as the rank and file, of his militias. He also included the Mosquito Coast territory as a central part of his political and economic plans and dreams for the future. These plans stood in stark contrast to those of the Nicaraguan governments of his time, which neglected the Mosquito Coast and used it as a fiscal windfall. These governments took taxes from the US extractive companies in the region and spent them disproportionately on governmental expenses in the Pacific region.[22] In the cycle of coup d'etat in Nicaraguan politics at the time, the Atlantic Coast (particularly Bluefields and Puerto Cabezas) was used as a temporary military safe haven and staging ground for assaults on the Pacific Coast. Few resources were allocated to equitably incorporating the region into national plans. Despite these contrasts, however, Sandino shared with his Pacific contemporaries an essentially colonialist approach to the region in which the preexisting interests of the inhabitants of the region (e.g., land claims as well as the willingness of Costeños to work as wage laborers for US extractive industries) were disregarded.

On a more symbolic level, Sandino's indigenist (or Indo-Hispanicist) valorization of Nicaraguan national imagery predisposed him to value the Mosquito Coast as a reservoir of cultural ammunition. This cultural ammunition could be employed in the symbolic war against what he and others of his political conviction regarded to be a debilitating Eurocentrism that plagued Latin America. This was the same Eurocentric malady that José Martí, Cuban poet and intellectual father of the nationalist Latin American left, eloquently identified at the turn of the century. While the Mosquito Coast represented the extant "Indo" half of the Indo-Hispanic formulation for Sandino, it also represented in a gendered and racialized fashion an unrefined, uncultivated, and uncivilized natural world, a perspective that invited a paternalistic and essentially colonialist approach to the region. After Sandino's assassination in 1933, the US companies in the region, which had been terrorized by Sandino's forces and which for this and other reasons had ceased large-scale lumber operations in 1931, enjoyed a period of uninterrupted domestic tranquillity that would last until 1979. This period had a profound impact on the development of ideologies of race and culture in the region.

SUMMARY AND CONCLUSION

The intensification of tensions brought about by the expanding role of US agro-industry, the US Marines, and the Nicaraguan government in the new port city of Puerto Cabezas took place in a cultural backdrop of deeply rooted Pacific/Atlantic and Spanish/English divisions. These divisions influenced the way in which capitalist penetration was received by the diverse actors who found themselves in the maelstrom that was Puerto Cabezas in the 1920s and 1930s. Costeño and Spanish ideologies regarding race, culture, modernity, progress, and the relationship between these factors played an important role in the upheaval of this period in Puerto Cabezas.

Costeño inhabitants of Puerto Cabezas invoked their Indian race and the rights that they argued went along with their status as Miskito Indians under the 1905 Harrison-Altamirano treaty in their efforts to resist the alienation of their lands at the hands of Bragman's Bluff Lumber Company and the Nicaraguan state. However, as their lands and labor increased in value on an international market, they found themselves increasingly unable to maintain authority over them. Once more, their strategies of resistance conflicted with the modernizing project of the Nicaraguan state that regarded the Indian, as well as the Afro-Caribbean worker, as an obstacle to national progress. Black West Indians found themselves in a hostile situation in which for ideological and structural reasons (i.e., their superior place in the job market) they were victimized both by the Nicaraguan government as well as Nicaraguan workers. This discrimination is one factor that helps explain the adoption by West Indians of the Creole, as well as the Miskito, racial label in subsequent generations.

Racial ideologies, phrased in the language of blood and civilization, played a major role in the politics of Puerto Cabezas in the 1920s and 1930s. Frutos Ruiz y Ruiz and Augusto Sandino engaged in a distinctively Spanish exoticization of the Atlantic Coast that invited a paternalistic and discriminatory approach to the conflicts in the region. Pacific Nicaraguans today continue to conflate the region's geography (perceived as forested and impenetrable) with its people, who are regarded as wild, savage and unrefined. These associations stand in direct opposition to Costeño self-perception as cosmopolitan and worldly. Understanding the specific nature of this exocitization is essential in understanding the ideological underpinnings of the historic and modern conflict in the region.

CHAPTER 4

Company Time

Puerto Cabezas is even more American than
Bluefields. It is an industrial village of some 1,200
people, situated on a broad, flat plain overlooking the
Caribbean. It looks and is precisely like a lumber mill
village in some southern US state. It is operated like a
tiny principality by the Standard Fruit Company and
its subsidiary, the Bragman's Bluff Lumber Company,
which possess vast banana and lumber lands in the
interior, tapped by a small privately owned railroad.
—Harold Denny 1929, 263[1]

FROM THE TIME of the establishment of Bragman's
Bluff Lumber Company until the Sandinista Revolution of 1979, which
effectively drove away North American enterprises, the port city of
Puerto Cabezas served as a base to a series of US and Canadian lumber,
mining, rubber, and fishing companies that operated in the "boom and
bust" (Helms 1971) economy of the region. The operation of these
resource-extracting industries radically transformed the natural environment of the Mosquito Coast within a short period of time. Lumber
companies left behind extensive grass-covered savannas littered with tree
stumps where extensive subtropical forest had once flourished. Mining
companies contaminated long stretches of Atlantic Coast rivers with
pollutants (T. Adams 1981). While the activities of these companies have
left at times irreversible reminders of their devastating impact, it is
perhaps more difficult to assess their social and cultural impact.

The companies' residential and labor practices served to institutionalize racial and ethnic categories and helped to channel collective action
within Costeño society into a racialized idiom. These practices and
the resulting "class-ethnic hierarchy" have been well documented by
researchers (Bourgois 1985, 209). But in addition to this centrifugal

effect that caused the entrenchment of racial categories, the activities of the companies also had a centripetal effect on the process of socio-racial group formation.[2] While contributing to the institutionalization of racial categories, the companies also transformed consumption patterns of all Porteños (inhabitants of Puerto Cabezas) regardless of their racial identification, thus creating a single overriding "consumer culture" that should play a key role in understanding the role of racial distinctions in the social life and conflicts in Puerto Cabezas, and the Mosquito Coast region as a whole, today.

From its inception, Puerto Cabezas fit the classic pattern of a US company town.[3] The company planned, built, owned, and managed every aspect of the city. Far beyond simply providing employment to its workers, the company provided government, transportation, entertainment, health care, recreation, infrastructure, police, and stores. Given that the company was so deeply involved in every aspect of social life in the city, it in many ways represented a so-called total institution not unlike the sugar plantations of the Caribbean. However, the economic system of Puerto Cabezas (unlike sugar plantation areas) relied both on the production of its work force and the work force's consumption of US products. This stage in Mosquito Coast history is now remembered as "company time"—a term commonly used by Costeños (in English and Miskitu alike) that refers to the period in which US companies were active in the city (1920–1979).

LABOR, MACHETE MEN, AND MUNICIPAL SELF-IMAGE

After having persuaded the Nicaraguan government to issue a grant of over 50,000 hectares of land, much of which had been claimed as "pasture land" by a number of Miskito Indian villages, Bragman's Bluff Lumber Company's next challenge was to bring laborers to the region and insure that they would continue to work in the region as long as the company needed them. At the level of management, the company used White American workers almost exclusively. At the height of company operations, White Americans never numbered more than two hundred workers and their families. The companies also sought "skilled" laborers in construction, railroads, sawmills, and creosote plants. They filled these positions primarily with Black West Indian workers, many of whom were recruited directly from the Panama Canal Zone and Jamaica at the company's expense. It also recruited a significant number of Black American workers who had experience in lumber and railroad companies. Nicaraguans performed the most physically demanding and poorly paid labor.

In the period between the mid-1930s and World War II, the banana industry dominated the economic life of the port. According to the US consulate that operated in Puerto Cabezas from 1931 to 1940, White workers (other than top managers and "superintendents") were divided into six occupations: overseers, timekeepers, foremen, stockmen, yardmen, and cooks. These workers were paid monthly in US dollars and worked on yearly contracts. The lowest and most poorly paid tasks, called "farm work," were carried out by about 1,500 laborers, almost all of whom were Nicaraguans (Costeños and "Spaniards") who were paid on a daily or weekly basis in cash or company script. The company did not recruit or house this reserve labor force, and the demand for these laborers fluctuated drastically. For example, in 1935, US Consul Eli Taylor in Puerto Cabezas noted that Bragman's Bluff Lumber Company reduced its labor force by 60 percent, "most of whom have returned to places of origin in the interior" (US Department of State Records, Correspondence of US Consulate—Puerto Cabezas, 1937).

"Farm work" was divided into six branches: (1) cutting and carrying fruit to the railroad, (2) cleaning the banana lands of weeds and brush, (3) making bridges over drains, (4) constructing "fruitroads" for mules, (5) constructing "corduroy roads" (used for access to the interior of plantations), and (6) digging drains (US Department of State Records, Correspondence of US Consulate—Puerto Cabezas, 1931) Not surprisingly, workers strove to acquire less grueling and more "skilled" jobs such as lower-level clerical and supervisory positions, as well as railroad and construction jobs. These mid-level jobs were often held by West Indian and Costeño workers who spoke English and had experience in the banana, railroad, and lumber industries—a fact that inspired resentment.

According to many of my older Porteño informants, "farm" workers were disparagingly referred to, in English, as "machete men."[4] They described "machete men" as illiterate agriculturalists from the interior of the country who, attracted by wage-labor opportunities, found their way to Puerto Cabezas. One of my informants, who worked as a carpenter and later a lumber-mill operator, described the "machete men" in the following way: "The company give job to bitcha [a lot of] machete men. Them boys work hard man . . . all day long in the plantation them swing machete and carry load like mule. I worked here in Port man, *tranquilo, sin problema.* Them boys no like Port . . . want to go back to their own place *cosechar* [to harvest] corn and all them things."

Although the skill of the "machete men" was legendary, Porteños did not envy the backbreaking and low-paid work that they performed. Porteños took pride in their ability to avoid this work and often attempted to involve themselves in the auxiliary industries that proliferated in the port to serve the companies' diverse needs. Also, many entered into commerce, opening stores that filled economic niches (such as providing loans and credit) that the company commissaries did not monopolize.

As the term indicates, "farm work" occurred not in the city but rather in banana plantations, owned and operated by the Standard Fruit Company, that lined the banks of the Wawa River. In the Wawa River area, the Standard Fruit Company attempted to control much of the productive process, from planting to weeding to transportation (O'Brien 1996, 71). This practice stood in contrast to the Coco River to the north, where smaller banana companies functioned primarily as buyers that purchased bananas from local villagers-cum-small-scale independent growers (Helms 1971, 113). To control the productive process, the company built a hundred-kilometer-long railroad line that connected Puerto Cabezas with inland "camps" located along the rail line that followed the Wawa River. Each camp had its own commissary and office. The camps were completely dependent on provisions sent from Puerto Cabezas by rail, and they were staffed by two kinds of workers: overseers who were based in Puerto Cabezas (Whites and mid-level Jamaicans and English-speaking Costeños), and a large and highly transitory body of "machete men" who stayed for long periods at a time in makeshift structures. Porteños who worked in the camps took pride in their ability to maintain a permanent residence in Port and looked down at "farm work."

I found in my interviews that Porteños (regardless of any self-identification as Black, Creole, Miskito, or Spanish—or any combination thereof) sharply distinguished themselves (and by extension their work) from "machete men" whom they viewed as rural peasants who were not suited or prepared for city life. As I will describe in greater detail in the next chapter, Porteños strongly valued their own identification with the jobs and lifestyle of city life in Puerto Cabezas. They have long perceived of themselves as a cosmopolitan people who enjoy the advantages of urban life, such as access to items of foreign manufacture and a consistent contact and exchange with the United States and the Caribbean. In their recollections of "company time," they contrasted their own cosmopolitanism ("good living") with the scarcity and self-reliance of peasant life.

According to the popular perception, Puerto Cabezas was a place where, as long as one had the money, any product could be acquired. In the countryside, on the other hand, peasants were viewed to be in the unenviable position of having to manufacture locally many of the goods that they consumed in their daily lives, such as soap, rope, baskets, brooms, and cheese. In the words of one Porteño informant, "Cuando Puerto realmente era Puerto, aqui se econtraba del todo" ("When Port was Port, you could find anything here."). I found that in the 1990s, the great majority of my informants, even young ones, agreed that "Port was no longer Port," by which they meant that after years of a war-imposed isolation, Puerto Cabezas no longer possessed an essential quality that had historically defined it: extensive commercial and cultural ties with the rest of the world, particularly the Caribbean and the United States.

In Puerto Cabezas the salaried work force was overwhelmingly male. As Cynthia Enloe has convincingly argued, banana plantation work, because it involved machete work and transportation to often-isolated camps, was regarded as "men's work" by US corporations (Enloe 1989, 133).[5] In her discussion of the role of gender in the banana plantation complex, Enloe wrote:

> One of the conditions that has pushed women off the banana republic stage has been the masculinization of the banana plantation. Banana-company executives imagined that most of the jobs on their large plantations could be done only by men. Banana plantations were carved out of wooded acres. Clearing the bush required workers who could use a machete, live in rude barracks, and who, once the plantation's trees were bearing fruit, could chop down the heavy bunches and carry them to central loading areas and from there to

the docks, to be loaded by the ton on to refrigerator ships. This was men's work. (ibid., 134)

Enloe emphasized that despite the absence of women's plantation labor in the first stages of development of banana regions, women's work played a key role in the overall banana plantation complex. This work, however, did not occur directly on the plantations.

There is an interesting paradox with regard to racial identification of "machete men" that arose during my interviews with Porteños about "company time." I found that, in what on the surface appeared to be contradictory statements, my informants identified "machete men" as both "Indians" and "Spaniards." Although they recognized that many "machete men" were Miskito Indians "from the communities," they also recognized that others of them were monoglot Spanish speakers "from the Pacific."[6] Because these non-Miskito "machete men" were from the Pacific and, for that reason, taken to be non-native to the region, Costeños described them as "Spaniards." But because they were also dark-skinned campesinos with rural skills and orientations, traits that Costeños associate with Indians, they also regarded them, somewhat disparagingly, as Indians. Thus Porteños described this contingent of "machete men" as being simultaneously "Indians" and "Spaniards," the term "Spaniard" serving primarily as a geographical referent to distinguish the Atlantic coast from the Pacific coast, and "Indian" being used as a term that in a complex way (particular to Costeños) indexed both race and class.

In the present, the term "Indian" connotes rurality—a rurality that contrasts with Porteño cosmopolitanism. Even Porteño informants who described themselves as Miskito or recognized their "Miskito blood" distinguished themselves from Indian "machete men" because they did not perform that sort of labor and because they did not have a rural orientation. In this sense, to be Porteño represented, and continues to represent in the present, a social identification that crosscuts ethnic identification. Within Costeño society it is perfectly reasonable for a campesino from the Pacific to be both a Spaniard and an Indian, and it is reasonable on the other hand for a Porteño to proudly "be" an Indian and disparage, in certain contexts, being Indian.

Bragman's Bluff Lumber Company and the companies that replaced it in the 1940s practiced a policy of strict residential segregation (Karnes

1978, 111). White American workers and their families lived inside a fenced area in well-constructed family housing with running water and electricity. (In the present, most residents of Puerto Cabezas do not have access to these amenities). The American area, known as the "zone," represented a distinguishing feature of the city that, in often very complex and controversial ways, stands out in the memory of present-day Porteños. The zone included both the industrial installations of the company and the residences and much of the "human resource" infrastructure (to use a term from modern-day corporate America) for US company employees. In my interviews with Porteños, they manifested a profound ambivalence with regard to the zone and, by extension, the role of US companies.

On the one hand, the massive installations of the zone embodied US wealth, progress, and technological prowess. When asked to describe Puerto Cabezas during "company time," Porteño informants universally mentioned the massive engineering and architectural projects initiated by US companies in and around Puerto Cabezas. They contrasted this technological and infrastructural advancement to the present *atraso* (backwardness). Informants explained how during "company time," the pier extended twice as far into the ocean as it does now and it accommodated large tankers. One informant nostalgically described these ships as the "biggest in the Caribbean" and contrasted them to the lamentable present situation in which "only lobster boats and Moskeeta *velas* [sailboats]" dock at the pier. For this informant, the small sailboats that Miskito fishermen use to catch and bring their haul of turtles, fish, and shrimp to market represented the polar opposite of the oceangoing tankers that during "company time" stopped at Puerto Cabezas: one was Indian, small, backward, and local (concepts that in the minds of Porteños, including self-proclaimed Miskitos, are in certain contexts closely associated); and the other was American, large, advanced, and international (also tightly associated concepts).

In the context of explaining to me the past importance of Puerto Cabezas, even young Porteños recalled nostalgically when the railroad tracks extended from the zone (situated on the bluff) down to the end of the pier. The rail line no longer functions in Puerto Cabezas and the rails were long ago removed from the pier. Today the pier continues to deteriorate to the point that it has become hazardous for its users. The government is unable to finance the maintenance of the pier. Now the government, in line with a long precedent of turning to foreign extractive industries for basic infrastructure, finds itself in a dispute with a US company that balked on its commitment repair the pier (López 2004; López and Urbina 2004).

In the present, severely rusted buildings and heavy machinery litter the area that used to be occupied by the zone. On walking tours of the area, Porteño informants brought my attention to these ruins in the context of illustrating to me the former grandeur of Puerto Cabezas and its present backwardness. In their presentations to me, planned and impromptu, my informants invariably referred to the irony of the present situation in which the great majority of the people of Puerto Cabezas lack the most basic infrastructure and services—infrastructure and services that were available (for some) thirty years ago. In a city that in the present can only be approached by two deteriorating dirt roads that accommodate only the most intrepid of vehicles, my informants showed me the gutted locomotives that once carried people and provisions a hundred kilometers into the interior. In a city in which only a small percentage of the population has access to running water, Porteños showed me the rusted and dangerously wobbly water tank that dominated the horizon of Puerto Cabezas and that once provided the water that poured out of chrome faucets in all the buildings of the zone.

Coincidentally, during my stay in Puerto Cabezas, this abandoned water tank finally fell to the ground in a windstorm, narrowly missing a family of squatters who had built a house in its shadow. The incident produced three principal responses in the city, the variations revealing the ambivalence of Porteños with regard to "company time." Some Porteños viewed the falling of the tank, which had not been functional for decades, as a symbolic marking of the end of US industrial influence in the city. This ending of US influence, in turn, signified the decline in the importance of Puerto Cabezas as a port city and a bustling hub of economic activity. The event signified for others the indifference of the present government that, in defiance of previous protests by concerned citizens, neglected to demolish the decaying structure in spite of the tank's threat to the public. The third reaction that I recorded was indignation on the part of Porteños who viewed the event as the most recent of a long line of negative consequences (such as the pollution from mining and the massive silting resulting from years of deforestation) that followed years of reckless exploitation at the hands of US companies. In a comment infused with bitter irony, one Porteño remarked to me that "the gringos aren't even here anymore but they continue to shit on us."[7]

Roberto Flores, the unabashedly Sandinista journalist of the leftist FM radio station in Puerto Cabezas, summed up the anti-US sentiment in a passionate radio broadcast in which he blamed the US companies for the near tragedy. In the broadcast Flores noted that US and Canadian mining companies whose Atlantic Coast properties had been nationalized by the Sandinista government were now petitioning the Nicaraguan government for indemnity. Flores regarded North American claims for indemnity shocking and absurd in light of the environmental and social destruction brought about by these companies. He vigorously protested that "the North American companies should pay the Costeños and the Nicaraguan people for all the damage that they did and not the other way around."[8] Flores insisted that the near tragedy of the fallen water tank was a product of the exploitation of Nicaraguans during "company time."

The large artificial ponds that are situated on the eastern edge of what was once the zone represent another distinguishing feature of Puerto Cabezas that was left by the companies and that continues to spark polemics.[9] In the 1990s, after fifteen years of rapid population growth caused by the influx of civil war refugees, the ponds lay at the center of densely populated neighborhoods. Porteños recall that during the heyday of the lumber industry in the region (in the 1950s and 1960s), the ponds were created and used by the US lumber company NIPCO (Nicaraguan Long Leaf Pine Company) to treat pine logs. NIPCO applied powerful chemicals to the logs to kill pests and prepare them for transportation.

One of my informants who had worked for NIPCO described the appearance of the ponds in the 1950s: "In those times those ponds were full of wood. You could have walked from one side to the other without getting wet walking only on pine logs. Later they brought mahogany and cedar. And right there to the side were the sawmills which in the high season for wood were working all day long making all that noise. In those times there was noise everywhere, with those big gringo trucks, not like the Soviet ones now which are worthless. Puerto Cabezas was like a beehive."[10]

In the present the rusted out metal frames of the old sawmills and newly-built one-room houses surround the ponds, which eerily lacks vegetation. Women can be seen in the morning and afternoons washing their clothes in their waters, disregarding warnings issued by institutions of public health. Like the water tanks, the ponds stand for both the best and the worst of "company time." They epitomize for Porteños the past importance of Puerto Cabezas and the technological defiance of the US companies against an unforgiving natural environment. At the other extreme they provide yet another example of the hazards callously left behind by US companies.

The examples of the water tank and the lumber treatment ponds illustrate the ambivalence of Porteños with regard to the historical role of US companies. Their accounts of "company time" were full of both approval and contempt. Porteños recall with awe and admiration the exploits of the companies, but they also recall, at times with acrimony, their second-class-citizen status vis-à-vis North Americans—a status that was most apparent in the zone. Some Porteños remember that Nicaraguans (Costeños and "Spaniards" alike) were not allowed in the zone unless they could demonstrate a good reason to be there. This was particularly true in the residential area of the zone, which overlooked the ocean to the north of the pier. Here, the "gringo bosses" lived in well-painted two-story wooden structures with screened-in second-story verandas. Mister Adams, one of my chief informants, a Belize-born "Hindu" man who had lived in Puerto Cabezas since the late 1940s, recalled:[11] "You know where the CIDCA house is? Well that was where the big boss man lived. Them people sit up there and drink gin and whiskey . . . they no like rum. They make big parties only for gringos . . . if you Nicaragua . . . no way, and if you black man . . . never. You can never go. They no like mix with no black man. You go to the zone only to work and when you finish you gone."[12] Other Porteños, aware of the common charge of racism leveled (in retrospect) against the companies, denied the severity of the segregation in Port during "company time."

Down the road a few hundred yards north of the American zone, the village of Bilwi swelled as Costeños, "Spaniards," and West Indians flooded the region. Workers, attracted by relatively high salaries, erected shacks. The companies housed many of the foreign workers in large company-owned barracks. On the opposite side of the zone lived a colony of American Blacks who had been brought in by the company to manage the mule trains and make railroad ties. As the years passed, these different areas of the nascent city acquired names, which have survived to the present as neighborhood names. However, after 1979 the Sandinista administration replaced many of the earlier neighborhood names with "revolutionary" neighborhood names. Some of my older informants recalled when American Blacks, or "American darkies," as they were called in Puerto Cabezas, lived close to the beach in "Mule Town." (While I was in Puerto Cabezas, Joe Taylor, a man that many reputed to be the last surviving American Black, died.) West Indian workers and other experienced workers stayed in a series of barracks on the opposite edge of the sawmill. Mid-level Pacific Nicaraguan workers were also housed in separate barracks and ate at segregated dining halls (Karnes 1978, 112).

"Mule Town" was bordered by "Spanish Town," another Black settlement populated originally by West Indian workers. "Spanish Town" apparently got its name from the Jamaican city and not from having "Spanish" inhabitants. As the city continued to grow, other neighborhoods, such as "Silver City" and "The Beach," emerged. In general, as the city grew in size, the company was no longer able or willing to pay to house workers, and so the strict residential segregation created in the company zone started to disintegrate.

Nevertheless, the rigid labor hierarchy in which Black Caribbean workers, some of whom were Nicaraguan citizens from Bluefields (headquarters of the United Fruit Company's Nicaraguan division), occupied a higher position than "Spaniard" workers became institutionalized and entrenched in other areas of port life. The institutions of the Standard Fruit Company contributed to the increase in the social salience and political ramifications of socio-racial identifications (Black, Indian, and Spaniard) in the daily lives of Costeños. This does not mean, however, that the company successfully erased competing categories of social differentiation, such as those based on regional, occupational, and linguistic differences.

One of the legacies of the company-dominated social configuration of the city of Puerto Cabezas was the persistence of separate leisure, recreational, and religious institutions for the different "races." For example, my informants recall that each "nation" in the city, with the exception of Miskito Indians, had its own social club. The White North Americans were members of the "Standard Club," which operated a bar, dance hall, and ice cream parlor, and which also hosted the "wives" bridge club (US Department of State Records, Consular Records, Puerto Cabezas, 1935). "Spaniards" participated in the "Social Club," which later became the "Club de Leones" (Lion's Club). West Indians founded the "Literary Society," which later became the "Atlantic Club." Interestingly, the club came to be known as a "Black man's" or Creole club, and not a West Indian or Jamaican club.

Indeed, by the 1950s the Afro-Caribbean population of Puerto Cabezas, the majority of whom had arrived within the last generation, increasingly identified itself as Creole, a category that was understood in the popular imagination to refer to the descendants of slaves brought to the Mosquito Coast by English colonists. Nevertheless, I almost never came across a "Creole" who did not trace at least one side of his or her family to twentieth-century immigrants from the West Indies. The same was true for many self-proclaimed Miskitos in Puerto Cabezas.

Even on those occasions when White women chose to live in Puerto Cabezas with their husbands, they rarely worked for wages in the zone. Very few other women accompanied their male family members to Puerto Cabezas. In addition to women's own productive work in their respective countries, they frequently received remittances from their distant husbands and brothers, who in most cases were contracted on a yearly basis and fully intended to return to their homes in Colón (Panama), Limón (Costa Rica), Jamaica, the Cayman Islands, and the Virgin Islands. The same was often the case with Nicaraguan workers from distant parts of the Atlantic and Pacific regions, who most frequently did not intend to place permanent roots in Puerto Cabezas. These workers, almost always men, used wage labor in Puerto Cabezas and the company "farms" as just one part of a larger, cyclical economic strategy that included subsistence farming and, in some cases, hunting and gathering in or near their respective homes.

Puerto Cabezas during "company time" was notorious for its abundance of brothels. The abundance of women employed as "sex workers" in a plantation and company-town setting is entirely consistent with other characterizations of similar social situations (Enloe 1989; Bourgois 1989).[13]

Company Commissaries and the Cultural Impact of Economic Dependence

Especially interesting is the use of script payment and company stores as means of inculcating consumer values, thus a desire to work for a wage, among laborers. The company consistently noted the tendency of the work force to develop a subsistence alternative and become unavailable as wage labor. It used movies, sports, advertising, and company newspapers as more subtle means of encouraging a worker consciousness suitable to its purposes. (Aviva Chomsky 1996, 11)

The Standard Fruit Company in Puerto Cabezas, like the more well-known United Fruit Company, consciously engaged in the creation of "consumer values" among its workforce as a way of shaping them, ideologically and physically, to most effectively suit the company's needs. In many ways the internalization of this "consumer culture" crosscut the different racial categories used by Porteños. By establishing a system in which workers were paid in company script redeemable at the company-owned commissary and discouraging the formation of an agricultural sector that might have served the food needs of the port, the company created a profound dependence among Porteños on goods imported from the United States and, later, the Coco River region. This dependence, in turn, became naturalized, resulting in Porteños actively valuing the cosmopolitan nature of the region and their own cosmopolitanism. This self-perception of cosmopolitanism stood in stark opposition to the Pacific Nicaraguan perception of the region as isolated and underdeveloped.

As many social scientists have observed, Costeños nostalgically recall the "golden age" (Helms 1971, 113) of the banana boom and the subsequent rubber, lumber, mining, and tuno booms (between the mid-1930s and the early 1960s) when cash and goods were relatively easily attainable from US companies and their commissaries operating throughout the Mosquito Coast (Helms 1971; Nietschmann 1973; Dennis 1981; Bourgois 1981; Jenkins Molieri 1986; Vilas 1989). Puerto

Cabezas was the international transportation hub of the northern Mosquito Coast region through which foreign goods entered and raw materials departed. In the twentieth century Puerto Cabezas eclipsed Bluefields, the historical cultural and political capital of the region, as the most important port of the region. Because of the lower availability of lumber and minerals in the southern region, as well as the shallowness of the Bluefields harbor, only US banana and fishing companies (industries that did not require a modern deep-water port) used the Bluefields port extensively.[14] Puerto Cabezas provided the deep-water port that was required by the North American mining and large-scale lumber companies that established themselves in the northern Mosquito Coast in the twentieth century. Puerto Cabezas became the most important and active port of the entire Mosquito Coast and one of the major ports of the Caribbean coastline of Central America. Given that Puerto Cabezas' raison d' être was to serve as an international port, it is not surprising that Porteños also regarded the agro-industrial boom periods of the twentieth century as "good times" in which life in the port city was best.

One of the defining features of US company towns in the Americas was the company commissary. From the perspective of the American bosses, the company store was a necessity in sparsely populated regions where local food and artisanal production was insufficient and no significant merchant class existed. It also made financial sense (in light of the high costs of transportation) to load bananas, lumber, and rubber for transport to the United States and to unload US products for sale.[15] In order to assure a market for its goods, the Standard Fruit Company followed the lead of many other banana companies of its day and paid workers in company script. Weekly steamships, only two days out of New Orleans, docked at the pier in Puerto Cabezas laden with provisions and food. Informants remember that during "company time," they ate bread made from American wheat, ate meat slaughtered in New Orleans, and enjoyed fresh vegetables from the farms of Louisiana. Country music, another import from the US South, continues to be the music of choice in Port.

The companies paid part of the earnings of their employees with a company script (known as "coupons") redeemable in the commissaries of the zone and the inland "camps" (Karnes 1978, 116). The remainders of the salaries were usually paid in US dollars. In some cases the company would advance merchandise to its workers and then subtract this amount from their weekly salaries (Vilas 1989, 48). Although at the time workers frequently opposed the "coupon" policy and protested the high prices and lack of variety in the company stores (ibid., 112), my modern Porteño informants generally regarded the stores as having played a positive role in the life of the city. One Porteño, who had worked as a mechanic during "company time," recalled: "Here in Port a person had everything. If the gringos didn't have it then the Chinos would have it on the commercial strip. Every week ships full of products came straight from the United States and they were good products . . . the same ones that the gringos used—rubber boots, soaps, shirts, you name it. And parts for motors? All kinds."[16]

German and Chinese immigrants established stores along the "Calle Commercial," which extended northward for a half-mile from the outer edge of the zone to the residential area of Bilwi.[17] Although these commercial outlets competed to some extent with the company commissaries, this competition was mitigated by the fact that they relied heavily on shipping lines controlled by the companies. The merchants of the Calle Commercial, in contrast to the itinerant North Americans, considered themselves "natives" of the city, and with the profits of their businesses came to represent a local bourgeoisie whose wealth is now legendary.

Porteños greatly valued the ease of communication with the United States, particularly in light of the difficulty of communication with the Pacific Coast. Until recently, no telephone, telegraph, radio, or all-weather road service existed between the Pacific and Atlantic coasts. Throughout the first half of the twentieth century, the primary mode of intra-regional communication took the form of a network of radio transmitters set up by US companies.[18] Porteños recall nostalgically the days in which letters to and from the United States would arrive at their destination in less then two weeks. A number of my older Porteño informants had taken advantage of the fast and easy contact with the United States to take mail-order courses that trained them to be electricians, mechanics, carpenters, and so on, all trades that qualified them for jobs in a semi-industrial port city. Porteños subscribed to US magazines and received reasonably current US newspapers. The loss of such ties to the United States and the Caribbean precipitated by the departure of US companies (punctuated by the foreign evacuations in response the Sandinista Revolution) has created, to modify Helms's term, an "ethic of isolation" among Porteños.[19]

At mid-century, regular steamship service existed between Puerto Cabezas and Bluefields on a vessel known as the *Bluefields Express*. This vessel has been immortalized by the song of the same name performed by the Costeño musical group Dimensión Costeña. The song, infused with an unmistakable Caribbean beat, has become part of the canon of Nicaraguan folkloric music (*música folklórica*). However, in contrast to Pacific Nicaraguan folkoric music, which has backward-looking rural themes and is played on the marimba by musicians dressed in peasant's clothing, the nationally-recognized "typical" music of the Atlantic Coast, sung in English and Miskitu by jazzily dressed Costeños, is performed on electric instruments and lyrically addresses themes that emphasize modernity and connection to the Caribbean.[20] The lyrics of "Bluefields Express" are as follows:

> Come take a ride on the Bluefields Express
> Check inside on the Bluefields Express
> She's coming down here quick
> She have a hot smoke coming out of the chimney
> She is throwing back smoke
> Come take a ride on the Bluefields Express.

During "company time" a rivalry developed between Puerto Cabezas and Bluefields. These cities were the two main ports of the Mosquito Coast and also were the base of operation of rival US fruit companies: Standard Fruit in Puerto Cabezas and United Fruit in Bluefields. The waxing and waning of the company labor rolls promoted a constant exchange of people between Puerto Cabezas and Bluefields. This resulted in the establishment of kin ties between the two port cities in which the "big families" of Bluefields (Hodgson, Downs, Cuthbert, Sujo, and Wilson among others) established themselves in Puerto Cabezas.

This lively rivalry manifested itself in the form of massively attended sporting tournaments (baseball and basketball) that were sponsored by the US companies, such as the "Serie del Atlántico" (Atlantic Series).

The trip aboard the *Bluefields Express* lasted less than five hours and people remembered that it was comfortable and safe. As one athlete recalled:

> Before Sandino time [the Sandinista Revolution of 1979] Port was *alegre*, man. The Bluefields boys them come up here to play, boy. They play good . . . Lagoon boys too. They come up here with all the *fanatico* them. And musicians come too. We play all day and dance all night, boy. All we want was to beat the Bluefields boys them. Nothing else matter. When we go to Bluefields they see about Port people. Next boys them bring their whole family on the boat, man. They bring food and rum and every damn thing. We all stay with our people in Bluefields—all the Port People have family in Bluefields.

The availability of fast, safe, and relatively inexpensive transportation between Puerto Cabezas and Bluefields (and to a lesser extent smaller villages such as Cape Gracias a Dios, Prinzapolka, Pearl Lagoon, and Greytown) made these cultural and athletic exchanges possible. The above quoted informant jokingly contrasted his memories of "company time" to the present, in which "you can't even go to Lamlaya [a small but important river port two kilometers from Puerto Cabezas] because the road so bad." The overland route to Managua, described by a journalist as a grueling *odisea* (odyssey), is an infamously difficult route (Treminio Urbina 2002).

Porteños recalled that Puerto Cabezas was an international city in which people of diverse nationalities mingled on a daily basis.[21] In the testimonies of my informants, the constant flux of people between Puerto Cabezas and distant ports of call was highly valued and was contrasted to the provincialism of the Pacific Coast, including Managua. Porteños described Puerto Cabezas as a strikingly multinational city that, in the idiom of Atlantic Coast, contained every kind of "race" and "nation." One Porteño stated: "During company time many people lived here . . . from the States, from Jamaica, from Germany, from Grand Cayman, from Panama, everything. Every nation came to Bilwi in order to work. Bilwi was a big city [*tawan tara*]."[22]

In both the English and Miskitu of the Mosquito Coast, the word "nation" does not correspond to its use in North American English. In the popular usage of the Mosquito Coast, "nation" is a term that can best be described as a fusion of the North American terms "nationality" and "ethnic group." Costeños generally recognize foreigners as members of their respective "nations" (in this case nationalities), but within Nicaragua they also recognize Indians, Blacks, and Spaniards as "nations."[23]

In sum, the distinctive feature of Puerto Cabezas, which Porteños most referred to in their narratives of "company time," was the level of "action" (in English) or *movimiento* (in Spanish) in the city. Although they recognized that work opportunities were unstable and that pay in the US companies was low, they valued the dynamism of the coastal economy. In their narrative of "company time," Porteños consistently emphasized the past "action" of Puerto Cabezas that contrasted with its present stagnation or "sadness" (*tristeza*). My informants constantly lamented that "el puerto esta palmado," or "the port is busted," and "No hay movimiento"—"there is no action." "Action" for Porteños signified the presence of a wide variety of international industrial and commercial interests that directly and indirectly resulted in economic opportunities for Porteños. The perception of action promoted in Porteños a highly valued sense of connection to the wider world.

North American ethnographers have noted that Costeños, particularly Miskito Indians, value their present and historical ties to the English-speaking Atlantic world and overestimate the importance and the centrality of their position within that world. Charles Hale and Edmund Gordon, for example, recognized what they respectively call "Anglo affinity" and "Anglo ideology" as central elements of Miskito and Creole worldviews (Hale 1994, 15; Gordon 1995, 6; 1998, 198).

Based on observations made during her fieldwork in the 1960s, Mary Helms claimed that the Miskito rejected the Hispanic "sphere of influence" and "imitated" the Anglo-American "sphere of influence" (Helms 1971, 221). She argued that the Miskito attempted "to feel psychologically a part of modern times," but that this created anxieties because "the Miskito do not fully understand the nature of the modern world" (Helms 1971, 220). She wrote:

For example, at the time of this study the news was heavy with the increasing military involvement of the United States in Vietnam. However, reports of fighting in the Far East were interpreted by the people of Asang to mean that the war would very likely soon affect them, because once they too experienced conflict on their river in which the United States was involved (the Sandino Affair), and if it happened once it could happen again. People talked incessantly about keeping an eye out for airplanes and awaiting an attack. Yet beneath the tension was a feeling that it was a mark of importance and recognition to have war on the river, or, in other words, if warfare were part of the modern world, the Miskito should be involved also. (Helms 1971, 221)

This phenomenon (a certain geopolitical self-importance that leads to an overestimation of their significance in world affairs) is related to the inevitable cultural impact of a regionally specific political economy in which exchange between Costeños and Anglo-Americans has created a profound dependency on interaction with more powerful external actors. This dependency and the ideologies that correspond with it need to be viewed as regionally specific, not ethnically specific.

The US-sponsored Bay of Pigs invasion of Cuba in the 1960s was launched from Puerto Cabezas (A. Adams 1992, 145). As a result of the close cold-war-era ties between the US government and the Somoza dictatorship, which was supported by the US-armed and US-trained Nicaraguan National Guard, the US military provided "aid" and "technical assistance" in the construction and maintenance of a paved airstrip on the outskirts of Puerto Cabezas.[24] The airstrip, which was long enough to support civilian and military cargo planes as well as fighter planes, was of strategic importance for the US and Nicaraguan militaries. For residents of Puerto Cabezas, whose precarious economic existence relied on the availability of transportation, the airstrip represented an important and valued link to national and international markets. Indeed, during my fieldwork the rumor that a major airline was going to make a stop in Puerto Cabezas on the main Miami-Managua route spread widely among excited but skeptical residents.

Porteños recalled the brief period before the Bay of Pigs invasion when Puerto Cabezas was filled with "action" as Cuban exiles and their US advisors prepared for the invasion of Cuba. The army provisions and supplies that were left behind at their departure (such as mattresses, tents, and weapons) filled the formal and informal markets of the city. In general, Porteños welcomed the infusion of goods and capital into the local economy that was caused by the buildup in Puerto Cabezas prior to the Bay of Pigs invasion of Cuba.

What was remarkable about my informants' recollection of the Bay of Pigs invasion was the matter-of-factness with which they regarded their city's brush with first-order geopolitical intrigue. It did not strike my informants as anomalous or fanciful that Puerto Cabezas should play a major role in an invasion that eventually led to a nuclear standoff between the United States and the Soviet Union. In this sense Porteños conformed to Helms's characterization (of the Miskito) in which she identified the exaggerated need "to feel psychologically a part of modern times" (Helms 1971, 220). Like the Miskito villagers with whom Helms worked on the Rio Coco in the 1960s, modern Porteños manifest what I prefer to call geopolitical self-importance that is absent from the Pacific region.

The Mosquito Coast region has in fact been drawn into the center of US foreign policy on many occasions in the twentieth century. From the US Marine occupation of region in the 1920s and 1930s, to the Bay of Pigs invasion of the 1960s, to the US sponsorship of Mosquito Coast Contras, to the current targeting of the Miskito Coast by the DEA (Drug Enforcement Administration) in the US "War on Drugs," Porteños have many compelling reasons to recognize their role in hemispheric politics.

BOOMS AND BUSTS: RACE AND POLITICAL ECONOMY IN THE MOSQUITO COAST

In contrast to the traditional sugar and tobacco regions of the Caribbean, where after emancipation ex-slaves and their descendants resisted working for wages on plantations and, whenever possible, attempted to engage in subsistence farming (becoming Sidney Mintz's "reconstituted peasantry"), a large-scale plantation or slave economy never operated on the Mosquito Coast. Porteños to this day devalue subsistence agriculture and take pride in the fact that they have urban-oriented jobs and lifestyles. Unlike other banana-growing areas like Costa Rica and Colombia, where the US companies occupied lands immediately adjacent to their corporate headquarters, the Standard Fruit and NIPCO banana and lumber lands, as well as the gold, silver, zinc, and lead mines of the interior, were relatively distant from Puerto Cabezas—a fact that discouraged workers from abandoning wage labor and reconstituting themselves as a peasantry.[25]

In the twentieth century, rural Costeños significantly increased their production of agricultural products for sale in local and regional markets. This change is particularly noteworthy because the region had historically lacked a significant peasantry.[26] The inhabitants of the Mosquito Coast, regardless of their putative ethnic or racial label, had for hundreds of years traded naturally occurring forest and marine products with Anglo-Americans for manufactured goods (including foods such as flour, cooking oil, and rum). In the trading ports of the region, the demand for food was filled by both regional and international trade; regionally traded products obtained from small-scale swidden agriculture (as well as hunting and gathering) were supplemented by imported international foodstuffs (Helms 1971, 4). In rural areas, Costeños satisfied their food needs by practicing a combination of swidden agriculture, fishing, hunting, and gathering. They regularly obtained manufactured items by participating in intermittent wage labor, barter, and the sale of forest and marine products such as turtle meat (Nietschmann 1973).

In the twentieth century, however, as large-scale lumber, banana, mining, rubber, tuno, and other companies established themselves in the Mosquito Coast, the demand for foodstuffs increased as the non-subsistence sector of the region's population rapidly grew. Consequently, the agricultural production increased as rural Costeños began to increase their production of "cash crops" destined for regional markets. These cash crops, primarily rice and beans, had not historically been incorporated into the diet of Costeños, who regarded rice and beans as "Spanish food."[27]

Helms, noting that this shift towards agricultural production for regional markets was relatively new, argued that despite this recent turn to peasant-like production, the Miskito Indians did not represent a classic Mesoamerican peasantry because the region had never been drawn into the surplus-extracting mechanisms of a nation-state. She wrote:

> From the point of view of the Miskito, the motivation to participate in such activities was not based on inescapable demands by state officials for a share in their energies and production, as is the case

with peasant-agrarian state relations. Instead it centered on a growing desire for the foreign material goods which quickly became cultural necessities for them over the years, a situation that Kroeber has termed "voluntary acculturation." Although the introduction of these goods came originally from the outside world, it was the increasing dependence on such items as manufactured cloth, iron tools, sewing machines, and rum that provided the impetus for continued Miskito involvement with the West. (Helms 1971, 6)

Helms observed that rural Costeños, particularly those living along the fertile banks of the Coco River, increasingly met their entrenched demand for foreign goods through the agricultural production of foodstuffs for sale in regional markets. In the decade from 1960 to 1970 this process accelerated as increasing number of Pacific campesinos immigrated to the region.[28]

Starting in the late 1940s, the populous Coco River region became the breadbasket of the Mosquito Coast, establishing itself as the major supplier of food to Puerto Cabezas (Vilas 1989, 48).[29] Waspám, a riverside city one hundred kilometers from Cape Gracias a Dios, became the *tawan tara* (big city) of the Coco River with a bustling *panga* (small motorboat) traffic that linked it the approximately seventy villages below and above it (Gomez 1991, 43).[30] Major US companies established offices at Waspám and made a major investment in the improvement and maintenance of the Puerto Cabezas–Waspám road. This road became the best and longest intra-regional road in the entire Mosquito Coast.

In the 1940s the US-based Rubber Reserve Corporation, based in Waspám, established more than forty commissaries on and around the Coco River. These commissaries supplied goods to as many as five thousand Costeño rubber collectors in addition to two hundred plant workers in Waspám (Vilas 1989, 48). By the 1960s the World War II–inspired rubber boom had expired as Southeast Asian rubber production returned to prewar levels. In the meantime, NIPCO had established a lumber-processing facility across the river from Waspám in the now-Honduran city of Leimus.[31] Pine extraction peaked in the mid-1950s, and by 1963 NIPCO abandoned Nicaragua.

In 1955 Wrigley's Gum Company of Chicago established a tuno processing plant in Waspám (Vilas 1989, 77).[32] The Wrigley company functioned primarily as a buyer and technical adviser to Coco River tuno collectors, who bled tuno trees throughout the region and brought their crudely treated blocks to Waspám for sale. Wrigley closed operations in 1979 due to the Sandinista revolution.

The final major company that opened in or around Waspám was ATCHEMCO of the United States. In the mid-1960s, ATCHEMCO (Atlantic Chemical Company) acquired and expanded a large resin and turpentine plant in a virtually uninhabited place twenty kilometers out of Waspám on the Puerto Cabezas-Waspám road (Rivera and Vernooy 1991, 22). ATCHEMCO used as its raw material the resin-rich tree stumps that NIPCO had left behind when it abandoned the region after twenty years of devastating logging of Nicaraguan pine stands (Jenkins Molieri 1986, 203).[33] The industrial complex at La Tronquera, which directly employed as many as five hundred Nicaraguan workers housed in company *barracones*, represented a "miniature social universe" (*micro universo social*) (Gomez 1991, 53) that in many ways conformed to the company-town pattern of Puerto Cabezas in the prewar era.[34] In the memories of Porteños, the "action" of Waspám in the early 1960s and 1970s rivaled the then-dwindling "action" of Puerto Cabezas. This turn of events was particularly galling for Porteños because they had long regarded the Coco River as an underdeveloped Indian backwater.

After the bust of the banana industry in the early 1940s, the second-most prominent extractive industry (behind logging) on the coast was mining. Three Canadian- and US-owned mines operated a hundred and fifty kilometers west of Puerto Cabezas in the jungle mining cities of Siuna, Rosita, and Bonanza. The economic void in Puerto Cabezas caused by the closing of NIPCO in 1963 was for the most part filled by mine-related commerce as Puerto Cabezas played an important role in the transfer of products and raw materials to and from "the mines" (the term used by Costeños).[35]

Like the Standard Fruit Company in Puerto Cabezas before World War II, the North American mining companies of the postwar period practiced a policy of residential segregation, dividing workers into neighborhoods based on their place in the labor hierarchy.[36] Given the undeniable correlation between the socio-racial identifications (as gringos, Creoles, Miskitos, and Mestizos) of workers and their place in the labor hierarchy, these neighborhoods were perceived to have a particular "ethnic" constitution (Jenkins Molieri 1986, 204). In the mining town of Siuna, for example, an area called "Jamaica Town" was known as a Creole neighborhood. Rural Costeños, most of whom went to the mines in search of seasonal wage labor, lived in the lowest-quality housing. American technicians lived in air conditioned homes on hillside compounds, complete with tennis courts and swimming pools. Nicaraguans were excluded from these "American zones."

The Costeño villagers of the region in effect formed a "reserve army" of laborers that could be hired and fired at will according to the vagaries of production (T. Adams 1981, 59). The lowest-level workers, who most frequently came from isolated rural Costeño villages that were considered Indian (Miskito and Sumu), seasonally migrated to the mines in search of wage labor. In the mines these workers suffered an alarmingly high rate of silicosis, a lethal lung disease (T. Adams 1981, 69–71).

North American management often favored English-speaking Costeños, many of whom already had work experience with North American companies, over monolingual (Miskitu-, Sumu-, and Spanish-speaking) Nicaraguans.[37] Costeños who possessed skills, experience, and sufficient fluency in English were often given higher-level positions such as office work or overseer. Given that proficiency in English as well as formal education were, in the racial ideology of the region, associated with the term Creole, Creoles were perceived to enjoy a privileged position vis-à-vis Indians and Spaniards. This division of labor, consciously promoted by foreign companies, undoubtedly contributed to the contextual hardening of the porous division between Creoles and Miskitos. This, of course, is not to say that people who primarily identified themselves as Miskito or Spaniard did not hold some of these positions. Indeed, my Porteño informants, some of whom identified themselves as Spaniards and Miskitos, worked at higher-level jobs in the mines. Although they did not use the term "Creole," they in effect passed as Creoles because by speaking English, coming from Puerto Cabezas, and having a trade or clerical skills, they could occupy the role that corresponded to Creoles. Clearly, ethnic identification in this context was not an inherent quality of an individual; rather, it intersected in complex and mutually constitutive ways with one's position within the larger political economy.

With regard to the relationship between education and socio-racial identifications, it is important to note that the official evangelizing strategies of the Moravian Church in the twentieth century recognized and incorporated the distinction between Creoles and Indians into their education policy. This is particularly significant given the fact that until the 1950s the Moravian Church and other missionary churches ran almost every school in the Mosquito Coast region.[38] In some cases the educational policies of the churches helped reinforce the so-called ethnic hierarchy in the North American industries of the region. Take, for example, the following North American Moravian missionary's description of the Moravian school at Wasla, a small Indian village: "The mission had begun an industrial school [in Wasla] as an experiment. A school which taught reading, writing and perhaps simple arithmetic was all right, but this seldom helped an Indian boy or girl get a job when he was older" (Borhek 1949, 27). The Moravian school taught shoe making to the children of Wasla because "shoes were important for work on plantations" (ibid.). Until the 1960s, the urban schools of Bluefields and Puerto Cabezas were "Creole schools" that used English and Spanish as the languages of instruction, and were superior to rural schools that generally used Miskitu as the language of instruction.[39] The above example represents a classic self-fulfilling prophecy in which rural Miskito children were educated to assume a subordinate position in the labor hierarchy.

What few government positions that did exist were almost exclusively occupied by Hispanic Nicaraguans, leaving Costeños politically disenfranchised. The highest-level political office normally held by Costeños was that of the village "headmen" or "*síndico*" who served as a link between the state and the local community. Under Nicaraguan rule each village acted as an autonomous unit within the state. The síndico was responsible for collecting relevant taxes and registering civil events such as marriage, divorce, births, and deaths (Helms 1971, 166).

Motivated by the postwar cotton boom and increasing concern about rapid resource depletion, the Nicaraguan government began to make greater efforts to integrate the region into the national governmental and economic structures. Viewed as a vast and underpopulated frontier, the region began to be used as an outlet for campesino migration from the Pacific. In the 1950s many Pacific campesinos, who had historically engaged in peasant agriculture, were forced from their lands by aggressive cotton producers. These cotton producers, driven by the favorable price of cotton on the world market, rapidly displaced campesinos from Pacific farmland (Vilas 1989, 60–97).

Pacific campesino migration was not a new phenomenon in the Atlantic Coast. Before 1950 many campesinos were attracted to the region by the opportunities for wage labor. However, never had migration occurred on such a large scale. From 1963 to 1971 the population of the Atlantic Coast increased 63 percent (from 88,963 to 145,508), while the overall population of Nicaragua increased only 22 percent (Vilas 1989, 72). The abundance of land and low population, which traditionally had allowed rural Costeños to retain their subsistence base in spite of the presence of capitalist enterprises, became challenged by the influx of the dispossessed peasantry of the Pacific region. This process of Pacific campesino penetration continues to this day, but after the Contra War, Miskito communities have fiercely guarded community lands, as the February 2004 forced eviction of forty campesino families by two hundred armed Miskito residents of Layasiksa (in the mining district) attests (Martinez 2004).

The developmentalist climate of the era deeply influenced the Nicaraguan government during the Somoza dictatorship. With the help of the World Bank, the Nicaraguan government created two organizations aimed at regulating the "colonization" of the region: INFONAC (Institute for National Development) and IAN (Nicaraguan Agrarian Institute). INFONAC initiated a reforestation project in which it created and took charge of immense forest reserves. INFONAC did not consult with the Costeño villagers of the region despite the fact that 12 percent of the reserve land overlapped with lands claimed (both collectively and individually) by Costeños living in villages that had received title to communal lands as a result of the land-titling process initiated by the Harrison-Altamirano Treaty of 1905 (Jenkins Molieri 1986, 290–292). INFONAC placed restrictions and taxes on the use of natural resources in these areas. This practice embittered Costeño villagers who had never experienced a comparable level of government interference with regard to these lands. The affected villagers, threatened by the new measures, set forest fires in protest. A remedy to this conflict was not attempted until the mid 1970s, when IAN gave land titles to sixteen villages that had been affected by INFONAC's reforestation projects (Jenkins Molieri 1986, 299–305).

Apart from the reforestation projects, the government attempted to carry out what it called an agrarian reform. However, it is clear that this agrarian reform represented mostly a mechanical transfer of population from west to east, as well as the increased regulation and taxation by the Nicaraguan government of foreign and national lumber companies operating in the region. In 1974 the Nicaraguan dictator Anastasio Somoza declared: "Once again I repeat to the young people of the countryside who are suffering because all the land is occupied, that here are the Atlantic Coast and the Coast people waiting for them to come to make it part of our country and to make the most progressive and the greatest agrarian reform in Latin America" (Vilas 1989, 78).

At first the government put campesino migrants to work primarily on transforming the western part of the region into a cattle-exporting zone. Later, campesino migrants continued to advance eastward, clearing land for farming. Inland Costeños, mainly Sumu Indians, were often driven from their lands. It has been approximated that during this period, about 300,000 acres of tropical forest were lost per year (ibid., 75). Between 1964 and 1973, IAN gave titles to 2,594,550 acres of land located in the Mosquito Coast to 16,000 families. Half of these grants were given to recent Pacific Nicaraguan campesinos migrants (ibid., 67). The majority of these campesinos cultivated crops for sale in the regional and national markets.

This increase in migration and agriculture was accompanied by a decrease in exports from the region. The 1960s were marked by a rapid decline in the production of wood and minerals as a result of the exhaustion of these natural resources. At the end of the 1960s copper mining virtually ended. This occurred only a few years after copper mining had been the Coast's most lucrative enterprise. Between 1963 and 1971, 60 percent of mining jobs were lost (approximately 1,800 workers) (ibid., 77). In the period from 1966 to 1975, copper, which in 1966 had represented 59 percent of the region's exports, declined to only 2 percent.

Seafood production (mostly for export to the United States) (ibid., 76) and resins (derived by ATCHEMCO from the tree stumps left by NIPCO) replaced minerals and wood as the major exports of the region. According to Vilas, in 1975 "shellfish and resin accounted for 75 percent of the exports of the region" (ibid., 83).

Major international oil companies, which previously manifested little interest in Nicaragua, received massive exploration concessions from the Nicaraguan government in the 1970s. More than 90 percent of these concessions were on the lands and waters of the Mosquito Coast (ibid., 77).

The wage labor opportunities offered by these new industries did not replace those lost by the "bust" of the previous industries. As I mentioned above, the unavailability of wage labor, and the associated lack of ability to purchase foreign goods, created an ethic of deprivation in cities and villages all over the region, not simply Miskito villages as the ethnographic literature seems to suggest.

THE RISE OF INDIAN INSTITUTIONS AND INDIAN COLLECTIVE ACTION

In the 1960s and 1970s the issue of communal land titles, which had been originally guaranteed for "Mosquito Indians" and "Creoles" by the Harrison-Altamirano Treaty of 1905, became a highly charged point of contention between Costeño communities, North American companies, and the national government. The land tenure situation became more contentious as a result of the following two factors: (1) many Nicaraguan Miskito Indian villagers were relocated within national territory when Nicaragua lost a large portion of territory (all in the Atlantic Coast region) to Honduras in a 1960 World Court ruling; and (2) in 1974 the IAN (Nicaraguan Agrarian Institute) granted titles to villages that lay on or near the huge "forest reserves," which, in the face of opposition by Costeños, were being demarcated in areas claimed by Costeño cities and villages (Jenkins Molieri 1986, 290–306).[40]

Despite the continued controversy surrounding the issue of land titles, political mobilization around this issue was limited, in almost all cases occurring on a village-by-village basis. That is to say, the ongoing struggles by Costeños to acquire and protect land titles did not rely on (1) a collective mobilization of villages claiming distinctiveness as Miskitos, Creoles, or any other "ethnic" category; or (2) any formal legal separation between Indian villages, Creole or for that matter campesino (Pacific Nicaraguan). Villages primarily made claims to land on the basis of having been established villages at the time of the Harrison-Altamirano Treaty or, as in the case of many Rio Coco communities in the early

1970s, on the basis of using land that fell within the forest reserves created by the Nicaraguan government at that time. Thus the individual village or "community" represented the key classification around which collective mobilization was exercised. Interestingly, as far as collective political mobilization was concerned, the racial identification of these villages, although in many contexts recognized, was not a particularly salient characteristic.

However, starting in the late 1960s, after at least forty years in which Costeños remained relatively apolitical, mobilization in the Atlantic Coast region increasingly came to be carried out along self-consciously ethnic and racial lines. During this period a number of organizations emerged that attempted to organize Miskito and Sumo Indians as Indians who shared a common collective interest above and beyond their local communities. Although North American missionary churches promoted these organizations, they represented a departure from the missionary church–dominated civil society characteristic of the twentieth-century post-reincorporation history.

Ironically, the Moravian Church during this period had been instrumental in inculcating both a pan-Costeño identification and providing the main institutional support for the salience of the division between Miskitos and Creoles. On the one hand, the very fact that the Moravian Church represented a Protestant missionary church that almost exclusively operated in the Atlantic Coast (in contrast to the Catholic Church, which had been firmly entrenched in the Pacific since the time of the conquest) helped to provide an institutional basis for Costeño self-identification as Costeños.[41] To be Moravian was to be Costeño, and profoundly not *español*. The Moravian Church held "provincial synod" meetings every three years in which pastors and religious representatives from villages with churches throughout the region would meet to deal with church matters.[42] Throughout the twentieth century these regional church meetings represented the primary event that, in addition to labor migration, allowed Costeños to tangibly experience their regional unity as a series of communities connected by a common faith and a common religious institution—an institution that was not shared by "Spaniards" from the Pacific.

On the other hand, the Moravian missionaries (whose skill and enthusiasm in learning "native" languages served them in the missionary activities throughout the Americas) quite consciously divided their missionary activities in two branches: the first aimed at Creoles and conducted in English; the second conducted in Miskitu and Sumu and aimed at Indians.[43]

The role of Miskito and Sumu organizations starting in the late 1960s differed from role of the Moravian Church in that they were explicitly Indian organizations that did not attempt to create a separate parallel organization among Creoles. ALPROMISU (Alianza para el Progreso de Sumus y Miskitos, Alliance for the Progress of the Miskito and Sumu) was formed in 1974 with the encouragement and guidance of North American Capuchin missionary priests, Moravian Church members (both North American and Costeño), and members of the Peace Corps.[44] Like ACARIC (Association of Agricultural Clubs of the Río Coco)[45] before it, a principal goal of ALPROMISU was to organize Coco River growers and collectors of foodstuffs and tuno[46] into marketing cooperatives that could demand better prices from regional merchants (mostly "españoles" and Chinese) who operated primarily out of Waspám, the capital city of the Coco River. The difficulty of navigating this river, in many ways a social and economic world to itself, often put cultivators (regardless of their ethnic identification) at the mercy of these merchants. In some cases villages that did not have storage facilities found themselves compelled to sell the majority of their rice and beans at harvest time at a low price, only to have to buy them back later at a much higher price. The folding of ACARIC (which in two years of existence had organized fifty-three Coco River communities) in 1972 provided the incentive to create ALPROMISU to continue to combat this process (CAPRI 1992, 58). In addition to this goal, ALPROMISU also aimed to advocate for the Indian villages whose lands were being engulfed by the new forestry projects of the national government.

The impulse to form such organizations was heightened by the economic crisis in the region. By this time the northern Atlantic Coast region was enduring a sustained economic "bust" in which foreign goods and wage opportunities were scarce as a result of the closing and curtailing of major foreign industries. Costeños tended to view their quality of life as having been much higher during the earlier "company time" and bemoaned their current situation in which they found themselves forced to find viable alternatives to the economic supplement previously provided by wage labor. Mary Helms, who conducted field-work at this time in an upriver village on the Coco River, described this Miskito reaction to the economic bust as an "ethic of poverty" (Helms 1971, 156). Given that Costeño representation in Nicaraguan governmental and nongovernmental organizations was almost nonexistent, Costeños turned to regional networks to attempt to address the economic and social problems faced by their communities.

Organizations such as ALPROMISU and ACARIC, although not run directly by churches, were promoted by the social service-oriented wings of religious organizations, many of which were heavily influenced by the Vatican II and "liberation theology" calls to address material poverty as well as spiritual and moral poverty (Hawley 1997, 120). In many ways the Vatican II calls for "social action" represented just one example of a larger shift towards greater economic engagement by both Catholic and Protestant denominations. In the case of ALPROMISU, the organization received funding from CEPAD (*Comité Ecuménico para el Desarollo*), an ecumenical organization devoted to economic development in the Atlantic Coast (Sanders 1985, 81).[47]

In May of 1974 ALPROMISU held its first annual meeting, in which five hundred participants from eighty-four Miskito and Sumu communities attended (Hale 1994, 127).[48] The meeting was held in Sisín, an inland village about twenty kilometers northwest of Puerto Cabezas.[49] Many of the leaders who participated in the first meeting were pastors in the Moravian Church, which after the 1974 Synod meeting held in Bluefields abruptly became an independently funded and locally run "associated province" of the international Moravian Church (C. García 1996, 100; A. Adams 1992, 174). Church facilities in Sisín, a community that at the time had no more than five hundred inhabitants, were used by the organization with full cooperation of the church authorities.

According to my informants, the meeting was very similar to the periodic pan-regional church meetings that occurred regularly in the region. Collective kitchens were set up at different homes in the region, and community members were asked to lodge delegates, many of whom had traveled for as long as two days by foot and by river. Christian prayers were offered at the beginning and end of each session, and at the conclusion of the meeting the delegates returned to their respective villages in order to provide a report to villagers during masses and services at the local village churches (Hawley 1997, 121; Hale 1994, 128).

The main feature that distinguished this meeting from the regular pan-regional church meetings was that it took place outside of the main cities of the region (Bluefields, Pearl Lagoon, Puerto Cabezas, Bilwaskarma, and Waspám) and delegates from southern English-speaking (Creole) villages were conspicuously absent. The location of this meeting was significant because on an ideological level Costeños identify Creoles with urban areas and Miskitos with rural areas. Within the Moravian Church, Miskitu-speaking pastors had long complained that their congregations were considered second class and that Miskito lacked representation in the church hierarchy (Hale 1994, 126, CAPRI 1992, 60). This complaint was grounded in the historical policy of the church to use English-speaking Creole pastors, often trained in the theological seminary in Costa Rica, to evangelize in Miskito regions (Wilson 1975).

It is interesting to note that many of these Creole pastors, most of who were from Bluefields, viewed themselves as superior to the Miskito and perceived their work in the northern (Miskito) regions as "missionary" work in a manner similar to that of North American Moravians performing missionary work among Costeños. To follow Susan Gal's use of the concept of recursivity, it could be said that from the Creole perspective, the Creole-Miskito relationship recursively mirrored the larger North American-Costeño relationship. This posture taken by English-speaking Creoles on one level would seem to represent an example of the alleged Creole over-identification with North Americans—what Gordon has labeled "Anglo ideology" (Gordon 1995, 6). However, there is an important geographic factor that must be considered.

In the course of my fieldwork I found that a number of Moravian pastors who were raised in Puerto Cabezas but primarily identified themselves as Miskitos also conceived of their service over the years in inland and riverine Miskito communities as "missionary" work: Missionary work among people not only less exposed to God's teaching but also less "prepared" and less "civilized" than themselves.[50] These Porteño Moravian pastors had been sent by the church to work in small and relatively remote Miskito villages in the 1950s and 1960s.

Their recollections of service in the "communities" were marked by a combination of nostalgia and a kind of ethnographic sensibility, both of which were infused with a deeply ingrained sense of superiority and paternalism. They recalled the "communities" as idyllic places of great natural beauty where life was easier and more tranquil. In contrast to the city, many vices such as thievery, drunkenness, and violence were absent. Also people were more friendly and approachable. In addition, they described the villagers as highly superstitious and unreflective in their Christianity. They viewed their experiences in the "communities" as an opportunity to learn about the "ways" of the rural villagers. Given that they considered themselves distanced from their Miskito "*raíces*" [roots], they welcomed the chance to have exposure to a village setting, the ideological center of Miskito life. However, while they and their families were in the field, they made sure that their children did not "mix" very much with the villagers, and they insisted that their children be educated in Puerto Cabezas and Managua so that they could become "prepared." An inherent part of their ethnological curiosity was a feeling of superiority as Moravian-educated Porteños, Porteños who also identified at some level as Miskitos.

How then are we to interpret this case? Clearly it suggests that some sort of identification with the civilizing project of the Anglo-American and Christian world has occurred among both Creoles and Miskitos, validating the Hale and Gordon notion of Creole "Anglo ideology" and Miskito "Anglo affinity." On the other hand, this case challenges the analytical value of positing a radical separation between the ideological world of Miskitos and Creoles. In addition to racial and ethnic ideologies, this case must also be understood in the context of regional status hierarchies—namely a rural-urban dynamic in which urbanism is associated with civilization, modernity, and cultural and racial hybridity, while ruralism is associated with a lack of refinement and Miskito cultural purity. It also provides an example of the importance Costeños give to formal education ("preparation"). The Miskito category is crosscut by regionally specific, status-based distinctions. It is precisely such an attention to status differentiation that has been so lacking in the writings on the region—writings that often have ignored these factors in favor of the reification of so-called ethnic distinctions.

The development of ALPROMISU's institutional philosophies and practices were deeply influenced by trends in both Catholic and Protestant missionary evangelization that took hold in the late 1960s. In addition to the renewed commitment to social action referred to above, missionaries in the region, influenced by Vatican II, the Episcopal Conference of Medellín, liberation theology, and Paolo Freire's "liberating education," devoted themselves to new kinds of culturally responsive methods of evangelization (Hawley 1997, 119). Responding to opponents who criticized missionary work as arrogant and paternalistic, missionaries began to adopt a rhetoric of cultural tolerance, an early version of today's multiculturalism. Catholic and Protestant missionaries, who in the Atlantic Coast region worked together to a surprising degree, attempted to heed Pope Paul VI's call to "evangelize cultures."[51]

Gregorio Smutko, a Capuchin Franciscan friar who worked for twenty-two years (starting in 1967) as a missionary in the region and who served as an adviser to ACARIC, ALPROMISU, and later MISURASATA, was a strong proponent of the need for such an approach that would integrate a group's culture and history into their evangelization. As an anthropologist with a master's degree from the University of Wisconsin, he represented an ideal candidate for enacting this approach in eastern Nicaragua among the Miskito Indians. As Indians and therefore as culture-bearing subjects, they fell under the jurisdiction of both missionaries and anthropologists. Smutko was both. He defined "inculturation," the term used by missiologists to describe this approach to evangelization, in the following manner: "Inculturation . . . is the incarnation of the message of Christ and the Christian life into a culture in such a way that the members of the culture do not consider Christian faith as an imposition from another culture, but rather compatible with the values of their own culture. . . . Gradually Christian values purify the counter values of the culture and a mutual enrichment takes place between cultures (Smutko 1992, 64).

For Smutko this approach was particularly "important in dealing with indigenous groups . . . where many are tempted to consider their culture inferior . . . [and] are tired of being told by outsiders what is wrong with their culture" (ibid., 65). In the name of the battle against intolerance and Euroamerican pretensions of superiority, Smutko strove to merge Christianity and anthropology into what he called "anthropological catechism" (Smutko 1983, 42). Consciously analyzing, describing and, in a word, objectifying Miskito culture and history as Miskito culture and history then became an integral part of the missionary evangelical project.[52]

In 1970 Smutko and other Catholic missionaries brought twenty-four "Miskito lay evangelists" from various Coco River villages for an interactive workshop (*cursillo*) titled the "Salvation History of the Miskito."[53] During the ten-day workshop the Miskito lay ministers were asked to identify the main features of their history and customs as a nation and then compare these to history and customs of the Hebrew nation as they appeared in the Old Testament. The objective of this exercise was to help the Miskito discover "the seeds of God's word in their own history" (Smutko 1983, 43). In turn, the Miskito lay ministers, by discovering the parallels between their own history and Biblical scriptures, would more "easily receive God's word and be seriously committed to better love and serve their communities" (ibid., 45). Smutko wrote: "We are convinced psychologically, anthropologically, theologically and pedagogically it is good to help the miskitos to discover the word of God written in the heart of their people and their ancestors and to discover the salvation history of the miskito nation and then reinforce it with reference to the Biblical similarities between the salvation history of the miskitos and that of the jews" (ibid.).

Clearly, this method took for granted the existence of a discrete Miskito culture and history that was separate from both biblical and modern Christian culture and history. So, for example, the Miskito belief in a single supreme deity called *Wan Aisa* or *Dawan* (a Miskito word probably derived from the English "The One God") was regarded by the missionaries as an independently derived parallel between indigenous Miskito religion and Christian monotheism (Smutko 1983, 47; also see Conzemius 1932, 129; and Sandoval 1957, 61 for a description of these concepts). The missionaries relied upon a definition of the Rio Coco villagers as an indigenous group (indeed an Indian nation) that possessed a discreet pre-Hispanic culture whose features could be readily discerned from European and Christian contaminants, thereby helping to inculcate in the Miskito a rhetoric of cultural difference and a sense of otherness.

The Miskito lay ministers in conjunction with the Capuchin missionaries constructed a fascinating two-column table, a version of which Smutko partially reprinted in his 1983 article, which visually represented the parallels between Hebrew history and Miskito history. In the Hebrew column, participants listed elements of Old Testament history, while in the Miskito column they listed the corresponding elements of Miskito culture. Just as the Hebrews "were unaware of their exact origin," the Miskitos were also said to be unaware of their exact origin (Smutko 1983, 46). Like the Hebrews who regarded Adam and Eve as the first man and woman, the Miskito regarded "Moris Davis" and "Awas Tara" as the first man and woman (ibid.).[54] Like Moses who led the Israelites from Egypt to the Promised Land, Miskut "came from Honduras with all his tribe to Sita Awala (Cabo Viejo)" (ibid.).[55] The Miskito multiracial heritage in which "the inhabitants of Sandy Bay (Tawira) mixed their blood with that of blacks, englishmen, etc." was compared to the biblical facts that "many Hebrews married canaanites" and "mixed with other nations [*pueblos*]" (ibid.). In general, Miskito lays ministers were, through participation in these exercises, being asked to both learn about their history from the missionaries and identify elements of the oral tradition of the region that they, in turn, presented as their own national history.

However, with regard to the issue of the increasing radicalization of Miskito consciousness, by far the most important history lesson that the Miskito lay ministers were supposed to take away from these sessions was that the Miskito not only represented a nation, but that also they had historically been an aggressive and expansive nation that had never been conquered by their Spanish Nicaraguan oppressors. Smutko, in addition to his anthropological and theological interests, was also a historian of the Mosquito Coast. In the 1980s he published a relatively secular history of the region titled *La Mosquitia: Historia y Cultura de la Costa Atlántica*. At the request of Miskito lay ministers who had participated in his 1987 workshop, the volume was re-published in Miskitu in 1989 (Smutko 1992, 64). During my fieldwork periods in Nicaragua, I noticed that a number of my informants proudly possessed a copy of this bright yellow book.[56]

The title of the Miskitu edition of the book is revealing: *Miskitu Nani Aiklabanka, Blasi Piua Wina 1850 Kat*, which can be translated as "The Battles of the Miskitos from the Beginning to the Year 1850." The participants in the 1970 workshops learned the dates and sites of eighteenth-century Miskito confrontations against "the Spanish invaders" that occurred in Pacific Nicaragua and other Spanish-controlled areas of

Central America (Smutko 1983, 46). They noted that just as King David and King Solomon had defeated enemy nations, the Miskitos "conquered more than 20 neighboring tribes" and bested Spanish armies. Eventually, the Miskito nation, of their own volition, "peacefully submitted to Nicaragua but no nation was ever able to conquer the miskitos" (ibid., 47). The 1970 workshop concluded with the following thought: "Nations that do not fight for progress and improvement are the slaves of others. The Miskito must continue fighting for their own progress" (ibid., 48). Although ultimately the goals of these workshops were to aid the missionaries in the lasting Christian conversion of the inhabitants of the region, their methods contributed to the increasing self-perception of Rio Coco villagers as an Indian nation, as well as their increasing self-presentation as culture-bearing subjects.

The Moravian Church (which along with the Catholic Capuchin missionaries in the Mosquito Coast was deeply influence by the current trends in what was called progressive pastoralism) immediately took an interest in the courses and methods developed by Smutko and his associates. These courses later became very popular among Moravian pastors and were offered throughout the 1970s (Hawley 1997, 120). This sharing of materials and strategies between long-time rivals was not surprising in this region where Catholic and Protestant missionaries had been cooperating closely for at least seventy years (Wilson 1983, 55). Based on the analysis of the accounts of ALPROMISU leaders with regard to the self-proclaimed "cultural revival" campaign that they initiated in the 1970s, it seems clear that the methods and ideas they used in their so-called (so-called by outside analysts) "ethnic" mobilization was almost indistinguishable from those used simultaneously in the religious mobilization of the region carried out by Catholic and Protestant churches, most importantly the Moravian church. The religious nature of modern Miskito resurgence is almost completely absent from the anti-Sandinista "essentialist" accounts, which I document in the next chapter, because these are perceived to be incongruous with "indigenous identity."

CULTURAL IDENTITY, GENDER,
AND POLITICAL ECONOMY

The extreme volatility of the regional economy prevented rural Costeños from completely abandoning subsistence and "cash crop" agriculture, thereby creating a contentious dual economy in Costeño villages in which, to quote geographer Bernard Nietschmann, a capitalistic mode of production deeply threatened the preexisting "domestic mode of production" (Nietschmann 1973, 193).[57] Male rural villagers of the region supplemented wage labor stints that were aimed at earning cash for the purchase of manufactured goods with agriculture on local village lands. The agricultural sector of rural village economies had "traditionally" relied on kin-based reciprocal exchange. However, in the twentieth century reciprocal exchange-based interactions were upset, as rural men became more deeply involved in an international capitalist economy as wage laborers and collectors and hunters of forest and marine products for sale to international buyers.

Although Nietschmann recognized the antiquity of Miskito trading ties with foreigners, he believed the "traditional subsistence system" was in danger of finally being entirely replaced by the "market economy" (ibid., 237). He wrote: "The relationship between subsistence primacy and subsidiary market sales is changing. Through the long history of economic contact between the Miskito and foreigners, the subsistence system was never replaced by a monetary system, yet this seems to be happening today" (ibid., 61).

In the case of Tasbapauni, a coastal fishing village closer to Bluefields than Puerto Cabezas that was Nietschmann's field site, the final blow to the subsistence system came in 1970 with the establishment in Bluefields and Puerto Cabezas of foreign-owned sea turtle-exporting companies that created an unlimited market for sea turtles in coastal villages (ibid., 199). As a consequence of this change, Miskito and Creole "turtle men," particularly the younger generation ("de younger race") (ibid., 201), overfished turtle stocks and reneged on their traditional (non-capitalistic) obligations to distribute turtle meat to kin and villagers.

In *Between Land and Water*, Nietschmann identified both Creoles and the "younger race" of Miskito men as the capitalistic sector of village society that rejected the domestic mode of production and so-called traditional reciprocal exchange. Although Nietschmann presented his work as a description of "Miskito culture," he recognized that the village in which he worked (Tasbapauni) had "four major ethnic groupings": Indian, mixed, Creole, and foreigner (ibid., 59). According to Nietschmann, a significant element of the distinction between Creoles and Indians was their economic orientation, particularly their respective level of adherence to "traditional social patterns." He wrote: "In many respects to the Miskito, Creoles personify the outside world with its different economic systems and social responses. The Indians consider the Creoles to be stingy, abrasive and mean, who sell rather than give, who hire people for agricultural work rather than exchange labor communally. If an Indian or a mixed does not honor traditional rules and expected behavior patterns, he or she is thought to have a 'Creole Way' in them" (ibid., 59).

By associating Miskito identity with tradition, he defined the Indian as a non-capitalistic group that stood in contrast to the presumably non-traditional Creoles. Nietschmann defined a Miskito villager as a person who "follows traditional customs" and a Creole as a person who "does not conform too rigidly to traditional cultural patterns" (ibid.).

Interestingly, Tasbapauni has come to be generally regarded as a Creole village (Hale 1994, 124). This shift in identification from Miskito to Creole would imply, if we were to accept the given ethnic characterizations at face value, that the economic orientations of the village should have radically changed from "traditional" reciprocity to "stingy" market principles. This does not appear to be the case. Tasbapauni is still a small fishing village that combines subsistence fishing and agriculture with "cash" fishing and turtling, an activity that did not lead to the extinction of the green turtle species and the breaking of all communal ties in the village.[58]

Charles Hale, who conducted fieldwork in the southern Atlantic Coast region in the 1980s, attributed this shift in self-identification of Tasbapauni villagers to the tendency of Costeños to shift their socio-racial identification from Indian to "one of the more privileged ethnic groups" (Creoles in the south and Mestizos in the north) as part of a "strategy of upward mobility" (Hale 1994, 123). He argued that the success in the late 1970s of Tasbapauni villagers in the regional lobster and turtle trade (some of them "acquired their own boats and developed direct relationships with companies in Bluefields and Corn Island") (ibid., 122) induced them to identify as Creole, a higher-status group. Citing Bourgois and Grunberg's 1980 study (CIERA 1981) of the Coco River villages, Hale made note of a similar phenomena in the northern region in which "upwardly mobile" Miskito villagers increasingly identify as Mestizo and "scorned Miskitu culture as backward and took every opportunity to emphasize their affinities with Spanish-speakers" (Hale 1994, 125).

In light of these shifts in socio-racial identification in response to socioeconomic success, Hale, with the benefit of twenty years of hindsight, critiqued Nietschmann's approach to race and ethnicity in Tasbapauni. He wrote: "By presenting ethnic categories as static, however, he misses the relationship between economic and ethnic change. As people 'made it' economically in southern Zelaya, they often came to increasingly to identify as Creole" (ibid., 124).

According to Hale, the ethnic switch of economically successful ex-Miskitos "deprived Miskitu people of middle-class allies and accentuated their sense of political-economic deprivation" (ibid.). In the Mosquito Coast village of Tasbapauni, upwardly mobile villagers, according to Hale, changed their race. This phenomenon speaks to the deep interpenetration of racial ideologies and political economic change in Tasbapauni and the Mosquito Coast in general. This case serves to demonstrate the porous nature of ethnic boundaries in the region— indeed the disutility of viewing ethnic and racial categories as corresponding neatly to culturally bounded social groups.

Whereas Nietschmann portrayed an entire "ethnic grouping," the Creoles, as the market-oriented sector of coastal society, Helms viewed a particular gender within Miskito society, Miskito men, as the market-oriented group. Working along the Coco River, Helms argued that women represented the last bulwark against the total erosion of the traditional economic system. Specifically, she argued that the agricultural work of women maintained the subsistence base of rural Costeño villages and allowed men to engage in "commercial ventures" such as seasonal wage labor, "cash crop" farming, and rubber, tuno, animal hide, or turtle hunting and collection (Helms 1971, 231). The continuous agricultural production of women mitigated, according to Helms, the disruptive negative effects of the boom and bust cycles of the region and allowed a gendered dual economy (which she labeled a "basic familial division of labor") to persist (ibid.). She wrote:

The very recurrence of economic cycles, what has at times led to insecurity, restricted sociability, and economic depression is perhaps also responsible for the maintenance of the Miskito subsistence economy. . . . The periodic return to depression conditions after more or less short-lived booms has meant that the Miskito have had to continue to fall back on their traditional economic practices to tide them over depression periods. The relative frequency with which boom-and-bust have followed each in the last sixty or seventy years has meant that there has not been an extended period of time such that an entire generation would be divorced from subsistence activities long enough to begin to forget relevant techniques. The division of labor between men and women makes this even more unlikely. As long as women remain relatively village-bound and are concerned primarily with agriculture, the subsistence cushion will in all likelihood remain. (ibid., 233)

Thus Helms associated the women-dominated agricultural sector with traditional non-capitalistic relations. This traditional sector allowed the Miskito to withstand the boom and bust cycles of the capitalist export-oriented sector, in effect subsidizing the US companies in the region by allowing them to have a standing reserve army of laborers.

Helms described women as the "conservative core" of Miskito society. Miskito women were able to retain "traditional Miskito culture" because they historically "did not come into contact with foreigners as much as men did" (ibid., 230).[59] She wrote:

Women's conservativism seems to have played an important role in maintaining a stable, definitely Miskito, cultural core, that is, in maintaining Miskito cultural identity. In addition to relative lack of direct contact, villages approximated a matrilocal settlement pattern, so that a nucleus of related women, mothers and daughters, formed the permanent element. Regardless of their husbands' wanderings, these women formed a stable consanguineal core in and of themselves. Therefore, all children born to Miskito women . . . grew up in a village where the Miskito language was spoken, and where traditional Miskito customs, many of them based on the duties and obligations of kinship, were taught and practiced by a close knit and cooperative group of related women. Whatever the nature of later contact with agents of change, and this applies especially to boys, there was a solid background of "Miskitoness" already firmly established. This organization pattern is an important reason why Miskito culture still remains viable today. (ibid.)

Although Helms recognized that the intensification of "cash crop" agriculture and wage labor during "company time" disrupted Miskito society, the fact that women remained in the villages practicing subsistence agriculture provided a "cultural cushion to balance the vagaries of Western demands" (ibid., 231). For Helms the role of women's labor within a regional economic system that relied on their surplus agricultural production caused them to serve as the "cultural cushion" of Miskito communities (ibid., 233).

In essence, both Nietschmann and Helms defined the Miskito as a traditional rigidly bounded social group that operated on non-capitalistic economic principles. They regarded Creole and Mestizo social life as operating under very different market-driven modern principles in which kinship was structurally less important. In light of the history of the region in which the group identification of Costeños as Africans and Indians has been highly politicized, contentious, and fluid, there exists a danger of mistaking discourses of African and Indian ethnic difference with the everyday practice of social life.

SUMMARY AND CONCLUSION

Costeños have developed a wide variety of economic and cultural adaptations to changing political and economic conditions over time— some more capitalistic than others. In the ethnographic record of the twentieth century, it is clear that Costeños in part understood and interpreted their world through a racial model in which there were parallel economies: an Indian one based on reciprocity and a Creole one based on market exchange. However, after hundreds of years of shared history (fostered, in part, by the geographic and ecological unity of the region as well as its distinctive colonial history vis-à-vis the Pacific Coast), inhabitants of the Mosquito Coast of Nicaragua forged themselves into a single society where, contrary to the prevailing social scientific approaches to the region, social "fault lines" did not occur solely on racial terrain (Smith 1996, 175).[60] Within this regional culture, racial ideologies (Costeño ideas about race) are inextricably linked to political economic conditions. These racial ideologies, at different moments in Mosquito Coast history, have become intensely politicized.

In the case of the Mosquito Coast, it is more productive to view racial categories as, to quote Lee Drummond, "symbols rather than signs." These categories do not function simply as labels that are attached to a concrete and uncontestable referent. Rather, these symbols (ideas about race and human difference) are integrated into larger ideological systems and "become ideas that men [and women] use to create a social world around them" (Drummond quoted in Brackette Williams 1991, 127). As I will continue to illustrate in subsequent chapters, individual actors, in turn, manipulate and contest ethnic stereotypes and symbols in their everyday status struggles. In the Mosquito Coast, ideologies of ethnic difference are used as after-the-fact rationalizations of class position and mobility, as the above analysis of Helms's and Nietschmann's work demonstrates.

It is important to note that the racial ideology that has developed in the Mosquito Coast associates urbanity (the consumption and work patterns of "city life") with the Creole ethnic category. The Indian category is generally associated with rurality, understood as subsistence production combined with low-level seasonal wage labor and trade.

Throughout the history of the region, all Costeños have adopted a common, but regionally varied, economic and cultural adaptation in which they have actively engaged in trade and labor exchanged with the Anglo-Caribbean world. The agro-industrial penetration in the region (in the form of capital-intensive and foreign-owned logging, banana, rubber, and mining industries) that started in the nineteenth century and greatly intensified in the twentieth century promoted the formation of a large segment of Costeño society that became dedicated to and dependent on their involvement with these extractive industries—most starkly in the port cities of Greytown, Bluefields, and Puerto Cabezas. As a result of the particularities of Mosquito Coast history, this segment of society came to be associated with the Creole category—a putatively Black racial category. To put it bluntly, to be Creole is to be a city dweller. In this sense the meanings of the racial categories in the region are and continue to be inextricably linked to the political economy of the region—a political economy profoundly shaped by the boom-and-bust cycles of North American extractive industries.

What then are the implications of the above conclusions for an understanding of the social life of Puerto Cabezas during "company time"? The most important feature of Puerto Cabezas that is relevant at this point in my analysis is undoubtedly the port city's extreme dependence on distant regional and international production and trade. Puerto Cabezas has from its inception been a consumer city created and propped up by its international resource-extracting industries. Porteños have in turn internalized their dependence on foreign capital as a positive collective trait that distinguishes them from both Pacific Nicaraguans and Indians. Unlike the iconic Indian of the Miskito woman in Helms's analysis or the traditional Miskito in Nietschmann's analysis, Porteños completely lack a "subsistence cushion" of any kind on which to fall back. Therefore, to live and work in Puerto Cabezas is at one level to live, consume, and work like a Creole (at least as Creole is defined in the popular imagination). In this sense, Puerto Cabezas had a strong ideological predisposition to identification as a Creole city, or "Black man city" as some Porteños call it.[61] For this and other reasons Puerto Cabezas has been known in the twentieth century as a center of Creole population.

In the next chapter I will explore the consequences of the tumultuous events of the 1980s, when the political economic underpinnings of Creole identification were rapidly withdrawn as a result of the Sandinista Revolution, in which all North American companies evacuated the Atlantic Coast, leaving Puerto Cabezas in its present "busted" state.

CHAPTER 5

Neighborhoods and Official Ethnicity

WHEN I FIRST STARTED FIELDWORK in puerto cabezas, I had hoped to focus my attention on the regional councils of the new autonomous regions and the ways in which race and culture were invoked within them. However, to my dismay I discovered that this forum was, for my purposes, remarkably ethnographically sterile as well as logistically frustrating. With regard to the logistical frustrations, I discovered that the national government, led by the UNO party, neglected to fund the regional councils. It also neglected to invest the regional councils with anything but the most limited governmental authority. For this reason the councils rarely met. When they did meet, the sessions were mired in protocol and factional posturing that I found to be anthropologically uninteresting.

After a great many frustrating interviews in which I found next to impossible to get more than the standard factional "party line," I decided to stop interviewing Costeño politicians. For this and other reason, I started to focus my attention on the behaviors and testimonies of a wider variety of Porteños rather than their regional representatives.

In my research I did not focus on the most obvious examples of cultural politics in the region, such as the Contra War itself and the subsequent formation of regional councils that were composed of representatives with an official ethnic label. Rather, I chose to focus on a series of more mundane expressions of the role of racial and cultural ideologies in the life of Puerto Cabezas. My findings are significant because they complicate our understanding of role of racial categories in Puerto Cabezas by demonstrating the complicated ways in which these categories intersect with regional and class-based distinctions that have specific meanings in Puerto Cabezas.

FROM COMPANY TIME TO SANDINO TIME

The 1979 overthrow of the Somoza dictatorship and the subsequent ascension to power of the FSLN abruptly marked the end of "company time" in Puerto Cabezas. Not coincidentally, the events of 1979 led to the emergence of Puerto Cabezas as a Miskito Indian city in the discourse of Costeños. Whereas during "company time" the political and economic environment of the city promoted Creole self-identification, "Sandino time" (as Costeños commonly refer to the period from 1979 to 1990) witnessed the rise of Indian self-identification. The upheavals of "Sandino time" also resulted in a political power shift away from Porteños and towards recent migrants from "the communities" who had been displaced by the Contra War. Given the nature of racial ideologies in the region, specifically with regard to extant rural-urban dynamics, the influx of war refugees into the city was perceived through a racial lens such that the influx of rural Costeños was experienced as a Miskitoization of the city. This perception was greatly sharpened by the fact that this influx of rural Costeños went hand in hand with the rapid decapitalization of resource-extracting industries, which had provided the material underpinning to the Creole identification.

The political and economic changes of "Sandino time" had an acute impact on the construction, transformation, and mobilization of racial ideologies in Puerto Cabezas. In the 1980s Puerto Cabezas became the political center of a self-proclaimed Miskito Indian resurgence-cum-insurgency that was understood internationally as quintessential cases of "ethnic conflict," "cultural clash," and the "national question." This conflict was presumed to have taken place as a result of the narrowly defined cultural differences between the Miskito Indians of the Atlantic Coast and the ethnically Latin American revolutionaries of the Pacific Coast. I argue that the opposition of Costeños to the revolutionary program should be understood as a product of cultural differences (when these are defined as language, religion, and customs), and also as the product of the perception that the revolutionary government would isolate the region and push it further away from its people's cosmopolitan ideal. This also can be seen as a kind of cultural clash, but not the sort posited in the literature on the period, which traced the conflict to culturally based, culturally rooted "misunderstandings" between Sandinistas and Miskitos.

A great deal of academic attention has been devoted to providing a more refined explanation for the causes of this conflict by incorporating so-called historical, ethnic, and cultural factors into the analysis. This effort suffers from the problem of diminishing return. Bluntly stated, the Mosquito Coast crisis of the 1980s resulted directly from the cold war geopolitical maneuvering of the US State Department and the Soviet Union. In this sense the causes of the crisis are not mysterious. Therefore, to set the analysis of culture and history to the interpretive task of revealing the underlying causes of the Mosquito Coast crisis represents, in the end, a misguided effort (unless, of course, it was the case that the gaze of this analysis was directed at the makers of the cold war in the Pentagon and the Kremlin). It is, however, a productive endeavor to shed light on the impact of the political and economic convulsions of the 1980s (only one of which was the Contra War) on the ways in which racial and cultural discourses were mobilized in Puerto Cabezas in the period from 1979 to the present.

DECAPITALIZATION AND ABANDONMENT

It is generally held, both inside and outside of Nicaragua, that the single most important factor in the ethnic conflict of the 1980s was the attempt by the national government in the Pacific to control and govern the Mosquito Coast region, which, through Pacific Nicaraguan neglect and self-interest, had never been fully integrated into Nicaraguan national life. This historical feature of Nicaraguan politics generated deeply rooted cultural differences between the inhabitants of the Pacific Coast and the inhabitants of the Atlantic Coast. These differences, in turn, were presumed to lie at the heart of Costeño resistance to Nicaraguan rule in the 1980s, as Costeños were presumed to have been intolerant of subordination at the hands of cultural and ethnic "others."

However, in the testimonies of my informants in 1992 and 1993, I found that the issues that Costeños found most intolerable were the economic deprivations and changes that had occurred after the Sandinista Revolution. They blamed most of these deprivations on the Revolution. The lack of wage labor opportunities, particularly in the agro-industrial sector, caused by the flight of North American companies stood out in the minds of my informants as the most prominent of these deprivations. Given the importance for Porteños of their collective self-image as a cosmopolitan people, the decapitalization in the region had significant social and cultural ramifications beyond the purely economic hardships that it produced.

In my interviews with Porteños about "Sandino time" in Puerto Cabezas, my informants consistently returned to, in one form or another, the theme of "abandonment." Whereas in their testimonies about Puerto Cabezas before the Revolution, they nostalgically emphasized the connection of the city to the wider world, as well as its "action" (*movimiento*), their post-revolutionary descriptions emphasized the feeling of isolation and stagnation that set in during the economic and political upheaval of the 1980s. In the minds of Porteños, Puerto Cabezas had become a forsaken place that despite its increasing population and nominal political and administrative importance no longer offered its residents the kind of life that they once enjoyed (and were perceived to have enjoyed) in the past. Porteños did not simply lament the high levels of unemployment that resulted from the flight of the resource-extracting foreign companies that had once pumped jobs and dollars into the regional economy. Equally prominent in their testimonies was the sense of being isolated and disconnected from the wider world. This isolation was evidenced by, among other things, their reference to the lack of activity on the pier, the disrepair of the city's houses, the immigration of the so-called "original Port People" to the United States, the unwillingness of these immigrants to return to Puerto Cabezas to visit, the absence of working foreigners in the city (as opposed to the leftist political tourists who visited the city throughout the 80s and 90s and almost always disappointed Porteños by their casual dress and their frugal spending habits), and also the chronic shortage of goods, particularly those goods that had been associated with company time. These goods included items such as clothes, appliances, flour, and small North American goods, from playing cards to flashlights.

Porteños unwaveringly described the situations in Puerto Cabezas as lamentable. In Spanish, one of the adjectives that my informants most frequently used to describe Puerto Cabezas was "*palmado*," which is a slang term that denotes destitution and poverty. In our endless conversations about the extreme levels of poverty and violence in the city, one of my key informants constantly used the refrain "*pobre Bilwí*" to describe the present state of affairs. In Miskitu, my informants described Puerto Cabezas during "Sandino time" as "*sari*" (sad) because there was no work and no money (*wark apu, lalah apu*). This sentiment did not change with the electoral defeat of the Sandinista administration in 1990. Puerto Cabezas continues to be *abandonado* (abandoned).

The fact that the hardships of the postrevolutionary period in Puerto Cabezas should have been experienced as abandonment speaks to the importance for Porteños of maintaining cultural, social, and economic ties with the rest of the world. This outward-looking orientation is a defining characteristic of Costeños that North American ethnographers have noted throughout the century, although they generally have recognized this as a Miskito trait (Conzemius 1932; Helms 1971; Dennis and Olien 1984). Costeños generally expect the events and actors of the international arena to affect their lives, and at times this clearly leads them to overestimate the degree to which these events are likely to impinge on their world.

Costeño receptiveness towards high-status outsiders has also been noted throughout the ethnographic literature, and nothing I observed in Puerto Cabezas contradicted this observation. Indeed, this trait proved to be enormously helpful during my research, as Porteños eagerly volunteered to speak with me (a Miskitu-speaking Latino gringo of "Spanish" Nicaraguan and Costa Rican parentage) without hesitation about topics that I expected to invite greater reticence. I also observed that despite the city's early history of racial violence and also despite Porteños near obsession with racial banter (particularly pertaining to skin color), the people of Puerto Cabezas and the Atlantic Coast are surprisingly racially tolerant. Porteños recognize that Puerto Cabezas had always been a place inhabited by many different "*razas*" and "*naciones*" (races and nations). Indeed, during "company time" the presence of people from near and far parts of world (Chinese, Turks, Italians, Japanese, Jamaicans, Hondurans, Mexicans, Germans, gringos and others) served as welcome indication to Porteños of the economic vitality of the port and of the region.[1]

As a consequence of the Revolution, the demography of the population of Puerto Cabezas radically changed as refugees from the Miskitu-speaking Coco River region entered the city by the thousands. Simultaneously, the Creole elite and Chinese merchants fled the city. Government administrators and soldiers from Managua (whose numbers had previously been far fewer) flooded the region, particularly Puerto Cabezas. The upshot of these changes was that Puerto Cabezas became far less international and racially diverse. My Porteño informants regarded this fact as symptomatic of the "abandonment" of the city.

Porteños distinguish themselves from other Costeños on the basis of their ability to speak Spanish and relate well with "Spaniards." They take pride in their own multilingualism (English, Spanish, and Miskitu), which they contrast to the monolingualism of English-speaking areas to the south and Miskitu-speaking areas to the west and north. Porteños universally recognize the importance of multilingualism and they regard this trait as being an integral part of being "prepared" (*preparada*), an important and commonly used term that can be translated as educated or sophisticated. To be "prepared" means to have the necessary education and formally acquired skills to succeed in a profession (*carrera*). Preparation, apart from being a mark of personal refinement, also places one in a position to attain a job of high prestige, which in Puerto Cabezas is defined as those jobs that spare one from routine manual labor. Hence, in Nicaragua, no matter how much folk knowledge a campesino may have with regard to agricultural techniques, he or she would never be described as preparada. Porteños view themselves as being more highly prepared than other Costeños on the basis of their multilingualism and their greater access to formal education and training given by foreign companies, missionary churches, and the Nicaraguan state.

Notwithstanding the abandonment of the region, Porteños view the relatively more advanced infrastructure (running water, electricity, roads, etc.) of the city in comparison to other regions of the Mosquito Coast as another indication of the privilege and, indeed, superiority, of Porteños. During my fieldwork in Puerto Cabezas, Porteños manifested this self-perception in a multitude of ways, including (as I illustrate in this chapter) popular jokes. The following case provides a clear illustration of this attitude, particularly as it relates to multilingualism.

THE ATLANTIC SERIES

During my stay in Puerto Cabezas I participated as a player in a number of sports leagues, and I came to establish good rapport with many of the athletes and athletic boosters of the city. For that reason, when the city organized its all-star baseball team to send to the annual

intra-regional championship, popularly known as the Serie del Atlántico, or Atlantic Series, I was allowed to tag along with the team as an
anthropologist/mascot.[2] That year the series was held in Pearl Lagoon,
a predominantly English-speaking commercial fishing-oriented city in
the southern region that is accessible only by canal and river.

During the eighteenth and nineteenth centuries, the city of Pearl
Lagoon was an important political center in Mosquito and the Mosquito
Reserve, and today is considered, next to Bluefields, which lies twenty
kilometers to the south, the second-most important city of the RAAS,
the South Atlantic Autonomous Region.[3] Pearl Lagoon has, since the
nineteenth century, generally been recognized as a distinctly Creole
town. The opportunity to travel with a large group of Porteños to Pearl
Lagoon provided an excellent opportunity to study regional ideologies
at work in a traditional and relatively depoliticized setting.

Since the late 1940s, the major cities of the Atlantic Coast region
organized and sent delegations to the Serie del Atlántico. The much-
celebrated tournament represented by far the most important sporting
event of the region and, indeed, was one of the few occasions in which
Costeños from all over the region gathered together in a social context.
In the expansive Atlantic Coast region, where north-south roads of any
kind do not exist and where the smallest overland journey can become a
swampy ordeal, the logistics of moving people and cargo in large volumes
has been historically only within the reach of large industrial and commercial interests. The "Synod" meetings of the Moravian Church, held
every three years and attended by delegates from Moravian congregations
throughout the Mosquito Coast, represented the only other civic event
of comparable scope and magnitude. In the 1980s the emergence of
meetings of the "Indigenous Assembly" has provided an example of a
pan-regional meeting that, significantly, is officially mono-ethnic in contrast to the ethnically unmarked Church meetings and sporting events.

In 1993, eight twenty-man baseball teams from Waspám, Rosita,
Puerto Cabezas, Karawala, Corn Island, Bluefields, Kukra Hill, and Pearl
Lagoon descended on Pearl Lagoon for a week of competition in the
Serie del Atlántico. In the months leading up to the tournament, rumors
had circulated in Puerto Cabezas that none of the northern delegations
would be able to attend the tournament because of the lack of "economic resources." The baseball "Federation," the committee composed

of leading citizens of the city who are known popularly as *"gente gruesa"* (literally, thick people), *"gente de billete"* (monied people), or *"upla tara"* (literally, big people in Miskitu), announced that it did not have the money to provide adequate uniforms, equipment, and, most importantly, transportation to Pearl Lagoon.

Porteños regarded this crisis as yet another example of the lamentable state of affairs of the port and of Nicaragua in general. They most commonly referred to this state of affairs simply as "the situation" or *"la situación."* They recalled that in the past, sports in the city had been financed largely by the foreign companies operating in the region. Also, commercial activity of the port during "company time" had allowed greater access to sporting equipment such as bats, balls, and uniforms. My older Porteño informants boasted that during "company time" their uniforms were as attractive as those used in the "Big Leagues" (US Major League Baseball) and they only used top-quality equipment.[4] They also recalled traveling to Bluefields and the south on comfortable transport ships at the expense of the companies.

However, in contrast to the general perception in the city that "Sandino time" brought hardship, Porteño athletes recalled that the conditions for them actually improved during the 1980s. On a number of occasions the Puerto Cabezas team was flown to the tournament on Soviet-donated transport planes flown by the Sandinista Air Force. Many Porteño athletes also reported fondly the experience of competing and receiving athletic and professional training in Cuba and Managua. In many ways, athletics during the Sandinista period was the one of the few areas in which Porteños did not feel "abandoned." In fact, apart from the much-despised military service, athletics represented one of the few avenues for young men and women from Puerto Cabezas to acquire "preparation" through scholarships and national and international travel.

In 1993, after last-second appeals by the Federation to citizens and institutions of the city, a foreign fishing company agreed to contribute the use of a shrimp-fishing boat on the condition that the Federation would provide fuel and crew. Despite the vociferous protests from the players, the players from the northern delegations (Waspám, Rosita, and Puerto Cabezas) and I piled into a small, diesel-powered boat that reeked of dead fish for a sixteen-hour trip, unprotected from the tropical sun and rains. In the meantime, government officials and wealthy merchants chartered planes for the thirty-minute plane flight to Pearl Lagoon.

Players and fans expressed to me at great length throughout the weeklong tournament the pathetic state of affairs in the region and the deprivations that they had to suffer as a result of the "situation." In their testimonies this current situation stood in sharp contrast to "company time" and "Sandino time," when, according to these athletes (many of whom were in their twenties or younger), sufficient resources were available to support athletes.

It became apparent immediately upon arriving in Bluefields and then Pearl Lagoon that English was the prestige language of the region's cities. My informants explained to me that the major cities of the region had few "Indians" and were populated mostly by English-speaking "Black people" ("*Negros*"). In the testimonies of the players and fans, the appeal to the distinction between "Indians" and "Blacks" was common. For example, it was common knowledge that the "Black man" teams were consistently the strongest and were not supposed to lose to "Indian teams." Two teams were generally referred to as Indian teams, Waspám from the North and Karawala, a southern community at the mouth of the Rio Grande. The fact that these teams possessed old and deteriorating uniforms and equipment was entirely consistent with the association, in the minds of Costeños, between material poverty and being Indian. The players from Waspám and Karawala primarily spoke Miskitu to one another but they were generally conversant in English. The team from Rosita (one of three interior mine cities that along with Siuna and Bonanza are known collectively as "the mines") was regarded as a Spaniard team, a perception that is also consistent with the official status of the mines as a Mestizo area of the RAAN.

On the other hand, the four remaining southern teams (Corn Island, Bluefields, Pearl Lagoon, and Kukra Hill) were regarded as "Black man" teams—a label that, in light of the regional association of relative material wealth and being Creole, was also consistent with their superior uniforms and equipment. The Black players and fans from Bluefields and Corn Island particularly distinguished themselves on the basis of possessing the latest Nike shoes, gold chains, and portable stereos with latest funk and rap music from the United States. My Porteño informants explained to me, somewhat enviously, that the "Bluefields boy them" have close ties to the big cities of the United States, such as

Miami, Houston, and New York. For that reason, in the words of one of my informants, they "think they are in Miami."

Interestingly, Porteños regarded their own team, their own city, and ultimately their own self as being fundamentally mixed. Among the players on the team it was generally accepted that all of the pitchers were "Indians from the communities" and that all the rest of the players were "Port boys." In fact the pitchers did come from nearby villages such as Kambla, Lamlaya, Sisín, and Twappi, communities that lie within the municipality of Puerto Cabezas. These pitchers told me that, although they received almost no money for playing baseball, they lived in Puerto Cabezas in order to play baseball at a more competitive level and to "pass time." Also they explained to me that there was little work or diversion in the communities, so they did not mind staying with their family members in Puerto Cabezas.[5] They all spoke Miskitu, some Spanish and English as well. Many of the self-proclaimed "Port boys" who distinguished themselves from the players "from the communities" also spoke fluent Miskitu and had kin ties throughout the region.

In formal and informal team meetings and conversations in which I participated, I noticed that the "Port boys" complained that the Indian pitchers lacked guile and sophistication in their pitching style. Many of them attributed the team's lack of success in the tournament to the inferior pitching of the pitching staff. They recognized that the pitchers had plenty of throwing velocity. Velocity is an essential talent that, like stature in basketball, is regarded to be innate. It was precisely on the basis of their demonstrated pitching velocity that they were chosen over the pitchers from Puerto Cabezas.

The criticisms that were made against the Indian pitchers corresponded to the racial stereotypes predominant in Puerto Cabezas. Namely, these criticisms corresponded with the historically rooted perception of the Indian as an unskilled laborer who, like a pack animal, makes a living from his or her brute force. In contrast, Porteños have throughout the century highly valued the ability to enter into more "skilled" positions within the regional economy. Consequently, Porteños perceive themselves as being more intelligent, worldly, and sophisticated in comparison to "simple" Indians. As I described in previous chapters, "from the communities" is a description that heavily implies Indianess, while being Porteño implies certain characteristics and lifestyles such as "preparation," intelligence, year-round skilled or semi-skilled work, and urbanity, which are more associated with being Black than with being Indian. Hence, when players appealed to stereotypes about the distinction between "Port boys" and pitchers "from the communities," they were simultaneously, yet not exclusively, invoking both race (Indian vs. Black and Spaniard) and culture (urban vs. rural, skilled vs. unskilled, civilized vs. uncivilized).

What is important to note about this case is that the same individuals who referred to the Indian pitchers as "*brutos*" (stupid) in a racialized way were themselves people who at some level proudly considered themselves Indians. Clearly, the ostensibly geographical categories of Porteño vs. "from the communities" were crosscut in complicated ways by racial and cultural categories that were deeply imbedded in the dynamic regional political economy.

I also observed that among Porteños the division of the Indian category along racial and cultural fault lines was paralleled by the division of the Black category as well. This phenomenon was most clearly illustrated by a series of jokes about the allegedly primitive people of Pearl Lagoon that were told by a self-proclaimed Black man of the Puerto Cabezas baseball team. Upon our return to Puerto Cabezas, I joined a group of young men who had gathered around Ted, a charismatic veteran baseball player, as he was describing in English his impressions of Pearl Lagoon. Ted remarked to the group how "primitive" life in Pearl Lagoon was in comparison to Puerto Cabezas. He noted that only a few cars existed in the entire city and he drew laughter from the crowd when he noted that all the streets were paved with grass. He also made fun of the sporadic and limited electrical service in the city that every evening left people from Pearl Lagoon talking on their porches in the darkness. The crowd received with much merriment his mimicry of a toothless elderly blind man swatting mosquitos in the darkness.

Continuing with the theme of the backwardness of Pearl Lagoon and its people, Ted went on to note that, in contrast to "Port people," the "Black men" of Pearl Lagoon spoke Spanish very poorly. He told the following two jokes, among others, as humorous illustrations of this phenomenon:[6]

A Spaniard went to Lagoon to visit one friend. When the Spaniard reached the woman house she said, "Que tal amiga?" [How are you, friend?]. The woman got vexed [angry] and said, "You come to *my* house and call me tall and meager!"

Later, another Spaniard gone to the house and said, "Como está?" And the old man on the porch turned round and said, "Eh, Esther someone looking you."

In both of these jokes the buffoon is the monolingual English speaker from Pearl Lagoon whose inability to understand basic Spanish causes an embarrassing misunderstanding. In the first joke, the person mistakes the Spanish words *tal amiga* for the English words "tall" and "meager" and therefore wrongly takes offense.[7] In the second, the old man mistakes *Como está?* for the English command, "Come Esther."

These jokes illustrate a series of widespread attitudes on the part of Porteños, the relevance of which has often been ignored in the accounts the region. First, Porteños highly value their own ability to speak Spanish, as well as English and Miskitu. This simple observation, trivial as it may seem, stands in contrast to the oversimplified view present in much of the social science and journalism about the region that contended that the crisis of the 1980s was caused by a cultural and linguistic clash in which the Pacific Nicaraguan government was rejected on the basis of the Costeño rejection of alien culture and language. Second, this case demonstrates the role of regionally based distinctions (in this case Porteño vs. non-Porteño) that crosscut racial categories (e.g., Creoles, Miskitos, and Spaniards). In much of the literature on the region, analysts have neglected the former and insisted on a reified and essentialist interpretation of the latter.

RACE AND MYTH IN INDIAN BILWI

When Porteños invoke ideas about the neighborhoods of the city of Puerto Cabezas in their quotidian dealings with one another and with powerful institutions, they reveal class distinctions and spatially based distinctions that intersect in complicated ways with racial and cultural ideologies. Neighborhoods in Puerto Cabezas are spatial divisions in the city that are frequently discussed. Porteños perceive certain neighborhoods as having particular racial compositions, and these racial compositions are believed to help determine the behaviors of its residents, as well as justify the historical and contemporary relationships between different groups in the city. In turn, Porteño ideologies of race are contested and transformed in the practice of daily life in Puerto Cabezas.

Although in the minds of present day Porteños, the founding of Puerto Cabezas is synonymous with the foundation of Bragman's Bluff Lumber Company, all recognize that the history of Puerto Cabezas predates the arrival of the company. Far from a matter of mere historical curiosity, the fact of Bilwi's Miskito Indian past impinges on the present of Puerto Cabezas on a daily basis. Although many deny it, others lament it, and still others glorify it, Bilwi was, and therefore is, "*indian tasbaika*"—a very charged Miskitu concept that means Indian land.

The city's Indian origin serves as a point of contention in a number of contexts. Most importantly, many residents of Puerto Cabezas, regardless of any ethnic affiliation that they may assert, must pay the community of Karatá, a Miskito Indian village fifteen kilometers to the south, a form of yearly rent. Karatá has since the 1920s successfully claimed that the land on which Puerto Cabezas now lies represents "pasture land" guaranteed to Karatá under the terms of the Harrison-Altamirano Treaty of 1905. The obligation to pay rent to Karatá creates a great deal of confusion and controversy in the city and is frequently the subject of debate. Specifically, the terms of this debate center on the issue of the validity of indigenous land claims. However, on a more general level this debate represents a matter of everyday relevance to Porteños through which they develop and contest ideologies of racial and ethnic worth.

Although Porteños take a wide variety of stances with regard to the legitimacy of Miskito, and especially Karatá Miskito, land claims in Puerto Cabezas, it remains a matter of uncontested collective memory that a Miskito man named Noah Columbus was the original inhabitant of Bilwi. During fieldwork in Puerto Cabezas, I collected many stories dealing with the first inhabitants of Bilwi, which I will refer to as "founding myths."[8] The content of some of these myths varied a great deal, while others contained a remarkable degree of consistency relative to one another regardless of any ethnic or geographic (Atlantic/Pacific) affiliation of the speaker.

A Costeño born in the Pacific who had resided for the majority of his fifty years in Puerto Cabezas explained to me the origins of the city of Puerto Cabezas: "Before the US company came there lived a family here. There was a Miskito named Noah Columbus. He lived out there by those tanks by the Moravian Hospital. Now that place is called El Cocal. But in those days they were the only people who lived in Bilwi. You know that this place is called Bilwi in Miskito? All this around where we are was bush. Over there in El Cocal is where Bilwi began."[9]

This quote expresses a number of common themes in the "founding myths" that I heard and collected in Puerto Cabezas. These founding myths all emphasize that Bilwi is the original name of the area, and that pre-company Bilwi had a small population, all of which was Miskito. Informants consistently portrayed Bilwi as having been an unimportant settlement with regard to both size and commerce. In fact, it is significant that many versions include the detail that Noah Columbus and his family members were the only inhabitants of Bilwi. It is also generally recognized that Noah Columbus lived in a place that has come to be known as a neighborhood of Puerto Cabezas called El Cocal.

Porteños regard El Cocal as a neighborhood that is overwhelmingly populated by Miskito Indians. Official surveys and census reflect this perception.[10] The neighborhood witnessed a dramatic rise of population in the early 1980s as communities along the Coco River were uprooted as a result of the Contra War and the forced evacuation of the region. Thus, Porteños, although recognizing that El Cocal has always possessed a high concentration of Miskito residents, view the majority of current residents of the neighborhood as being recent immigrants from rural and riverine communities. Given that Porteños, regardless of any and all ethnic identifications they may adopt, associate Indianness with rurality and with backwardness, it is not surprising to find that El Cocal carries the reputation of being an impoverished, unsanitary, and unsafe neighborhood.

During my stay in Puerto Cabezas, radio reports frequently decried the increase of crime in the city that began at the end of the Contra War, presumably as a result of the demobilization of Contra and Sandinista troops. These reports often singled out El Cocal as the most crime-ridden of neighborhoods. I was frequently warned to avoid El Cocal at night because "los Miskitos de allá" (those Miskitos) assault and rob people indiscriminately. A frequent explanation given to me for this per-ceived peril was that El Cocal contained a lot of "bush people" or "gente de las comunidades" (from the communities) or "upla sinskas" (ignorant people in Miskitu) who had fought in the civil war and had retained their weapons.

The concept of the "community" [Costeño settlement or village] is a salient native category that carries many highly charged associations, both negative and positive, for Costeños. Spanish speakers use the term *comunidad* and this term is also sometimes used in Miskitu but with the distinctive Miskitu pronunciation that stresses the first syllable of every word, thus *cómunidad*. However, the most common equivalent term used by Miskitu speakers is *tawan*, a word that is probably based on the English word "town." In the Atlantic Coast this term refers specifically to Costeño villages, not Spanish-speaking campesino villages. Both of these terms distinguish small, relatively isolated settlements from larger cities that have had more ties with Pacific Nicaragua and the Caribbean, such as Puerto Cabezas, Bluefields, Waspám, Rosita, and Siuna.

The fear of Miskitos from the communities represents a new popular perception of Miskitos that undoubtedly resulted from the Contra War, in which community residents, especially those along the Coco River, were recruited and trained (at times forcibly) by the Contras and the CIA in Honduras to attack Nicaraguan targets. Those Costeños who fought for the Contras came predominantly from inland rural villages close to the Honduran border and not from coastal areas farther to the south, such as Puerto Cabezas. The process of demilitarization and disarmament posed serious problems for the UNO (Unión Nacional Opositora, National Opposition Union) government in the Atlantic Coast, and indeed all of the country. The fact that many civilians in the RAAN (the North Atlantic Autonomous Region) have remained armed creates an environment of uncertainty and unease among Porteños. This unease is heightened by the frequent reports of supply trucks from the Pacific being hijacked by roving bands of Miskito ex-combatants on the remote dirt roads that lead to Puerto Cabezas.

This general feeling of insecurity, whose root lies in the foreign-sponsored Contra War of the 1980s, manifests itself in the form of ethnic, racial, and rural-urban stereotypes and epithets that have proliferated in the city. Porteños, including Miskitu-speakers, reminisce about the days before the people from "the communities" arrived, allegedly bringing with them violent behaviors. Other individuals find fodder for arguments about the innate savagery and brutality of Indians in general. José, a Puerto Cabezas-born self-proclaimed Miskito, told me: "Before people would fight with their fists . . . sometimes with knives if it was serious. But now with these Miskitos if you fight with one of them they go home and return to kill you in the street with an AKA [automatic rifle]."[11]

I commonly received warnings such as the following from longtime residents of the city: "Miskito man them BAD! You better watch your ass, Barón." Many Porteños harkened back to the days when there were fewer "bush people" and Miskito people knew their place. Residents created for themselves an idealized past in which Miskito were docile and respectful, which contrasts with the present where they are perceived to be violent and uppity. The end result has been that in Puerto Cabezas, rural and Miskito has in some contexts come to be ideologically associated with armed and dangerous. Although levels of violent crime have no doubt risen in the aftermath of the Contra War, in many ways this proliferation of negative stereotypes of community-born Miskitos reflect more a resentment of the increased political power and aspirations of Miskito organizations by Porteños rather than an actual rise in violent crimes perpetuated by Miskitos of rural origins living in El Cocal.

Apart from attributing criminal traits to residents of El Cocal, many Porteños also characterize them as ignorant and uncivilized. In direct response to my questions, informants portrayed the neighborhood extremely negatively. In addition, I found that in social-group contexts, El Cocal had the unfortunate distinction of being the target of jokes and teasing related to supposed ignorance and barbarity. Statements like "What a stupid thing to do, he must be from El Cocal" abounded. The widespread and closely related prejudices against both Indian and rural origins found specific expression in negative characterizations of El Cocal residents. That is to say, in Puerto Cabezas (including among people who either shun or embrace identification as Miskito) those negative images of what it means to be Miskito and to be from a community cohere around these negative characterizations of El Cocal. As a neighborhood within a larger city, El Cocal has come to stand for, to embody, those negative characteristics that are at times attributed to rural people and Miskito people respectively, thereby ideologically inscribing prejudice on the urban landscape.

Returning to the founding myths, it is interesting to note that the folklore of the city locates the founder of Bilwi in El Cocal, a neighborhood that since the Contra War has come to evoke otherness for Porteños. The most crucial, and undisputed, detail of the Puerto Cabezas founding myth is that Noah Columbus was a Miskito man. The myth functions to unequivocally establish Bilwi in pre-company time as an Indian place. Yet ironically, as a result of the influx of rural, particularly Wangki (Coco River) Miskito, El Cocal, which before had stood for and reinforced Miskito nativist claims, now has come to be associated with the unfamiliar and uncultivated Miskito. Within this new ideological landscape, the efficacy of El Cocal and Noah Columbus as symbols continues to be transformed and challenged.

However, by far the most controversial issue that relates to the foundation of Puerto Cabezas deals not with the relationship between the gringos, Miskitos, and Spaniards; rather, it deals with relationship between Bilwi and Karatá, two villages that have historically be regarded as Indian. As I mentioned above, all Porteños cannot help but be aware, given that many must pay rent to Karatá, that the community of Karatá exercises special land rights in Puerto Cabezas. Most are unaware of the obscure juridical base of this relationship. However, many of the founding myths provide an explanation for this state of affairs—a state of affairs that many Porteños regard as particularly unjust. The following narrative related to me in Miskitu by a middle-aged Porteño approximates the most common version of such a myth that I encountered.

> This is how it was. In the first time Noah Columbus lived here with his family. He was the leader of Bilwi . . . he had the title. Everything was good, lots of food, lots of turtle, no Spaniards. But he liked to drink rum. One day the boss of Karatá came and as they started to play cards he brought out some bottles of rum. Noah Columbus got really drunk—*blocked up, man.* He kept on losing, he lost a lot of money. That's how he lost the title to Bilwi. The boss from Karatá went home happy. The next morning when Noah woke up he said, "Oh, shit!"[12]

The key feature of this story, one that is repeated in many others, is that Noah Columbus had possessed a legal title that documented his personal ownership of Bilwi, and this was lost to people from Karatá as a result of drunken folly. In other versions, informants emphasized that the title had come from the Miskito King or the British. In still other versions, Noah Columbus is said to have gotten drunk off American whiskey, implying Karatá's complicity with US companies. In other versions he is said to have lost the title to Bilwi either after or before the arrival of Bragman's Bluff Lumber Company.

For those Porteños who are hostile to Karatá land rights, the story of Noah Columbus losing the land title exemplifies the arbitrariness of Indian land claims, because ownership of the land was so frivolously alienated. For these people, the story also exemplifies the child-like vulnerability that they attribute to Indian people. For anti-Indian Porteños in general, the story serves to confirm the commonly held position that Indians are savage, uncivilized, and unable to care for themselves in an urban setting. Specifically, the story confirms another commonly held prejudice against Miskito men that claims they are unable to "control their liquor" (*tienen mal guaro* in Spanish).

On the other hand, for those who support Indian land claims, the story reinforces the conviction that the region is rightfully *Indian tasbaika* regardless of which community holds title to the land. Similarly, the story serves to reinforce the notion that each Miskito community has at one time possessed a legal document that guarantees possession of the land that it occupies from encroachment by the Nicaraguan government. Those versions that mention that Noah Columbus received the title from the British government serve to legitimize Miskito land claims by appealing to the authority of a country regarded as more important than Nicaragua. Many Porteños recognize that at some point in the past, the Miskito King and the British government exercised an alliance in opposition to the Nicaraguan and Spanish governments.

Nevertheless, I found the issue of the role of the British was not viewed as particularly important or controversial. For most, *King taim* (Miskitu for the period in which the Miskito King, in collaboration with the British, ruled the region) is viewed as a distant age whose legacy does not impinge on modern times. The US banana and lumber companies, rather than the governments of Nicaragua, Great Britain, the United States, or Mosquito, represent by far the most important actors in the historical imagination of Porteños.

THE BEACH: CREOLE NEIGHBORHOOD
OR INDIGENOUS COMMUNITY?

Reference to the Noah Columbus local folklore plays a significant role in current land disputes. Viewing these ongoing local disputes as a form of social practice allows us to see the ways in which ideologies of race and culture are formed and transformed in the context of everyday life. During my fieldwork, a land dispute arose between a group of so-called squatter families and a government institution in Puerto Cabezas.[13] I conducted interviews with many of the parties involved, attended community meetings, and observed the activities taking place on the land in question. What immediately drew my attention to the case was that although it ostensibly concerned land tenure, it also simultaneously exposed with great clarity a broad range of crosscutting contradictions and cleavages within Porteño society—particularly those based on race (Miskito vs. Creole), class, and political affiliation (Contras vs. Sandinistas).

The dispute pitted the Port Authority (ENAP—Empresa Naciónal de Puertos) of Puerto Cabezas, a public institution created by the Sandinista administration and directed as an agency of the national government in Managua, against residents of the neighborhood known as The Beach. Tensions began to simmer in late 1991 when the Port Authority permitted a small fishing company to build a fish-processing facility directly in front of The Beach in a largely vacant area of land directly between the city pier on the east and the Port Authority headquarters that lies on high ground to the west. Residents, who for many years had disputed the Port Authority's claim to the vacant strip of land to the west of the pier, protested that they were never consulted about the building of the plant on the disputed land. They also lodged the general complaint that the Port Authority did not take their interests into account.

In October of 1992 certain residents of The Beach started to dig the postholes for houses that they planned to build in the disputed area. The news of the defiant groundbreaking on the disputed site spread rapidly throughout Puerto Cabezas, provoking a great deal of speculation and a general mood of tense anticipation. Both parties issued threats and both parties looked for allies to fortify their respective claim. On a number of occasions armed standoffs and vandalism occurred, but during my stay the contest remained in stalemate.

The Beach, a particularly large and impoverished neighborhood of Puerto Cabezas, occupies a low-lying coastal strip extending approximately one kilometer along the beach south of the city. During the 1980s the Sandinista government imposed Spanish names, El Muelle (The Pier) in the case of The Beach, on the neighborhoods of Puerto Cabezas as part of its revolutionary restructuring of government—a restructuring that in Puerto Cabezas, in contrast to the Pacific Coast, represented an unapologetic Hispanicization program. The pier, built in the 1920s by Bragman's Bluff Lumber Company, and the main road that connects it to the interior marked the northern boundary of The Beach. The majority of the city of Puerto Cabezas occupies a bluff to the north of the pier that rises five to twenty meters above sea level and protects the majority of the city against hurricanes and flooding. The Beach lies on the lowlands to the south of the bluff and is thus geographically separated from the rest of the city. Large portions of The Beach neighborhood lie directly on swampland and are flooded almost year round, a situation that aggravates health problems related to mosquitoes and the lack of a clean water supply.

For this and other reasons, city planners during the Sandinista administration of the 1980s recommended relocating the entire neighborhood to higher ground in the city. This heavy-handed plan, reminiscent of the massive evacuation of the Coco River during the same period, greatly embittered relations between so-called Beach People and the Sandinistas. After fierce opposition, the Sandinistas abandoned the plan.

The racial composition of The Beach defies categorization within the official system of ethnic categorization that identifies three main ethnic groups (*étnias* in Spanish) in the region: Creole, Miskito, and Mestizo. More than any other neighborhood in Puerto Cabezas, trilingualism is the norm in Beach households.[14] I found that in my conversations with Beach People, only few would positively identify themselves as a "member" of any ethnic group. It was never my intention to try to categorize my informants within a system of categorization that they did not accept, but on those occasions when I did bluntly ask a person if he or she was Miskito, Creole, or Mestizo, the most common response was "mix" (a word used in both English and Miskitu).[15] Porteños who did not live in The Beach often referred to the residents of The Beach as Blacks, Negros, and *Nikru* (in Miskitu), and recognized that English was the most commonly spoken language. However, there existed no uniformly accepted convention for labeling the race or ethnicity of the residents of the neighborhood.

Beach People derive the majority of their income and subsistence from the sea. The main wage-earning activity for young Beach men is lobster diving, a profession in which they are disproportionately represented in comparison to other neighborhoods of Puerto Cabezas. Lobster diving on foreign-owned (Honduran and Colombian) lobster boats, which sell to a recently opened US-owned lobster exporting company, is by far the highest-paying form of manual labor in the city. Unfortunately, the work is also extremely dangerous and physically demanding. *Busos* (lobster divers) rarely are able to endure the rigors of diving full time for more than a few years. After a few years, if shark attack or decompression sickness has not injured them, they invariably suffer from dizziness and loss of hearing. Nevertheless, divers are able to earn as much as $500 (paid in US dollars) in a two-week voyage—a salary that very favorably compares to the $100 that a schoolteacher earns monthly. Beach People, particularly men, also engage in artisanal fishing and turtling (turtle hunting) for money and food. Women rarely engage in wage-labor activities. When they do earn money, it is usually through small front-yard stores (*ventas* in Spanish).

The dispute between the Beach People and the Port Authority resulted from the desire of a group of young men and women to establish households of their own. The majority of the men worked as divers, and had children with women who either lived with their mothers or lived with the young men in the men's mothers' houses. These couples longed for the privacy and comfort of their own house, while also desiring the communal and familial support offered by locating their prospective house within the neighborhood. For most young people in Puerto Cabezas, the goal of marrying and living in a separate residence ("*independizarse*") is a valued luxury that few can afford. Although the ideal of conjugal neolocality exists in the minds of young Porteños, the harsh realities of a severely depressed economy and residential overcrowding usually prevent the attainment of this goal in practice. In the case of the young divers in question, they had through hard labor saved enough money to buy building materials but could find no adequate site to build within the traditional residential areas of the neighborhood. They therefore turned to the vacant lot between the pier and the Port Authority headquarters as a place in which they should rightfully be allowed to erect a house.

Immediately upon their digging the first postholes, Port Authority officials informed them that they were trespassing on Port Authority land.[16] Officials threatened to use the police to stop construction and ordered the men to remove all building materials from the site. The men flatly refused, arguing that the land was not being used by the Port Authority and ironically (given that they shared the pro-Contra tendencies of their neighbors) borrowed a Sandinista agrarian reform slogan stating that the "land belonged to those who would work it." They also organized themselves into an ad hoc commission, called the Comisión del Barrio El Muelle, which was composed of seventeen families.[17] The Port Authority, hoping for a quick and unequivocal resolution to the matter, beseeched the police to evict the families, but for a number of reasons, which I will now outline, this strategic appeal to police authority did not work.

After the election of 1990, which was won by the anti-Sandinista UNO party, the issue of the partisan nature of the army and police represented one of the most serious challenges to peace in Nicaragua.[18] This issue was particularly explosive in the northern Atlantic region, adjacent to Honduras, where Contra activity had been strongest and where the civil war had been most bitter. Contra leadership agreed to demobilize and return to Nicaragua only on the condition that they be allowed to join and at times lead the police forces in the areas in which they planned to return to. Some factions of the UNO party even demanded that President Chamorro dissolve the EPS (Sandinista Popular Army) and replace it with an entirely new army and police force consisting of ex-Contras and new recruits. Many feared at this time that if Chamorro were to take such an extreme measure, the EPS would rebel and choose to not serve the new administration—in effect launching another civil war. Nicaraguans also feared that the opposing forces would carry out bloody vendettas against one another once they were united as civilians within Nicaraguan territory. Chamorro adopted a conciliatory tactic, reducing the EPS from about 80,000 to 20,000 soldiers and reappointing Humberto Ortega, brother of former President Daniel Ortega, as its leader on the condition that he resign from the Sandinista

Directorate and swear to obey the authority of the popularly elected UNO government.

In Puerto Cabezas, the capital of the North Atlantic Autonomous Region (RAAN), ex-Contra leaders took top positions within the police force, and many ex-Contra soldiers joined a special new armed force formed with the help of the UN and the OAS (Organization of American States) called the Disarmament Brigade. The UNO government drastically reduced the size of the EPS in the region but did not significantly change its leadership or attempt to incorporate Contra elements within it. Thus, the police force, which contained high-ranking officers from the ranks of the EPS as well as ex-Contra combatants, represented the only government-sanctioned armed body in the region that incorporated both Sandinista and Contra elements, although Contras held the highest positions. Men and women, who months before had stood on opposite sides of a ten-year civil war, now intermingled in the police station of Puerto Cabezas. Fortunately, in this case, this polarization within the police force greatly hampered the ability of the institution to make decisions and act uniformly.

The two political affiliations contributed to the police force's unwillingness to use force or other types of influence to resolve the matter. In general, the UNO party favored returning to the original owner land that had been expropriated by the Sandinistas. The Sandinistas had confiscated and nationalized the Port Authority in 1980, and the institution continued to be associated with and controlled by individuals with Sandinista affiliations. In addition, many of the Beach People in question had Contra leanings or indeed had at one point either served in the Contra forces or lived as refugees in Honduras. Thus the Contra-led mixed police force was hesitant to act to protect Sandinista-tainted interests against the pro-Contra residents of the neighborhood. Members of the Comisión del Barrio El Muelle explained to me that they made every attempt in their dealings with the police to bring this contradiction to the fore as they appealed to other shared Contra loyalties. This initial strategy proved successful, as the Port Authority ceased to threaten police action and agreed to form a special commission that would investigate the matter. Such an appeal to political affiliation was related to, but not wholly dependent upon, ethnic or racial affiliation.

In the meantime, residents approached the local YATAMA office for assistance. (YATAMA is Yapti Tasba Masraka Nani Alsatakanka in Miskitu, translated as "Descendants of Mother Earth.") YATAMA, composed mainly of ex-combatants within the Miskito wing of the Contra armies, emerged after the war as an aggressively indigenous Miskito political organization. A number of officials from YATAMA agreed to advocate for the residents and immediately sent a letter to the police in which they urged restraint and emphasized that the land dispute was not a simple squatter problem, but rather it was a problem related to indigenous rights. At a meeting called by the Port Authority and attended by local and national civil and military leaders, Rigoberto Carpentier, a YATAMA official representing the "17 families," proclaimed that "The Beach is not a neighborhood [*barrio*] rather it is an indigenous community." He explained that the Harrison-Altamirano Treaty guaranteed that Miskito communities would have legal title to their traditional lands. The Standard Fruit Company, according to him, recognized these rights and rented lands from the indigenous community. Later, when the company ceased operation, the Nicaraguan government took possession of the lands around the pier, but neither the government nor the Standard Fruit Company ever owned this land. It was "*Indian tasbaika*" (Indian land) and therefore belonged to the residents of The Beach, which he now redefined as an indigenous community.

Pedro Martinez, a high-ranking official from the national office of the Port Authority who had been sent from Managua to take charge of the situation, followed Carpentier's speech with a speech defending the position of the Port Authority. He argued somewhat contradictorily that any arguments based on turn-of-the-century treaties were legally irrelevant, while simultaneously delegitimizing The Beach's land claims on the grounds that the majority of Beach residents leased or bought their land from the community of Karatá and therefore did not represent an indigenous community which possessed special land rights. The contradiction here rested in the fact that the rights of the community of Karatá were based on the very Harrison-Altamirano Treaty that he flatly rejected as inapplicable. He stated:

This is a difficult problem . . . very difficult because many years and many governments have gone by and an adequate solution has never been given to this problem. We hope that with our presence [the national directorate of the Port Authority] . . . we are sure that we are not going to solve the whole problem but we hope our presence will at least begin a regional dialogue so that the central government, the local authorities, as well as the very Autonomy Law and the communities can arrive on an integral solution to this problem—the problem of land ownership. We already were aware of the majority of the information that our friend Carpentier indicated with respect to the history of these lands. We even studied the Harrison-Altamirano Treaty and we looked up the history in order to better understand this problem. We made a series of interviews and we collected documentation etc. in order to solve this problem. It is not necessary to look at the land history nor even at the Harrison-Altamirano Treaty, rather more contemporaneously we as a corporation claim to be the owners of these lands. What I have with me is a map, a groundplot . . . where it indicates in accordance with the land documents which are duly registered in Bluefields, which is where this kind of property is registered, that this is a polygon here [pointing to the map] that clearly belongs to the Port Authority. . . . According to the people we have interviewed, all say that they have negotiated with the community of Karawala [sic] particularly with Mr. Chico Francis. . . . So then what is the reality as such of these lands? More than 90 percent of them have been taken. Some [residents] argue that the lands have been given to them by City Hall, others claim that they have been given by the Port Authority, but the great majority indicate that they have bought or leased the land by the community of Karatá. So in this sense I would correct a bit of what Carpentier said about Karatá . . . only until recently has a conflict emerged in the Beach. The people with which at different moments we [the Port Authority] have had a relationship has been the community of Karatá. . . . But if you speak with the people around the Cayuco [a bar located in The Beach] they show you documents given by the community of Karatá.[19]

This speech revealed a number of telling contradictions and ambivalent attitudes with regard to Indian land claims expressed by a Pacific Nicaraguan government official. Martinez indicated that appeals to turn-of-the-century history were not legally valid in this case because the Port Authority possessed relatively recent legally binding documents, all of which had been generated after 1980 as a result of the confusion brought about by the rapid flight of foreign companies and Somocista government officials. Yet he admitted that the Port Authority had continued to honor Karatá land claims. He recognized this policy without mentioning the fact that Karatá land claims were originally based on the Harrison-Altamirano Treaty, whose relevance he had just denied. Martinez refused to accept the argument that The Beach constituted an indigenous community because he felt that their status as Indians was contradicted by their traditional role as paying tenants on lands claimed by Karatá Indians. Here Martinez mistakenly presumed that Miskito Indian land rights were held by Miskito Indians as a general class of people rather than as inhabitants of specific communities that had formally acquired title to their land at the turn of the century, as was actually the case. This perspective betrayed his unawareness or indifference with regard to the established indigenous land tenure system in the city in which all persons, including non-Karatá Miskito, whose houses lie on land claimed by Karatá must make lease payments to the community of Karatá. He also refused to accept The Beach's bid, which he acknowledged had only recently emerged, to be able to act as both a communal and indigenous collective entity.

In an interview that I conducted with Carpentier later that week, he explained in greater detail the arguments that he and the community were asserting. He recounted to me an interesting variant of the Puerto Cabezas founding myth. According to him, what is now Puerto Cabezas used to be called "Bilwi—Mosquitia." Originally Bilwi comprised three, not one, Miskito communities. The one that was led by Noah Columbus occupied the area where El Cocal now finds itself. The other was called Mule Town and occupied the area that is now known as Barrio San Luis. The Beach was the third community and a man called Casanova led it. He claimed that he had formerly possessed documentation that proved this, but that the Sandinistas had confiscated and destroyed these documents during the civil war.

In general, residents of The Beach appreciated and realized the necessity of the efforts made on their behalf by YATAMA, but manifested rather different arguments as to the legitimacy of their claim to the disputed land. Many confirmed the claim that the original inhabitant of the neighborhood was named Casanova but acknowledged that they were not accustomed to referring to the neighborhood as an "indigenous community."

In an interview that I conducted with Ronald Villarreal, one of the leaders of the seventeen families, he denied the centrality the arguments made by YATAMA. He regarded these as obscure and trivial historical arguments. This is not to say that he denied their validity; rather, he simply did not accept the current relevance of an old and, most importantly, complicated history. For him, there existed two principal reasons that he and his neighbors should have access to the land. First, the Port Authority did not currently use the land in question; and second, the land belonged to the neighborhood by virtue of its proximity—only a dirt road leading down to the pier separated The Beach from the disputed land.

Villarreal resented what he perceived as the Port Authority's indifference with regard to the welfare and rights of the neighborhood. Here he cited among other grievances the Port Authority's refusal to consult the residents of The Beach before making decisions about the disputed land. This refusal had most recently manifested itself in the case of the fish-processing plant. He also complained that the Port Authority rarely hired Beach People on the docks and made no attempt to improve the infrastructure of the neighborhood. For him, this indifference was typical of the relationship between the "poor people" of The Beach and the "rich people" that run the "companies" and "governments." In this relationship, Beach People find themselves powerless and easily victimized. He stated, clearly with the current struggle in mind, that rich people "can always pay someone to draw up a map but poor people can't." The majority of the members of the seventeen families with whom I spoke shared Villarreal's disappointment and indignation, and also expressed a great deal of pessimism with regard to their ability as poor Beach People to openly confront the authorities in the city. They did, however, take heart in the fact that they were united, armed, and willing to fight.

Ultimately, what lay at the core of Villarreal and his neighbors' claim to the land was the notion that they as poor inhabitants of The Beach had been neglected by the government and the Port Authority, and therefore had no obligation to respect the authority of these institutions. The land history of Bilwi was in this context only important in the sense that it was complicated and obscure enough to question the validity of the claims of any party. Throughout the confrontation between the police and the seventeen families, it became very apparent that the neighborhood came to represent the most important communal identification around which collective action was mobilized. The families asserted their right to build homes as Beach families. They did not assert their rights as Nicaraguan families or as Porteño families. Their defense of their rights was thus clearly phrased and conceived in terms of communal rights as a neighborhood within a city. From this point, claiming indigenous communal identity was a step that could easily follow.

This case illustrates the complex ways in which ideologies of race and culture intersect with regional and class-based divisions. Contrary to many of the accounts of the region by journalists and social scientists, the so-called ethnic groups of the region are not monolithic entities, nor do they reflect fixed and unalterable identities. In this sense, it is important to heed Charles Hale's call to problematize the increasingly popular concept of identity (Hale 1997, 571). The categorical distinction between Creole and Miskito is part of a wider vocabulary through which Porteños understand and act upon their social world. In the practice of acting upon that world, Porteños in turn rework and transform these categories.

The case of the land conflict in The Beach also speaks to the disutility of interpreting the self-conscious assertion of identity as a phenomenon that can only be understood from the perspective of the so-called ethnic group (Smith 1996). If viewed in isolation, the fact that residents of The Beach, a neighborhood mainly composed of English-speakers who trace at least part of their origin to the West Indies (particularly Jamaica and the Cayman Islands), should claim indigenous identity in the context of a land dispute might lead one to question the authenticity of such a claim. Indeed, many people in Puerto Cabezas did question the motives of Beach families in this case. On the other hand, to view this case as the organic reemergence of a latent indigenous identity by authentic Indians would be equally problematic. In actuality it was through their participation in the land conflict that Beach residents actively asserted and simultaneously reevaluated the nature of their communal ties. Identity in Puerto Cabezas must be understood within contexts in which individuals and other social actors challenge and transform social categories in practice.

LINGUISTIC IDEOLOGY AND OFFICIAL
ETHNICITY IN THE RAAN

The practice of ethnic and racial identification in Puerto Cabezas also must be understood in the context of official attempts by the Nicaraguan government to create ethnic policy. In 1987 the Nicaraguan government, in an attempt to address the long-standing problem of political, economic, and social discord between the eastern and western halves of the country, approved the Statute of Regional Autonomy, which created a legal and legislative basis for a limited amount of political decentralization within the Nicaraguan polity. The Autonomy Statute replaced the former Atlantic Coast department of Zelaya with two new administrative units (known as autonomous regions), RAAN and RAAS, and it also chartered the formation of elected legislative bodies in each region.[20]

Although generally welcomed by Costeño political leaders, the statute has been criticized for its lack of clarity with regard to the juridical and administrative relationship between the autonomous regions and the national government. After the election of 1990, in which the first representatives to the regional assemblies were elected, Costeños on both the left and right questioned the national government's commitment to respecting the spirit of the Autonomy Statute. The implementation (*la reglamentación*) of the Autonomy Statute has since that time emerged as the single most important political project in the region, as regional leaders have universally recognized that in its current form the statute lacks the capability to provide for anything more than a token autonomy. Although completely lacking in muscle with regard to political and economic matters, the statute makes, according to many Costeño leaders, important and novel provisions with regard to cultural matters.

The Autonomy Statute, rather than delineating the duties, rights, and powers of the regional government with respect to the national government, devotes itself primarily to recognizing the social heterogeneity of the region and guaranteeing inhabitants the right to maintain their distinctiveness on an individual and communal level. In order to identify and define the nature of this social heterogeneity, the statute uses a set of terms, and the underlying assumptions on which these terms are based, which taken together form what I call "official ethnicity." Key concepts within official ethnicity include culture, identity, ethnic identity, and ethnic group (*cultura, identidad, identidad étnica, y étnia* in Spanish). The specific nature of the official recognition and use of these terms represents a new development in the relationship between the Central American national governments and the indigenous and minority groups that inhabit these countries. Official ethnicity is based on a specific kind of analysis of the social diversity in the region—an analysis whose introduction has been relatively recent and is in many ways at odds with Costeño ways of understanding and characterizing this diversity.

The Autonomy Statute guarantees the right of all inhabitants of the autonomous regions to "preserve and develop their languages, religions and cultures" (for the full text see Anuario Indigenista 1987, 106–117). The statute explicitly protects the ethnic and cultural rights of the inhabitants of the Atlantic Coast—rights that have not explicitly been extended to the rest of the nation's population. The high concentration of so-called ethnic communities (*comunidades étnicas*) in the Atlantic Coast is the demographic feature that clearly motivated the government's decisions to extend these special rights to Costeños (CAPRI 1992, 230).

The implicit assumption behind enacting such legislation in the Atlantic region as opposed to the Pacific region is that, in contrast to Nicaraguans from the Pacific Coast, Costeño groups were viewed to manifest a culture and ethnic identity that warranted specific governmental consideration. The social variation within the Pacific Coast was not recognized as ethnic or cultural because the common presumption within Nicaragua is that the Pacific Coast does not contain significant indigenous populations or ethnic communities. This perspective reflects what Gould (referring to the Pacific Coast) calls the "myth of a Mestizo Nicaragua," which he defines as "a collective belief that Nicaragua has been an ethnically homogenous society since the nineteenth century" (Gould 1993a, 394). The myth of mestizaje (in which Nicaraguans emphasize the mixed, neither solely Indian nor solely European, nature of the nation) represents an official discourse that has penetrated in one form or another all levels of Nicaraguan society.

The text of the Autonomy Statute lays out what amounts to a demographic analysis of the population of the Atlantic Coast region, an analysis that operates under the assumptions of official ethnicity. The statute declares that, given that distinct ethnic communities populate the Atlantic Coast, Nicaragua must be considered a "multi-ethnic, pluri-cultural and multi-lingual" country.[21] In contrast to the Pacific region, each inhabitant of the Atlantic is associated with one of the so-called ethnic groups identified in the statute. Article II of the document states:

> The Atlantic region of Nicaragua constitutes approximately 50 per-cent of the territorial patrimony of the nation and close to three hundred thousand inhabitants, representing 9.5 percent of the national population, which are distributed in: one hundred eighty-two thousand Mestizos who speak Spanish; seventy-five thousand Misquitos who speak their own language and twenty-six thousand Creoles who speak English; one thousand seven hundred Garífonas the majority of which have lost their language and eight hundred fifty Ramas of which only thirty-five conserve their language. (CAPRI 1992, 229)

The most striking feature of the classificatory system elaborated in the statute is its comprehensiveness. That is to say, the statute implicitly identifies a single genus or category (ethnicity) containing species or headings (e.g. Miskito, Creole, etc.) with which each and every Costeño can be exclusively associated. Thus, official ethnicity submits ethnicity not just as a limited classificatory scheme, such as, for example, occupa-tion (a category that is not expected to manifest itself in every member of a society), but rather as an all-encompassing system such as gender, which is applied to all people. The official ethnicity as manifested in the Autonomy Statute confidently asserts its own universal applicability.

Not only does the statute correlate every Costeño with one of the mentioned ethnic groups, it also associates each ethnic group with a particular language (Mestizo, Spanish; Creole, English; Miskito, Miskitu). The European-derived languages are referred to by name in the text, while each indigenous language is referred to as the possession of the ethnic group to which it presumably pertains. This way of referring to the languages of the region, far from trivial, betrays a significant feature of official and unofficial linguistic ideologies. Pacific Nicaraguans in general manifest a clear ideological distinction between European language and indigenous languages, the former being considered intrinsically superior. It is a common practice, even in the Atlantic Coast, for Spanish and English speakers to refer to Miskitu and Sumu as "dialects" within an ideological framework that ranks languages vs. dialects on a superior-inferior scale. In contrast to speakers of European languages, speakers of indigenous languages are viewed to have a proprietary relationship with these languages as ethnic groups. The statute tacitly postulates an inextricable link between a specific ethnic population and a specific indigenous language. Thus the Miskito, Sumu, and Garífonas possess "their language" (*"su lengua"*).[22]

I found that Porteños frequently engage, often vehemently, in debates as to whether Miskitu is a language or dialect. Many Porteños refuse to grant Miskitu status as a language and instead disparage it as only a dialect. The negative associations that are attached to indigenous "dialects" do not go uncontested, however. Particularly in postwar Puerto Cabezas, Miskitu is witnessing something of a linguistic renaissance. Many of my Miskitu-speaking informants confessed to me that in the past they had been ashamed to speak Miskitu, especially when they found themselves in Managua. Now Miskitu is defiantly spoken in official places, where in the past its use had been considered inappropriate. For example, in the offices of the municipal government of Puerto Cabezas, only Miskitu can be heard. The current mayor of the city, elected in 2004, is Elizabeth Enrique, a Miskito woman from the YATAMA party. Miskitu leaders, all of whom speak Spanish and English, now insist on speaking Miskitu for at least part of their public appearances in places such as schools and sporting events.

Some Miskitu speakers attempt to counter the claim to the superiority of the English language by criticizing Mosquito Coast English as *"inglis saura"* (bad English). A number of my Porteño informants, defensive of the negative characterizations of Miskitu by English-speakers, disparagingly referred to *"cus inglis"* ("coast English" in Miskitu) as *"plas untara"* (from the banana plantation). In order to learn Miskitu in Puerto Cabezas, I frequently exchanged conversation practice in Miskitu for conversation practice in English. Many of my Miskitu teachers/informants expressed their enthusiasm about learning *"inglis pain"* (good English), which they perceived as being far superior to the Mosquito Coast English that many of them spoke to varying degrees.

On the surface, these linguistic ideologies could be interpreted as indications of the deeply rooted ethnic divisions between Creoles and Miskitos that are presumed to exist in the region. For example, the derision of Mosquito Coast English by Miskitu speakers in response to the claim to superiority of European languages (Spanish and English) over Indian languages might be interpreted as an illustration of ethnic rivalry. In this ethnic rivalry, each group would be perceived to have its own distinct cultural expressions that it defends against the foreign cultural expressions of another group. This sort of interpretation would certainly be consistent with the perspectives that are prominent in journalism and scholarship, as well as the official stances of the Nicaraguan government.

However, it is important to note that non-Miskitu-speaking English speakers also express very ambivalent attitudes about the alleged quality of their English. During fieldwork in Puerto Cabezas, I noticed that some English-speakers were reticent to speak English with me and preferred to speak Spanish with me in one-on-one settings. When I asked about this, they explained that their English was hard for North Americans to understand and that it was "bad English." These people were usually younger English speakers who had less access to the traditional sources of knowledge of North American English (e.g., the Moravian Church and US companies). Older Porteños, in contrast, often relished the opportunity to converse in "good English" (some Porteños even defined good English as "the Queen's English") with a person from the United States. They took pride in their ability to speak both good English and Mosquito Coast English.

In Puerto Cabezas in the 1990s, the primary source of good English was the Moravian Church, where church services in the so-called Creole Church are held in an idiom that more closely approximates North American English. In fact, one of my young informants told me that she preferred to attend Moravian services at the Beach church, which conducted services in Miskitu, because she could not read English and she did not understand much of the English spoken in the Creole Church. Although she insisted that she spoke "Coast

English" better than Miskitu, she said that reading Miskitu was easier for her than reading English.

In the face of the perceived threat to Creole power in the city in the postwar period, the issue of the nature of the differences between Creole and Miskito has become highly politicized. This has resulted in the attempt by leaders and non-leaders alike to consciously remove perceived mutual influences from their language and culture. This push towards purification, however, stands in the face of the long-standing value of cosmopolitanism that has predominated in the region.

English speakers who identify themselves as Creoles often deny or downplay their command of Miskitu. The act of denying speaking Miskitu was interpreted as an assertion of social status on the part of such a person. So, for example, among a multiethnic, multilingual group of friends that I spent time with, Lutz (a self-proclaimed Creole) was chided for being "*fachente*" (conceited in English and Spanish) for claiming that he did not speak Miskitu. Many Creoles admitted to picking up some Miskitu "in the street" but denied any real fluency. This denial of Miskitu fluency and refusal to speak Miskitu can be interpreted as a manifestation of "second order indexicality" in which the linguistic performance of speakers serves primarily as a way of marking social identity rather than simply communicating information (Graham 2002, 203).

Among Miskitu speakers, I frequently came across the conscious rejection of English loan words that were perceived to be nonnative to Miskitu. From a philological point of view, such a rejection is a very tricky proposition in light of the deep interpenetration of Miskitu and English due to the historical alliance between the British and the Miskito that was a precondition for the expansion of the Miskitu language in the seventeenth and eighteenth centuries. Nevertheless, I witnessed the impulse among Miskitu speakers to purify Miskitu of English influence.

During interviews with Miskito political leaders, I noticed that it had become a common practice when dealing with outsiders (particularly so-called *internacionalistas* such as myself) for party leaders to conduct the interview in Miskitu with Spanish translation, despite the fact that all Miskito leaders in Puerto Cabezas were fluent in Spanish. This practice, also a kind of linguistic indexicality, has become common among indigenous leaders in Latin America as a way of establishing their authority as indigenous leaders and performing difference (see Graham 2002).

I often surprised my informants with my ability to speak Miskitu that steadily increased as my fieldwork progressed. This was always a pleasant surprise for my interviewees, who typically spoke with foreign researchers and journalists who were making brief visits to the region and did not speak Miskitu. They were flattered that an English-speaking North American would take the time to learn the language, and they would often shift the tone of the interaction away from formal and dramatic to informal and pedantic. They would evaluate my abilities, question me about how I went about learning Miskitu, and educate me about the subtleties and varieties of Miskitu.

On many occasions I was corrected for using terms that my informants stated were truly English. For example, it is the norm in the Miskitu of Puerto Cabezas to seamlessly use the words "want" and "like" without marking them as loan words. So "*Plun* [food] *piaia* [to eat] *want* [want] *sna* [I am]" means "I want to eat food." I was informed, however, that the true Miskitu way to express this idea of wanting was to use "*brih ai duakaia*"—a more cumbersome term that I found was used infrequently.

In general, Miskito leaders and others lamented what they perceived as the heightening contamination of the language that had been precipitated by the Miskitu displacement from the Wangki River (the ideological core of Miskito culture and language) to the English-speaking and Creole city of Puerto Cabezas. Although Miskitu had been spoken continuously in the city since well before its foundation as Puerto Cabezas in the 1920s, it was commonly believed that the varieties of Miskitu spoken along the Wangki River were the pure representatives of the language that had resisted the English influences of city life.

I also spent time attending rehearsals and performances of a Miskitu dance group that was headed by the sister of a major Miskito political leader. In one of my conversation with her, she suggested that I should not use the term "*dans pulaia*" to describe what they do, given that "dance" is an English loan word. She explained that they simply practice "*pulaia*," a word that means play. Her group performed in tuno (pounded bark) outfits, the official traditional fabric of the Miskito, and as a director she was actively interested in trying to present authentic

Miskito culture. With regard to the style of dance, she instructed her dancers that to dance as a Miskito was to dance in truncated hopping motions (she used the Spanish term *brincadito*). She distinguished the brincadito style from what she called the Black style of dancing, which used the hips and was sexually suggestive. This distinction was in line with the common belief in Afro-Caribbean hypersexuality, as well as a broader Latin American belief in the moral purity of Indians in contrast to non-Indians.

Continuing with the issue of language, linguistic ideology, and cultural purity, the case of the Rama Indians is revealing on the same score. According to the Autonomy Statute, the Ramas are a group that has all but lost their language. According to the historical and anthropological work done in the region, the inhabitants of Rama Key (a small island in Bluefields Bay) and its surroundings have to different degrees spoken both Rama and Mosquito Coast English since the colonial period. Researchers speculate that the geographical territory of the Rama language has shrunk drastically from the seventeenth century to the present, having been replaced by both Miskitu and English (Craig 1992; Salamanca 1993). Historically speaking, Creole and Rama ethnic identities have not been mutually exclusive, nor have they been plainly linked to the English or Rama language. The boundary between a Rama Indian and a Creole, when these identifiers have been used at all, has always been porous.

Historically, there exist many examples of people with strong familial ties to the inhabitants of the Rama Keys who used a Creole label and the English language in their political dealings with Britain and the Mosquito Government (see Hale 1987a). Yet according to the reasoning of the Autonomy Statute, a Rama Indian who no longer speaks English (in favor of Spanish for example) would be not be considered to have lost their language because Rama identity is rigidly defined as being linked to the Rama language, not English.

In practice the assumptions of the official ethnicity of the Autonomy Statute come into conflict with systems of racial categorization that exist among people. The case of the Mestizo provides an example of such dissonance between official and popular racial vocabularies. Generally, in Latin America the word "Mestizo" refers to a person of mixed race. In the Pacific regions of Nicaragua, "Mestizo" functions as an intermediate category in a system of racial classification in which Indian and European occupy opposite poles. As mentioned earlier, the Nicaraguan "myth of mestizaje" claims that Nicaragua's population is dominated by Mestizos.

Nevertheless the word "Mestizo" in both the Pacific region as well as the Atlantic region is not a commonly used term for self-identification. In the Pacific region, rural Nicaraguans (more than half of the population) predominantly identify themselves as campesinos (peasants) in order to distinguish themselves from city dwellers. In terms of racial terminology, Nicaraguans most commonly situate themselves within a skin-color spectrum (dark-skinned to light-skinned, *moreno* to *claro* or *blanco*) rather than in terms of a racial continuum (Indian to European).[23]

In the Atlantic Coast, the word "Mestizo" functions differently. In this region it not only refers to a presumed mixed ancestry but also to one's presumed place of origin. This is to say that in the Atlantic Coast, a Mestizo is a person who is considered to have come, at some indeterminate point in history, from the Pacific part of country. Thus, within the system of racial classification in the Atlantic Coast, Mestizo carries a strong geographical component in addition to the strictly racial one. It is telling that a person of mixed Miskito and Creole/Black ancestry is not considered a Mestizo despite the fact that they are of undeniably mixed ancestry. When the Autonomy Statute speaks of " one hundred eighty-two thousand Mestizos" who inhabit the region, it is not referring to all those people who are considered to be of mixed race. Rather, it refers to those people who in some sense are not considered to be native to the region. The Mestizo category of the Autonomy Statute corresponds to a set of commonly used Costeño terms that refer to people from the Pacific.

Using a telling anachronism that dramatizes the deeply rooted divisions established by European colonialism between the Atlantic and Pacific regions, Creole English refers to Pacific Nicaraguans and Pacific Coast Central Americans in general as "Spaniards" and "Spanish," while Miskitu uses an equivalent term, *ispail*. When Spanish speakers in the Atlantic coast want to distinguish themselves from the Miskito or Creole, they rarely use the term "Mestizo"; rather, they affirm that they or their family, at some real or mythical point in time, was "*del Pacífico*" (from the Pacific). I found that it was very common for Spanish-speakers born in the region to identify themselves as being "del Pacífico" and later feel obligated to clarify that they were born in the Atlantic Coast: "*Yo soy del Pacífico . . . bueno yo nací aqui pero mi familia es del lado del Pacífico.*" ("I am from the Pacific . . . well, I was born here but my family is from the Pacific side.") Thus, a term that has an ostensibly geographical referent functions within nominally racial- or color-based vocabularies of social differentiation.

The classificatory scheme of the Autonomy Statute eliminates the disharmonic term "del Pacífico." It substitutes "Mestizo," a term with a clear racial referent but which is rarely used in the daily life of Costeños, for "del Pacífico" or "Español" (Spaniard.) Within the popular Costeño classificatory system, to assert that one is "del Pacífico" is a way of resisting identification as a Creole or Miskito. In this sense it is a negative or leftover category that functions as a distancing mechanism from the positive or better established terms of Miskito and Creole. Yet the Autonomy Statute recognizes its official substitute, Mestizo, as an ethnic group, which can be identified according to the same kind of characteristics as the other ethnic groups of the region.

What, then, does this imply about the principles of official ethnicity as embodied in the Autonomy Statute? What kind of social grouping does the official ethnicity presume an ethnic group to be? In addition to the identification of an ethnic group with its native language, the statute presumes that each "ethnic group" can be identified and defined according to its particular "culture," "traditions," "values," "art," "social organizations," and "communal, collective and individual property standards."[24] In addition to language, these are the supposedly objective criteria that distinguish one group from another. The Autonomy Statute assumes that the Mestizo category indexes an ethnic group in the same sense as other ethnic groups of the region. The ethnic discourse thus necessarily defines all ethnic groups as being inherently parallel, self-evident, social formations. Thus, according to the Autonomy Statute, the ethnic group is the product of a set of presumably objective characteristics, all regarded as being, in one way or another, cultural.

CHAPTER 6

Costeño Warriors and
Contra Rebels

NATURE, CULTURE, AND ETHNIC CONFLICT

THE CONTRA WAR and the Costeño-Sandinista confrontation received a great deal of attention from scholars and journalists, particularly because it represented a hot spot in the tense cold-war standoff between the United States and the Soviet Union. For leftists around the world, the Sandinista Revolution became a symbol of hope in the losing struggle against unfettered global capitalism. Within the hemisphere the revolution stood for the power of popular nationalist movements against dictators and their traditional US patrons. For the right, the revolution invoked the fear of the domino effect in a region in a perpetual state of brutal civil war in which related national liberation fronts fought against unpopular right-wing governments.

Countering the hostility of the US government against the Sandinistas, an outpouring of support came from leftists throughout the world, including social scientists—some of whom took posts in the new government or offered their services as consultants. The US government turned to right-wing scholars and journalists, enlisting their services in the battle of world opinion that was waged with the pen. The cold-war polarization that characterized this time was, not surprisingly, reflected in the theoretical models of social scientists and others in their analyses of the conflict.

In the Mosquito Coast, the fall of the Somoza dictatorship and the triumph of the FSLN (Frente Sandinista de Liberación Nacional, Sanadinista National Liberation Front) in 1979 initiated a series of events in Nicaragua that eventually led to the proliferation of, at times, highly

organized and, at times, heavily armed social movements. These movements expressed Costeño aspirations to exercise greater control over
regional affairs, as well as their dissatisfaction with the changes brought
about by the revolutionary government.[1] Initially, Costeños expressed
these aspirations primarily through civil organizations that had some
degree of continuity with prerevolutionary groups, as well as Sandinista-
sanctioned "revolutionary" organizations promoted by the FSLN throughout the country. Later, however, many Costeños began to organize
themselves into anti-Sandinista armed groups. The US government
promoted the formation of these groups as part of its destabilization
campaign against the government of Nicaragua.

As the civil war escalated in 1981–1984, thousands of Costeños fled
to refugee camps in Honduras and Costa Rica (Americas Watch Committee 1986, 5).[2] The budding civil war and the unrest that accompanied
it received a tremendous amount of international attention. The assort-
ment of counterrevolutionary armed groups that began to form in and
around Nicaragua came to be referred to collectively as the Contras.

Internationally and nationally, the confrontation between the Sandinista government and the Contras was presented as a military and
political question related to the continuance of the Nicaraguan National
Guard that for almost fifty years had propped up the Somoza dictatorship. However, the armed rebellion of Costeño groups was viewed as an
ethnic and indigenous question that was related to the so-called cultural
and historical differences between the Pacific and Atlantic regions of
Nicaragua. In an environment of increasing polarization, Sandinistas and
their allies labeled the Contras as "*Somocistas*" (Somoza loyalists) and
"*vendepatrias*" (traitors), whose behavior could be explained by purely
political factors such as political patronage and foreign intervention.
Meanwhile, the same pro-Sandinistas applied the label "separatists" to
the insurgent Costeños whose behavior, in their view, needed to be
explained by cultural factors.

On the other hand, ardent pro-Contra groups commonly referred
to the Contras as pro-Democracy rebels and even (to use the term dis-
seminated by the propaganda machine of the Reagan Administration)
"freedom fighters" that were fighting for enlightened principles such
as democracy and freedom.[3] Costeño combatants, in contrast, were
referred to as warriors and members of separate nations and ethnic

groups who were fighting for "tribal" rights (Nietschmann 1984a; US Department of State 1986b, 193). Their behavior needed to be understood as a manifestation of deeply rooted identification with the land rather than abstract ideals. Whereas both sides predictably leveled accusations of military atrocities, the Reagan administration referred to atrocities allegedly committed on the Atlantic Coast as genocide.[4]

Clearly, both sides (pro-Sandinista and anti-Sandinista) mobilized a rhetoric that made a consistent and clear set of distinctions between politics vs. culture and ideology vs. identity, and applied this to the geographical distinction of Pacific Coast vs. Atlantic Coast. Thus, culture and identity were perceived to motivate the Indians and ethnic groups of the Atlantic Coast, while politics, patronage, and ideological conviction motivated the northern campesinos (the rank and file of the Contras). The status of the Mosquito Coast, in contrast to the Pacific Coast, as a place inhabited by Indians contributed to use of an exoticizing lens through which to view the conflict.

Undoubtedly, this dual perspective was adopted at least in part as a response to the discourse of Costeño leaders and their advisers, who increasingly couched their aspirations in the language of ethnicity and cultural difference. The tone of the meetings and negotiations between Costeño and Sandinista leaders, beginning in November of 1979, initially expressed hope and mutual accommodation in which commonalities between the Sandinista program and Costeño aspirations were stressed. Costeños, for example, actively accepted the literacy campaign that the Sandinistas promoted nationwide, but they insisted that it be conducted in the languages of the region, Miskitu, Sumu, and English (Shapiro 1987). However, despite this initial accommodation, within two years negotiations became confrontational and polarized as Costeño leaders, disappointed with developments in the region, stressed the need for the national government to respect indigenous and minority demands to territory and political power as ethnic groups and Indians.

Costeños increasingly justified their demands on the grounds of cultural differences that entitled them to particular rights. For example, with the aid of indigenous rights groups in the United States (particularly Cultural Survival of Boston), MISURASATA (the newly reconstituted Costeño Indian organization) demanded control of about one- third of what the Sandinistas considered national lands (CIDCA

1984, 23). MISURASATA did not make this demand as part of the Sandinista agrarian reform that distributed large amounts of lands to both individual peasants and cooperatives in the Pacific. Rather, they demanded the land as "indigenous peoples" who were "descended from the original inhabitants of the area" and possessed a "communal [collective] style of life" that was in a "harmonious ecological equilibrium" with nature (Ohland and Schnieder 1983, 163). MISURASATA affirmed that the "right of the indigenous nations over the territory of their communities holds more importance than the right over the territory by the state" (ibid.).

The Sandinista government, threatened by statements such as these that it interpreted as "separatist," reacted by jailing MISURASATA leaders, an action that resulted in massive Costeño flight from the region and a surge of Costeño participation in the counterrevolution. Thus, the confrontation between Sandinistas and Costeños was paralleled by the increasing self-assertiveness of Costeño leaders as indigenous peoples and ethnic minorities whose rights devolved from their closeness to nature ("aboriginal rights") rather than simply from their rights as citizens of Nicaragua.[5] For a country that had historically presented itself as ethnically homogeneous, the fact that the Sandinista government found itself at odds with an indigenous and ethnic movement was both unexpected and enigmatic.

ANTHROPOLOGY ON THE WARPATH IN
NICARAGUA: COLD-WAR THEORIZING[6]

The so-called ethnic conflict in Nicaragua attracted the attention of social scientists throughout the world. Given that cultural and historical elements were considered to be at work in the Atlantic Coast (and presumably not in the Pacific Coast), anthropologists, historians, and geographers (in sum, those social scientists under whose jurisdiction culture and Indians usually fall) focused their attention on the crisis in the Atlantic Coast. Social scientists served as advisers to both the Sandinista government and the Costeño Contra forces, and therefore some of their opinions, analyses, theoretical approaches, and recommendations, far from a matter of purely academic interest, influenced the parties involved in the conflict. For this reason, the following analysis of social-science writing on the Atlantic Coast crisis represents a review of the perspectives of parties that in more conventional circumstances would be outside analysts but in this case were inside actors in the events involved.

Not surprisingly, pro-Sandinista social scientists employed theoretical and conceptual approaches that were different from those of anti-Sandinista social scientists. Within the anti-Sandinista camp, I identify two approaches: anticommunist and Indianist. The pro-Sandinistas adopted a "deconstructionist" approach that established as its main interpretive problem the explanation of Costeño false consciousness. On the other hand, the anticommunists and Indianists generally adopted an essentialist framework that relied on stereotypical notions of an ahistorical and unchanging Indian identity.

Socialist-leaning analysts in the pro-Sandinista camp, many of whom volunteered to work for the government in Nicaragua as part of an outpouring of international solidarity for the revolution, approached the crisis in the Atlantic Coast as being rooted in the combination of residual effects of British and US colonialism and neo-colonialism, along with the modern manipulations of the US State Department and its Contra proxy army. They stressed the role of exterior factors in predisposing the region to anti-governmental mobilization. These factors included, for example, the British government's indirect rule of the area during the colonial period, repeated US Marine invasions, the quasi-governmental role of US banana, mining, and lumber companies, the indoctrination of German and North American Moravian missionaries, and the neglect and corruption of the US-backed Somoza dictatorship.

With regard to the actions of the Sandinistas, they echoed the Sandinista government position that recognized that the FSLN had simply made "mistakes" in the region, and that by talking into account the cultural particularities of the region, it would be able to avoid repeating these mistakes. According to the Sandinista government, these mistakes stemmed from their inability to understand and be prepared for Nicaragua's "national question"—the term for ethnic conflict used in the Marxian tradition. Pro-Sandinista social scientists downplayed the severity of alleged Sandinista human rights violations. Inasmuch as they held the Sandinista government responsible for the crisis, they argued that the Sandinistas' dogged insistence on viewing the Nicaraguan reality through a class-tinged lens that obscured the importance of ethnic identities was the fatal error of the Sandinistas.[7] They encouraged reconciliation and offered regional autonomy as a solution to the crisis.

Paradoxically, pro-CIA/anticommunist cold warriors found themselves allied with supporters of indigenous rights and human rights, if only in their mutual opposition to the Sandinista policies in the Atlantic Coast (Buvollen 1987, 597). This placed the United States (a country with a far-from-stellar record regarding indigenous groups, not to mention human rights in Central America) in the highly ironic position of nominally supporting Indian rights. Meanwhile, human-rights groups and Indian-rights groups (such as Americas Watch and Cultural Survival), as well as Indian groups themselves (e.g., Mohawk Nation, Indian Law Resource Center, and the World Council of Indigenous Peoples), voiced protests and goals similar to those of the Pentagon.

North American Indians were themselves divided over the issue of the Sandinista policies toward the Indians of the Atlantic Coast (Hale 1994b, 272; Dunbar Ortiz 1983). Some Indian organizations, such as the International Indian Treaty Council (IITC), supported Sandinista policies, while others were extremely hostile to the revolution. Clem Chartier (then president of the World Council of Indigenous Peoples) traveled to Nicaragua in 1986 as part of an armed delegation that engaged Sandinista army forces. The trip was later condemned by the WCIP and Chartier was removed as president. Russell Means, hero of the Wounded Knee uprising, was part of this delegation.[8] Means had at one point petitioned the help of the US State Department to recruit and train North American Indian veterans to fight in Nicaragua (Buvollen 1987, 597).

Individuals and organizations that normally would be identified with the left and that under other circumstances would have been more inclined to favor a popular and "anti-imperialist" (to use the Sandinista term) socialist revolution, found themselves divided over the issues of human rights and indigenous rights in Nicaragua. They maintained that the issue of indigenous identity did not fit within paradigmatic cold war oppositions such as left vs. right or socialist vs. capitalist. In their opinion, a completely different vector, which pitted minority and indigenous group claims against those of the bullying central government of a divided country, added a new dimension to these polarized cold-war oppositions.

WARRIORS AND COLD WARRIORS:
THE ANTICOMMUNIST POSITION

Anticommunists (such as the Contras and the US State Department and their supporters) portrayed the confrontation between Costeños and Sandinistas as being the result of the attempt of a totalitarian state to assert absolute control over an unwilling population: "From the start, the Sandinistas could not tolerate individual expression, whether in the form of a newspaper article that disagreed with their position, or the desire of Indian populations to follow cultural traditions . . ." (US Department of State 1986a, 13). This quotation illustrates a dual perspective with regard to perceptions of Costeño resistance to the revolution vis-à-vis Pacific Nicaraguan resistance to the revolution. Whereas opposition to Sandinista despotism in the Pacific Coast was said to have galvanized around issues such as press censorship (a consummate civil right), in the Atlantic Coast among Indian populations opposition was claimed to have arisen around the necessity to follow vaguely defined cultural traditions. In general, anticommunists focused on the allegedly oppressive policies of the Sandinistas that they argued were the conscious product of aggressive and authoritarian intentions. Not merely a matter of reacting to "mistakes" unthinkingly committed by a young, idealistic, and inexperienced government, the opposition to the Sandinistas directly resulted, according to this perspective, from the automatic and inevitable resistance to authoritarianism.

According to anticommunists, the Nicaraguan government was attempting to reorganize Costeño society away from their idyllic "communal lifestyle" towards Cuban and Soviet communist models (US Department of State 1986a, 3). One anticommunist publication explained: "Historically, there has been little understanding between the peoples of the east and west coasts of Nicaragua. Under the Sandinista National Liberation Front (FSLN), relations have not only gotten worse, but they have evolved into open warfare. Shortly after the revolution, the government insisted that Cuban-style block committees replace tribal councils, that religion be supplanted with allegiance to the FSLN, and that Indian lands belong to the state, instead of to community farmers" (ibid., 1).

In this quotation, anticommunists invoked the heuristic value of the region's separate history and traditions, in this case, tribal councils and community farming.[9] Miskito Indian "cultural identity," which according to this perspective was inherently incompatible with communism, predisposed them to resist Sandinista programs. Communist-inspired Sandinista collective entities such as the Comites de Defensa Sandinista— militant Sandinista neighborhood organizations built on the Cuban model—clashed with the corresponding Costeño collective entities such as tribal councils that provided the similar function of local self-administration and which were an entrenched part of Miskito culture. Within this framework these Miskito cultural forms were endorsed on the grounds that they were both traditional (therefore legitimate) as well as non-oppressive. (For another example of this approach, see Ortega 1991, 42–45.) For these reasons, anticommunists generally discouraged Miskito negotiation with the Sandinistas. In fact, the Reagan administrations used funds illegally garnered in the Middle East as part of the Iran-Contra affair to pay Miskito Indian leaders to withdraw from negotiations (Lernoux 1985a, 1985b; Pichirallo 1987, 1, 16).

The late Bernard Nietschmann, a cultural geographer from the University of California at Berkeley whose pre-Revolution work in the cultural ecology of coastal Miskito communities was well known, loudly condemned what he called Sandinista "Indian policy." His criticism reached far beyond the confines of academic ivory towers. In fact, he served as an expert witness to Congress and the Organization of American States, as well as a chief advisor to the Miskito armed insurgency. He also published extensively on the Miskito-Sandinista conflict in academic and popular journals.[10] During the tense years of Miskito-Sandinista armed confrontation, he championed the cause of the nation of "Yapti Tasba," a name for the "Miskito nation" that came into limited use in the 1980s (see B. Rivera 1988, 95–120). He adamantly discouraged Miskito leaders from negotiating with the Nicaraguan government. Rather, he advised "Indian warriors" to settle for nothing less than complete sovereignty and the expulsion of all "invaders in Yapti Tasba" (Nietschmann 1989, 15). Nietschmann's agenda extended far beyond the Miskito nationalist movement. He supported the armed uprising of all indigenous nations, which constituted "40% of Central America," because "indigenous nations are a territorial and cultural firebreak to the spread of communism . . ." (ibid., 52).[11]

In contrast to his theoretically more sophisticated and empirically grounded earlier work, Nietschmann's post-revolutionary work adopted a crude and conjectural approach to culture and identity—an approach that was firmly grounded in essentialist principles. For Nietschmann, the Miskito-Sandinista struggle represented just one example of a larger phenomena (which he called the "Third World War") in which indigenous nations, which he estimated number from 3,000 to 5,000 worldwide, struggle to resist incorporation into the "168 states" (Nietschmann 1987, 2). This confrontation between indigenous nations and modern states represented the most important cause of war in the modern world and also the most important threat to indigenous nations. Each of these indigenous nations represented, for Nietschmann, a clearly bounded and easily definable group that could be identified on the basis of objective cultural criteria. He wrote: "Nations are geographically bounded territories of a common people. A nation is made up of communities of people who see themselves as 'one people' on the basis of common ancestry, history, society, institutions, ideology, language, territory and (often) religion. Nation peoples distinguish themselves and their countries from other adjacent and distant people and countries. The existence of nations is ancient" (ibid., 1).

The indigenous nation for Nietschmann thus represented an unchanging and transhistorical entity that finds itself threatened by the encroachment of states that aspire to strip members of these nations of their collective identity. The boundaries, both physical and sociological, of these nations were thoroughly unproblematic for Nietschmann.

Regarding the case of the Mosquito Coast, he insisted that the Miskito people fit in every respect his definition of a nation and therefore they should enjoy self-determination. He regarded as unproblematic the fact that the Miskito represent only one population among many in the Atlantic Coast. He also took for granted that those people whom he identified as the Miskito nation should necessarily possess a separate and distinct culture from their Costeño counterparts. It is precisely the centrality that he gives to this simple-minded equation between culture and social group (not his strident support of the Miskito cause as he defined it) that is most objectionable in his work. Predictably, this flawed theoretical framework spilled over into his analysis of the Costeño-Sandinista conflict:

> The Indian peoples had their own distinct national systems of identity, economy and property that were different from those of the

Sandinista invaders. What the Sandinistas saw as the 'Indian Problem,' the Miskitos saw as 'the Sandinista Problem.' Limited by class-based Marxism, the Sandinistas have been unable to comprehend an identity and a resistance based on culture. Culture and homeland unify a people more strongly than do ideology, class, or adherence to a particular political-economic system or group of leaders. (Nietschmann 1989, 28)

Nietschmann's framework obliged him to view the clash between the Sandinista government and the Miskito people as having resulted from fundamental and absolute cultural differences between the Mestizo Nicaraguan state and Miskito Indians. According to Nietschmann these differences automatically prevented collaboration and understanding between Miskitos and the Sandinista government. What remained absent from this framework that fetishized cultural difference and group identity was a treatment of the interests of the multiple actors (not just the so-called ethnic groups) involved. Also, in postulating a unified and homogenous identity for the Miskito nation, he ignored the tremendous differentiation within the Miskito category, as well as those cultural features that are shared by Costeños.

INDIANISTS, INDIAN RIGHTS, AND THE MISKITO MORAL ECONOMY

Indianists, the second subgroup of anti-Sandinistas, made similar claims about the nature of the Costeño-Sandinista crisis as did their anticommunist counterparts. Their motivations, however, were very different. Among the Indianist anti-Sandinistas, I include Harvard-based Cultural Survival (along with other indigenous rights organizations), various so-called Fourth-World organizations such as the World Council of Indigenous Peoples and the Indian Law Resource Center, North American Indian organizations (such as the American Indian Movement), and North American Indian tribes themselves (such as the Mohawk Nation). Throughout the 1980s, Cultural Survival and the Mohawk Nation published articles and updates (which included articles by Nicaraguans as well as North Americans) about the conflict in their respective publications, *Cultural Survival Quarterly* and *Akwesasne Notes*.[12]

Although Indianists by no means adopted the same position with regard to the conflict, they did share the view that the Sandinista government, regardless of what may have been benign initial intentions, enacted programs and policies that had harmful effects on the indigenous peoples and ethnic minorities of the Atlantic Coast. They argued that these policies threatened both the "way of life" as well as the well-being of Atlantic Coast peoples, particularly the Miskitu and Sumu Indians.

During the 1970s, Costeños, who had long been used to calling themselves and being called Indians in certain contexts, entered into contact with a new kind of "pan-Indian" ideology that was being developed in Canada, Mexico, and the United States. Before the revolution, ALPROMISU joined the World Council of Indigenous Peoples, which had been formed in the early 1970s as a self-proclaimed Fourth-World organization. The WCIP promoted a progressive "pan-Indianism" that, it argued, stood in opposition to prevailing doctrines of paternalism and integrationism held by national governments and development agencies. The WCIP and other organizations like it emerged with the explicit goal of defending indigenous peoples and their cultures from destruction at the hands of an economic model relying on modernization and industrialization. These organizations contrasted subordinate and oppressed Indian cultures to oppressive Western cultures. Their philosophy associated indigenous peoples with a distinctive pan-hemispheric Indian ethic, typified by, among other things, harmony with the environment and a communal way of life. In general, firmly anti-imperialist and anticapitalist, pan-Indian ideology saw itself as at odds with Marxism, which was integrationist and ignored and devalued ethnicity (Mohawk 1981; Dunbar Ortiz 1983, 79–87).[13]

Indianist anti-Sandinistas did not necessarily oppose the heavy-handed integrative programs of the Sandinista government solely because they were communist. Rather, they opposed the Sandinistas on the grounds that the government, regardless of its revolutionary rhetoric, was unwilling negotiate on the issues most crucial to Nicaraguan Indians—specifically the issue of "independent Indian self-determination" (Macdonald 1988, 143; also see IACHR 1984, 126). Notwithstanding the Sandinista accusations to the contrary, Indianist groups and human rights groups (and most importantly Costeños themselves, some of which I include here among Indianists) were well aware that the non-Costeño Contras would be no more willing to negotiate on these issues. Immediately as Sandinista-Miskito relations began to sour, *Akwesasne Notes*, whose editors were in contact with Costeño rebels, expressed its ambivalence over denouncing the Sandinista treatment of Nicaraguan Indians:

> The NOTES reports on this situation with some reservation. The position by Native peoples that they constitute real nations and their continued struggle for international recognition as such—is a difficult one for nation/states to entertain. That this conflict should come to the point of eruption in recently-liberated Nicaragua, and at this particularly dangerous time for the beleaguered revolution there is unfortunate. Certainly, the counter-revolutionary forces inside Nicaragua (and in the neighboring countries and North America as well) could find much to manipulate in it. . . . Nobody wants to play into the hands of the US war machine, least of all in this instance. (Akwesasne Notes 1981, 11)

For *Akwesasne Notes*, a Contra victory would not necessarily represent a solution to the fundamental Indian problem in Nicaragua. The unwillingness of states, regardless of their official ideologies, to modify a rigid conception of rights and citizenship, linked to Western notions of democracy, society, and personhood, lay at the root of the indigenous problem not only in Nicaragua but all over the Americas, according to Indianists (ibid., 11).

Indianists endeavored to elaborate a third position that, in their view, would not fall within any of the political spectrums that were being employed nationally and internationally: neither left nor right, neither east nor west, neither Contra nor Sandinista. In their opinion other analysts committed the error of forcing the Indian position within foreign, and ultimately Western, models that left no room for a true Indian perspective. Everyone, according to Indianists, tended to downplay the agency of Miskito actors, thereby reproducing stereotypical images of the passive Indian who is easily manipulated by outside agents. The left and the right portrayed "genuine leaders as either putty or puppets, molded and manipulated by outside interests" (Macdonald 1988, 111).

Theodore Macdonald, projects director of Cultural Survival (an organization that had contact with Miskito organizations), expressed such an Indianist critique: "Concerned primarily with the political symbolism of the Nicaraguan revolution, many observers chose to portray the Indians as either dupes of imperialist advances or victims of Communist totalitarianism; their perceptions were influenced more by their image of the Nicaraguan revolution than by any analysis of the Indians' actual condition" (Macdonald 1988, 107). According to this position, both Sandinistas and Contras equally misrepresented the Indians of Nicaragua, and each was, or would be, resistant to considering Miskito demands. The Indianist position of the Miskito insurgency attempted to claim immunity from cold-war biases because the insurgents as Indians championed an agenda that transcended cold-war oppositions.

Macdonald, borrowing from James Scott's notion of the moral economy, traced the roots of Indian resistance in the Mosquito Coast to "a different understanding of their past and somewhat divergent aspirations for the future." He described Nicaragua as a plural society that was deeply divided on cultural lines (ibid., 111).[14] He attributed the ultimate cause of the civil war in Nicaragua to these cultural differences between Miskitos and Sandinistas. He postulated ethnic identity as a real and tangible possession of the Miskito, the potential loss of which sparked the Miskito Indians to rebellion. Because the "Miskito moral economy," which consisted of "both subsistence rights and deep emotional concerns regarding land rights and resource rights" (ibid., 122), had never previously been violated, the Miskito had never risen up against the US companies or the Nicaraguan government. He wrote: "Subsistence security was never threatened. So, despite periods of undeniably intensive expropriation, feelings of exploitation were not particularly strong" (ibid., 114). The reason, according to Macdonald, that the Miskito rebelled in the 1980s was that the Sandinista government placed this moral economy in jeopardy and did not respect Miskito ethnic identity.

Referring to the Sandinista hostility to ethnic organizations, as well as their insistence on viewing the history of the Atlantic Coast through the lens of class struggle, Macdonald argued that one of the main goals of the Sandinistas was the "dissolution of ethnic identity." Upon arriving at the view that their ethnic identity was in danger, the Miskito took up arms. Macdonald explained: "Ethnicity is not simply the cause of racism and discrimination, it is also the source of a unique, vital self-identity; it is something that Indians will not relinquish simply on the promise of improved social and economic conditions" (ibid., 111). Thus Macdonald incorporated the concept of ethnic identity (specifically Indian identity) into the center of his analysis of the causes of the Costeño-Sandinista crisis. Given the fluid and contextual nature of self-identification in the region, which I have outlined in the previous chapters, Macdonald's reliance on the concept of identity was limiting. Macdonald and his Indianist colleagues fell into the trap of reifying the boundaries of the social groups in the region to a degree that was not warranted.

Sandinista Social Science I: The Ethnic Prism, False Consciousness, and Dogmatic Marxism

In an often-quoted interview that appeared in a Mexican magazine soon after the escalation of the crisis in the Atlantic Coast in 1981, Tomas Borge (FSLN cofounder and Nicaraguan Minister of the Interior during the Sandinista administration) attributed the problems in the Mosquito Coast to the political, economic, and social "backwardness" of Costeños. In his opinion the Mosquito Coast's unique colonial and post-colonial history lay at the root of this backwardness (Ohland and Schneider 1983, 189–192). He stated: "It is very difficult to fight against backwardness, and this is an extremely backward zone. . . . We are decolonising them. So we are taking roads to them, telephones, medical care, literacy, television; for the first time in their lives they have seen a television image; but two years is a very short time in which to overcome the prejudices, the religious fanaticism, the ignorance, the apathy of centuries" (ibid., 191).

In the eyes of the revolutionary leaders the Atlantic Coast represented a glaring example of the disastrous effects of imperialism.[15] Indeed, the region represented a paradox for the Sandinista leaders: it was a region that had the greatest direct exposure to world capitalism (particularly to wage labor and proletarianization) as well as the most extreme levels of poverty, and yet its inhabitants demonstrated the least revolutionary potential of all segments of Nicaraguan society. Sandinista social scientists became trapped in a limiting paradigm in which they devoted their interpretive energies to addressing this alleged paradox.

Generally, Sandinista analysts employed a two-pronged model that included a deterministic structure-oriented approach and a voluntaristic agency-oriented approach (Hale 1994b, 17). During the crisis in the 1980s, a structure-oriented approach was applied to the historical roots of Costeño ethnic identity, while an agency-oriented approach was employed to explain the increasing ethnic militancy of Costeños, particularly Miskitos. Sandinista analysts brought to the fore the process through which US and British extractive industries created an ethnically based labor hierarchy that pitted ethnic groups against one another in a competition for scarce opportunities and resources (Vilas 1989, 7; Hale 1987a). Also, the Moravian Church's policy of providing education and proselytization to Creoles in English and to Miskitos in Miskitu drove wedges between Creoles, Miskitos, and Catholic Mestizos. Over time, both of these factors caused ethnic differences to deepen within the Costeño worldview, obscuring the material base of ethnicity, which was regarded as a "superstructural" ideology within the Marxist theoretical tradition. CIDCA (Centro de Investigación y Documentación de la Costa Atlántica), a social science research institute commissioned in the early 1980s by the Sandinista government, identified this propensity to view the world through an ethnic lens as being a crucial feature of Costeño culture that predisposed them to counterrevolution. CIDCA investigators labeled this process, by which Costeños misrecognized the true class basis of their exploitation, the "ethnic prism" (CIDCA 1984, 17).

With regard to the causes of contemporary ethnic radicalization, Sandinista social scientists highlighted the duplicity of Miskito leaders, who manipulated ethnic and indigenous rhetoric in order to promote their personal agendas (as well as, of course, the agendas of US imperialism) at the expense of the great majority of Costeños (Vilas 1989, 132–135; Gurdián 1987, 175; Jenkins Molieri 1986, 315–318). These investigators put their social science theories to the primary task of invalidating the legitimacy and representativeness of the "ethnic discourse" that Costeño leaders developed during the crisis.[16] Many Sandinista social scientists placed themselves, and their science, in the highly paternalistic position of demonstrating to Costeños that their cultural movement was both false and ingenuous.

Although Sandinista social scientists explicitly distanced their own interpretations from "dogmatic Marxism" and its alleged reliance on economic determinism (Gurdián 1987, 172; Hale 1994b, 15), all asserted, in one way or another, that Costeño consciousness (particularly that part of it that predisposed Costeños to oppose the revolution as ethnic groups and Indians) was at some level false. According to Sandinista social scientists, the fact that Costeños organized themselves along ethnic lines indicated that they operated under the assumption that their problems stemmed from their marginalization as ethnic minorities within a country, rather than as workers within a national and international capitalistic economy that exploited them. In this sense, their uprising was based on a fallacious interpretation of their situation because it was based on an ethnic model rather than a class model.

In the following passage, Galio Gurdián, a Nicaraguan anthropologist working at CIDCA who later took a PhD from the University of Texas, clearly expressed this insistence on the primacy of class analysis: "Ethnicity, within this position, should be seen as one particular dimension of social structure, as a form of organization of certain social groups that have a clear class nature, however. In complex societies, ethnic groups are neither distinct from nor independent of the class structure, but are rather the way in which certain classes or class sectors are differentiated in terms of different socio-cultural elements" (Gurdián 1987, 177). Given that ethnicity was an epiphenomenon of class, Costeños drew attention away from, according to Gurdián, the true nature of their exploitation by asserting ethnic demands. Although Sandinista social scientists granted the importance of recognizing ethnic and cultural differences within the nation, they stood by the claim that Costeño ethnic discourse was both politically harmful and ideologically incorrect.

Many Sandinista social scientists made little attempt to hide their contempt for Costeño ethnic discourse. Vilas labeled the positions taken by MISURASATA as "ethnic chauvinism." He defined this term as "a kind of reductionism that privileges ethnic elements in the analysis of a given social group, including the mystification of its own history." He added that the main characteristics of Miskito "ethnic chauvinism" include an "oversimplified view of reality and a simplistic, black-and-white schema of confrontation" (Vilas 1989, 126). According to Vilas, ethnic chauvinism had "very little to do with Miskito culture" and was used by Miskito leaders motivated only by the desire to attract international attention and to appeal to Miskito followers. Vilas's unabashed paternalism is most apparent when, on a conciliatory note, he conceded that similar kinds of claims are "also found in other social groups in the first stages of their consciousness of themselves as a distinctive social entity" (ibid., 127).

Other Sandinista social scientists manifested similar antipathy towards what they perceived as radical demands by Costeño organizations. They attempted to deconstruct and delegitimize Costeño ethnic discourse. Gurdián, for example, reprimanded Miskito leaders for engaging in an "ethnicist" rhetoric that "preaches an almost mystical exaltation of ethnic traits" (Gurdián 1987, 177). He described this position, which he lamented was "gaining ground in Latin America," in the following manner: "It is based on an ahistorical romantic vision of ethnicity: on the one hand, it affirms the existence of a millenary ethnic nucleus, invariable in its essence and uncontaminated by the historical process; on the other hand, the 'superior' nature of ethnic traits is affirmed in contrast to the decadent nature of all things Western" (ibid.).

Jorge Jenkins Molieri (Nicaraguan anthropologist and *militante Sandinista*) launched an equally belligerent salvo at Miskito ethnic discourse:

> The ethnicist romanticism of this proposal [MISURASATA's "Plan 1981"] is rooted in the fact that it does not recognize, or portends to not recognize, the general situation of oppression and misery that the Nicaraguan peasantry has lived, not to mention the other disadvantaged classes, as a result of the capitalist development imposed on the country by the liberal-conservative regimes in complicity with imperialism. They claim that being an Indian in itself confers supranational, incontrovertible and self-evident rights which are above history and social processes—a kind of divine grace that, removed from humanity and its struggles, turns its back on the achievements of national liberation. The infantility of the proposal made by these leaders can only be matched by the religious idea of judgment day—in which they would be seated on the best balcony. (Jenkins Molieri 1986, 313)

For Jenkins Molieri the history of the Miskito was a history of exploitation and manipulation at the hands of British and later North American capitalism. His book on this crisis consisted of an extended discussion of the negative ideological and social effects this foreign presence had on the Miskito people. This history of foreign exploitation robbed them of the possibility of assuming their true Nicaraguan "national sentiment" (ibid., 22). It also created mutual resentment between "the indigene of the Atlantic and the ladino of the Pacific" (ibid., 23).

A particularly glaring irony of this history for Jenkins Molieri was that foreigners "made the indigene believe in the goodwill [*bondad*] of his exploiters" (ibid., 26). The inability of the Miskito to recognize the objective fact that they were "brutally exploited" was rooted in two idiosyncratic features of the region's history: (1) "its early articulation in the english mercantile and colonialist economy," and (2) "fundamental elements in the ideological formation of the indigene, particularly the interiorization of the moravian religion" (ibid., 238). It was precisely this aspect of Miskito consciousness (part of what he called their "social backwardness") that caused them to mis-recognize the boon represented by the Sandinista revolution. Instead they rebelled, thereby failing the revolutionary challenge to "improve the conditions of their pathetic existence" (ibid., 23).

For Jenkins Molieri, Miskito people's long historical ties to the capitalist world economy and its English and North American agents molded them as a distinctly modern people—a modernity that he argued contradicted their status as Indians. He chided Miskito leaders and their supporters for appealing to indigenous rights because, according to his analysis, this appeal flew in the face of hundreds of years of capitalist exploitation as wage workers. Referring to the Miskito activism of the post-revolutionary period, he stated: "The real problem, which has always been the exploitation of the indigene's labor and the permanent alienation of his territory, was hidden craftily behind a mask of idyllic ethnicism promoted even by the paternalistic and philanthropic attitudes of anthropologists and religious leaders" (ibid., 239).

The romantic notion of the Indians' "idyllic" existence, promoted by the self-romanticizing Miskito leaders and their religious and anthropological advisers, was directly contradicted and indeed undermined, in Jenkins Molieri's view, by their historical exploitation as workers.[17] According to Jenkins Molieri's formulation, Sandinista social science provided a corrective to the tendency of Miskito leaders and indigenists to exoticize and "idealize" their own history (ibid., 22). Clearly, his version of this social science operated on the assumption that Indianness is innately pre-modern and pre-capitalist. Departing from this primitivist set of assumptions, he critiqued the genuineness of the assertion of indigenous identity by Costeños, whom he viewed as proletarianized, and therefore un-Indian, Nicaraguans.

It is crucial to note that although Jenkins Molieri aggressively attacked Miskito appeals to rights as Indians on the grounds that these were romanticized and ahistorical, he simultaneously assumed some of the very assumptions about Miskito history and culture on which he argued these appeals were based. He limited his analysis exclusively to *indígenas* (primarily referring to Miskitos), a category whose boundedness he leaves unquestioned. By relying on the unqualified salience of this term, he unwittingly adopted a fundamental assumption of the position he was trying to deconstruct—namely that the Miskito Indians represent a bounded social group united by race, language, and culture. Despite consistently emphasizing the impact of foreign influence on the Miskito, he nevertheless adopted primitivist language to describe the social structure that resulted from this interaction. That is to say, in his analysis of the Miskito he embraced stereotypical characteristics commonly associated with Indians, such as communal living, harmony with the environment, closeness to nature, and having distinct culture and traditions. He wrote:

> In the face of the irrational plunder of the natural resources and the destruction of their environment the Miskitos almost instinctively reacted by maintaining the steadfastness of their communal life, exchange relationships, reciprocity, kinship ties, customs, traditions and language. Granted all of these characteristics were blended with enormous european, north american and caribbean influences in such a way that this group [the miskito] took shape as a motley culture with multiple manifestations but with the stamp of an authentic cultural continuity in continual change. (ibid., 28)

Jenkins Molieri countered Miskito claims to cultural purity and indigenous essence by focusing on their victimization within the world economy. However, in the process he constructed a reconfigured Miskito essence based on stereotypically Indian features. Thus, although

Jenkins Molieri engaged in a deconstructionist project aimed at delegitimizing Miskito claims to indigenous rights, ultimately this project incorporated key elements of these claims within the analysis.

SANDINISTA SOCIAL SCIENCE II:
THE INVENTION OF TRADITION,
CONTRADICTORY CONSCIOUSNESS,
AND THE ANTHROPOLOGY OF LIBERATION

The late Martin Diskin, an MIT anthropologist, published a number of articles that also operated within a modified deconstructionist mode (Diskin 1987, 1989, 1991). In these articles Diskin dedicated himself to examining two separate but related phenomena: (1) the challenge to anthropology represented by the increasing importance of "native self-representation" (Diskin 1991, 157); and (2) the "manipulation of indigenous struggles" by outside actors (e.g., the United States).[18] Diskin argued that these phenomena were integrally related (particularly in the Miskito case) because modern "ethnic discourse" (or "native self-representation") has become highly politicized as indigenous groups have altered, invented, and reshaped their self-representations in response to external actors and external paradigms of self-representation (Diskin 1989, 11).[19] Echoing Clifford Geertz's 1960s work on ethnic bloc formation and primordial loyalties in the so-called New Nations (Geertz 1963), Diskin characterized the emergence of ethnic discourse as a creative, modern, and undeniably strategic and tactical tool that is used by formerly isolated or sheltered societies that, caught in the maelstrom of global politics, find themselves being drawn into self-consciously multi-ethnic states.[20]

With regard to the specifics of the Costeño-Sandinista conflict, Diskin concentrated on what he perceived to be the increasingly radical ethnic discourse of Miskito organizations and their leaders, a discourse that he described as a "new voice" in the region. For Diskin, the claim to native and Indian status by Miskito leaders represented an instrumentally motivated attempt to maximize their access to national and international resources. In response to the radical changes in their world (e.g., the Sandinista revolution, pan-Indian activism, and the US support of the Contras), Costeños simply chose to adopt and propagate an ethnic identity that suited them best in that moment. Diskin wrote: "In the example of Nicaraguan Costeños, ethnic discourse is employed to alter the historic image of coastal peoples and argue for specific guaranteed rights from the central government. The ethnic discourse, a tool in ongoing social negotiation, is therefore eminently situational. . . . The identities chosen may shift depending on the group's allies and adversaries of the moment, the resources they seek, and, of course, timing" (Diskin 1991, 157). In his view of the role of ethnic identity formation, Diskin clearly assumed that the modern politicized version of Miskito self-representation (i.e., situational and shifting) departed from a pre-crisis true self-presentation that was devoid of such elements. Armed with this assumption, he went about the business of citing the alleged reality from which Miskito ethnic discourse diverged.

According to Diskin, Costeño ethnic discourse consisted of the claims to: (1) the primacy of ethnic identity over other identities; (2) the Indian identity and nationhood of coastal peoples; (3) the spiritual and cultural identifications of these nations with their land; (4) their communitarian nature; and, finally, (5) their right to self-determination. All of these, he argued were, at best, recent reformulations and reshapings of Costeño ethnic identity. At worst they were, from the privileged perspective of the social scientist, patently false.

For example, Diskin criticized MISURASATA pronouncements (at one point he referred to these as "ideological statements" [Diskin 1989, 20]) in which Miskito leaders referred to the Atlantic Coast Indians as the "original inhabitants" of the region. He explained that "this characterization often ignored the history of coastal people's interaction with the Caribbean, especially with the British Naval Force" (ibid., 19). Diskin noted that Miskito claims to a history of self-rule and cultural continuity "contradicts other [scholarly] accounts" (Diskin 1991, 169). For example, he reported that the Miskito leaders of MISURASATA refer to the "council of elders" as a distinctly Miskito form of self-governing that they continued to respect during the 1980s. Citing his knowledge of the anthropological scholarship on Nicaragua, he objected that this "group of decision makers, are simply not recorded in the literature." He added that only the Moravian Church (a consummate outside influence) could have provided any "centralized form of governance" to the alleged Miskito nation, but "that is hardly an aboriginal pattern of governance" (Diskin 1991, 170).

Citing Hale, he insisted that Miskito pretensions of having had a long history of communal land tenure is undermined by the fact that at the turn of the century a British agent actually initiated the practice of communal land claims in order to ease his work load. At the turn of the century, the culturally informed inclination of the Miskito, according to Diskin, was to claim lands as individuals—a fact that Diskin believed delegitimized modern Miskito claims to communal lands. He used Helms's ethnographic data from her 1971 book, *Asang*, on individually owned cash-producing lands to support the conclusion that "communal subsistence activities are not as widespread as the ethnic discourse insists" (ibid.). These factual inconsistencies, according to the deconstructionist logic of Diskin, are due in large part to Miskito leaders' contact with indigenous advocacy groups that support a "maximalist statement of indigenous rights" and which were responsible, at least ideologically, for the "consistency and increasing sophistication of Indian demands and maneuvers" (Diskin 1989, 19).

The main problem with Diskin's approach was not his critical stance towards Miskito ethnic discourse. There can be no doubt that Miskito leaders geared their descriptions of themselves and their culture to suit, or counter, the expectations of outsiders. And there also can be no doubt that the details of these self-descriptions in some cases had very little to do with how the majority of Costeños live and describe their lives. The problem was that Diskin implicitly assumed that there existed a more authentic Miskito ethnic identity prior to the 1980s that became polluted and distorted by the outside interference brought about as a result of the crisis. He assumed that premodern self-representations (ethnic identity) are more genuine because the Indian societies that produced them lacked an analytical sense of self-awareness. This self-awareness, then, only results from the attempt of modern states to insert marginalized Indians into national society as ethnic groups (Hill 1996). Diskin took the newness of this post-revolutionary Costeño cultural production as prima facie evidence of its illegitimacy, the case for which he ironically dedicated his "engaged science of liberation" to prove (Diskin 1991, 17). In his insistence on deconstructing Costeño ethnic discourse, he neglected to analyze this discourse on its own terms in order to understand how it worked within Costeño society.

Although other Sandinista social scientists refrained from frontal assaults on Miskito ideology (like those of Vilas, Gurdián, and Jenkins

Molieri), all of them, in one form or another, worked within an interpretive framework geared towards explaining the paradox of Costeño cultural and political backwardness. Charles Hale, a North American anthropologist who during the 1980s worked with CIDCA and conducted fieldwork in Nicaragua for his PhD dissertation at Stanford University, provided a much more subtle analysis of "Miskitu consciousness" in his dissertation and subsequent book and other publications, but even these teeter at the brink of this paternalistic interpretive trap (Hale 1990, 1991, 1994b). As a self-proclaimed "politically engaged anthropologist" (Hale 1994b, 217) and "quasi-insider within what might be called the revolutionary establishment," Hale made no attempt to disguise his solidarity with the FSLN and its goals of revolutionary social transformation (ibid., 9). Due to the antigovernment hostilities in the region, Hale found himself in the uncomfortable position (particularly for a North American anthropologist committed to "research, theory and political practice of a radical bent") of supporting, and working for, a government that was hostile to an anti-state subaltern uprising (albeit a subaltern uprising that temporarily had a powerful ally in the form of the US State Department) with which the majority of his informants in his field site harbored sympathy and with which many directly and indirectly participated (ibid., 7).[21] The task then became managing to maintain theoretical and practical sympathy for the Miskito while at the same time supporting a Sandinista interpretation of (and solution to) the conflict.

Hale attempted to distance himself from what he described as "structural" explanations of the conflict that ignored Miskito agency and focused exclusively "either on the intrusive, repressive character of the Sandinista state or on the interventionist policies of the United States." Such structural analysis was incomplete because "it offered at best a vague and deductive sense of what Miskitu people understood themselves to be doing" (Hale 1994b, 17). On the other hand, he regarded the "Indian perspective" to suffer from an over-reliance on "people's motivations." He stated: "Accounts that began from the 'Indian perspective' tended to caricature the structural determinants of the conflict, to portray Miskitu culture in a vacuum, and to neglect how structural conditions had shaped Miskitu people's consciousness" (ibid., 17). For Hale, the dilemma between focusing on Miskito consciousness in a vacuum and focusing on structural factors that played a crucial role in shaping this consciousness was symptomatic of a larger theoretical tension in the social sciences between "voluntaristic and deterministic types of theory" (ibid.,18).

On a practical level, his solution to this dilemma was to work as an agent of "conflict resolution" by contributing research that supported the Sandinista-initiated autonomy project (Hale 1994b, 217). On a theoretical level, Hale argued for a compromise in which Miskito consciousness was regarded both as an ideological apparatus with which to resist oppression and a hegemonic ideology that exposed them to other forms of oppression. Miskito insurgency could then be viewed at some level as being rooted in a rational response to real threats as well as a misguided rejection of real opportunities. Both right and wrong, both nearsighted and farsighted, the Miskito were, according to Hale, driven by what he called (inspired by Gramsci's discussions of hegemony) "contradictory consciousness."

Miskito contradictory consciousness was composed of two competing and partially intertwined elements that he labeled (1) Anglo affinity and (2) ethnic militancy. Miskito Anglo affinity referred to their historical over-identification with the Anglo-American world. Anglo affinity, more than simply a product of a strategic alliance with English and Americans, manifested itself in a series of beliefs that venerated Anglo-Americans, their cultures, and their companies. As a result of extended contact with Anglo-American institutions and the traders, soldiers, ministers, and managers that led these institutions, the Miskito people "came to accept some of those institutions' self-justifying premises as their own" (Hale 1994b, 83). Thus, to be Miskito meant to believe that "Americans were benevolent allies, that North American companies brought unmitigated benefits . . . that white people are superior in phenotypes and intelligence" (ibid.).

Miskito ethnic militancy, which emerged and gained strength during the confrontation with the Sandinistas, represented that part of the Miskito worldview that opposed subordination to a "Spanish" central government. According to Hale, Miskito demands for control over eastern Nicaragua stemmed from their ethnic militancy (ibid., 81).

The status of Anglo affinity as an analytical concept remained nebulous throughout his analysis. Distancing himself from the "class/ethnic dichotomy" of some of his Sandinista colleagues, he insisted that this aspect of Miskito consciousness was not false. He explained that it

consisted "of ideas, values and notions of common sense" but was not a
"discrete variable or attribute" nor "a set of ideas—much less an ideology." However this ambiguous concept was defined, Hale found himself
in the awkward position of being a White North American anthropologist (and a self-proclaimed radical one at that) who was placing the term
"Anglo affinity" at the center of an analysis of a rebellious Indian group.[22]

Hale argued (in opposition to those who criticized the Indian
movement and Indian ideology as false) that Miskito ethnic militancy
actually was at one level very rational. Following Paul Willis's analysis of
the role of hegemony among working-class high school children in
England, Hale argued that the Miskitos' analysis of their situation and
the reasons for their plight contained true and important "penetrations"
as to the causes of their plight (Hale 1994b, 25). He stated: "I contend
that the ethnic militancy of the 1980s contained a perceptive critique of
the dominant society, an eloquent series of insights into the structural
and historical factors underlying Miskitu oppression. It entailed an
understanding of the workings of the system and gave rise both to profound feelings of empowerment and an explosive inclination for collective action" (ibid., 83).

On the other hand, these "penetrations" simultaneously manifested
"limitations," where the process of resisting one type of oppression
causes one to embrace another form of oppression. Precisely in this
Gramscian formulation of hegemony, in which resistance to one form of
domination creates susceptibility to another form of domination, Hale
offered his solution to the dilemma. An analysis that would incorporate
hegemony (so defined) could both explain Miskito so-called backwardness (within a Sandinista framework) and positively analyze the Miskito
worldview on its own terms.

Hale incorporated hegemony into his explanation of the Miskito/
Sandinista clash of the 1980s in the following manner. The Miskito were
historically caught up in two separate "spheres of inequality": (1) North
American-dominated economy and civil society, and (2) the oppressive
Nicaraguan state (Hale 1990, 22). The Miskito had never openly resisted the Nicaraguan government on a large scale because, from the
moment of Nicaraguan annexation of the region in 1894, the government had been complicit with United States companies and the United
States government. This partnership between their historical allies

(North Americans) and their historical enemies (the Spanish Nicaraguans) caused Miskito ethnic militancy to remain dormant because their Anglo affinity stood in the way of the Miskito developing a critique of their economic situation that would have included the role of the US companies.

After the triumph of the Sandinistas in 1979, who came to power with an outspoken critique of "Yankee imperialism" (to quote the Sandinista epithet), North American capital fled and quickly relations between the Sandinistas and the US government soured. Miskito Anglo affinity no longer stood in the way of the Miskito resisting the Nicaraguan government. In the 1980s they aggressively asserted themselves in defiance of their oppression—an oppression that they now were able to attribute (albeit mistakenly for Hale) to communism and Pacific Nicaraguan oppression, and not North American capitalism. In this process, however, they could not help but "'lock' themselves into a cultural form that lacked the basis for critique of ongoing Anglo-American domination" (ibid., 23).

Although providing a more-nuanced explanation of Costeño rebellion against the Sandinista government, Hale's analysis remained caught up in the Sandinista social science paradigm that posited Costeño backwardness as the key interpretive problem. Ultimately, his elaborate analysis of Miskito consciousness was aimed at demonstrating the irrationality of Miskito rebellion against the Sandinista state. He conceded that Miskito ethnic militancy responded to a real appraisal of a historical pattern of Nicaraguan governmental neglect and marginalization of the region that in part was supported by racist beliefs of Pacific Nicaraguans towards the Miskito (Hale 1994b, 82). However, by resisting this neglect and marginalization through forming affinities with the Anglo-American world, the Miskito exposed themselves to another, equally detrimental, form of oppression—namely, manipulation at the hands of the CIA and the US State Department. Modern Miskito militancy suffered acutely, according to Hale, from "the absence of a critical orientation toward the United States" (Hale 1991, 128). Its negative response to a perceived communist threat was the product of a misguided and thoroughly colonized worldview; to quote the provocative title of Hale's contribution in a volume titled *Decolonizing Anthropology*, "They exploited us, but we didn't feel it."

It is ironic that Hale, who worked as an anthropologist for a Sandinista government that he admitted often treated the region as an internal colony and that was at war with his subjects during fieldwork (Hale
1994b, 13), should be included in a volume devoted to an "anthropology of liberation" that condemns, in the words of the editor, "anthropology's collusion with and complicity in colonial and imperialist
domination" (Harrison 1991, 1).[23]

Hale's 1994 book, *Resistance and Contradiction: Miskitu Indians and the
Nicaraguan State, 1894–1987*, was widely praised, and many reviewers
focused their commendations on his handling of the professional and ethical contradictions of his role in Nicaragua (Diskin 1995; Gudmundson
1995; Herlihy 1994; Weiss 1995). Indiana University's Jeffrey Gould, for
example, wrote that it "should become a model for politically engaged
scholarship" (Gould 1995). However, anthropologist Mary Helms, who
worked in the Mosquito Coast before the revolution and strongly
opposed the Sandinista policies vis-à-vis the Miskito Indians, did not join
in the chorus of praise for Hale's political engagement. She wrote that
"Hale's Sandinista sympathies seem to have led him largely to ignore the
most destructive aspects of Sandinista militancy particularly . . . where
some forty Miskitu and Sumu communities were totally destroyed and
their populations forced to flee in order to create a 'sanitized' zone"
(Helms 1995).

The case of engaged anthropology in the Nicaraguan revolutionary
context puts into uncomfortable focus the much-debated relationship
between engaged activism and scientific detachment. Particularly telling
is the critique leveled against the activist camp within this debate, to the
effect that one anthropologist's activism is another's imperialism.

SUMMARY AND CONCLUSION

With regard to the crisis in the Atlantic Coast of Nicaragua in the
1980s, social scientists and journalists, many of whom joined the groups
involved as members or advisers, found themselves divided along cold-
war lines. Pro-Sandinistas at times provided an apologist position for the
so-called mistakes committed by the revolutionary government. These
mistakes were said to be rooted in an alleged Marxian over-reliance on
class analysis by Sandinista leaders—a bias that blinded them to the
salience of ethnic factors. On a practical level, pro-Sandinistas supported

a reconciliation that would include provisions allowing for regional autonomy. On the level of theory, pro-Sandinistas employed a deconstructionist approach that endeavored to explain the reasons that the Miskito failed to understand the true sources of their exploitation. Pro-Sandinistas fell into a paternalistic interpretive trap in which they uncritically accepted the dilemma of Costeño "backwardness" as a key interpretive problem. Emphasizing the situational and changing nature of the Miskitos' ethnic identity assertion, they critiqued what they regarded as essentialist approaches to ethnicity on the part of the Miskito and their supporters.

However, this approach did not sufficiently question the boundedness of the ethnic categories in question. In this sense, pro-Sandinistas fell prey to the same sort of essentialism that they vigorously critiqued. Pro-Sandinistas, some more than others, often neglected to fundamentally interrogate the assumption that the Mosquito Coast was divided into separate ethnic groups that each manifest distinct culture. Although many Sandinistas were remarkably sympathetic to the Miskito cause, the use of this deconstructionist theoretical approach was designed at least in part to discredit Costeño and Miskito aspirations.

On the other hand, anti-Sandinistas were divided into two camps that had very distinct motivations but shared a similar essentialist approach. The first camp, anticommunists, attributed Costeño resistance to Sandinista authoritarianism and the incompatibility of communist programs and Costeño culture. In practice, anticommunists made great efforts to prevent Sandinista-Costeño reconciliation.

The second camp, Indianists, opposed the integrative revolution of the Sandinistas on the grounds that, despite ideological differences with traditional nonrevolutionary nation-building projects, the Sandinistas program for the Atlantic Coast reproduced integrationist policies that were typical of governments in the Americas.[24] They tended to admire the fear and respect inspired by Costeño bellicosity, which according to them stood in the face of five hundred years of Indian and African defeat at the hands of European and European-descended society. Wary of classic "regional autonomy" governmental arrangements, which had been routinely practiced with varying degrees of success in regions of the Soviet Union with significant ethnic minorities, they encouraged negotiation with the Sandinistas, but only negotiations that would put true indigenous self-determination on the negotiating table.

Despite their divergent ideological and political motivations, anti-communists and Indianists constructed a similar framework that relied on romantic stereotypes of native societies. Each camp placed at the center of their respective analyses a set of stereotypical qualities that they presumed to be inherent to native societies. These qualities counterproductively reified ethnic boundaries to the point of ignoring other crucial elements of Costeño society. Rather than attempting to explain the ways in which seemingly "false" Costeño ideological structures (such as Anglo affinity or simply ethnic identity itself) worked themselves out in practice, Sandinista social scientists strove to delegitimize Costeño cultural self-representation.

CHAPTER 7

Conclusion

There are, I am informed, about thirty English families residing here [the Mosquito Coast], who possess lands granted to them by the Indians, and have begun to settle plantations; but the quantity of that produce they have hitherto manufactured has not been considerable enough for exportation. Of other commodities sufficient is collected to load a large annual ship for Great-Britain; besides several small ships belonging to Jamaica. . . . But, however extensively these articles may be attended to by the European settlers, I think that more capital advantages might be obtained by striking out such employments for the native Indians as they would be willing to enter into, and pursue to the mutual gain of themselves and great Britain. Preparatory to this, some degree of civilization is necessary; without which, their consumption of British manufactures cannot reach to any great extent. They are rather of an indolent temper; and will not labour, unless when indigent and compelled to it by want. . . . The better to attract these Indians to such objects, it is necessary to open a market, where their crops might find a ready price, and yield a quick return. . . . Their wants will undoubtedly increase in proportion as they grow more civilized; and, in order to gain the costlier articles of dress and convenience, they may soon be taught, that nothing is requisite on their part, than an advancement of skill, and redoubled diligence in selecting and procuring commodities of superior value; or larger collections of the same kind, for carrying on their barter, and due payment of their annual balance.

—Edward Long, *The History of Jamaica*
(Long 1774, 318)

A few miles up the main river live the Woolvas and
Cuckeras Indians. Mr. Henry Corrin, of Jamaica,
settled here in 1752, and acquired a large fortune from
the luxuriant productions of this district. He exported
great quantities of mahogany, tortoise-shell, &c. to
Jamaica, and the Northern colonies. He likewise took
some pains to civilize the neighboring Indians; for, on
his first coming to reside here, they lived in a savage
state, and had very little commerce either with the
Spaniards or English. This example of success, from
the endeavours of a private person, may lead us to
conclude on the proportionately greater advantages to
be gained by establishing a regular colony in these
parts, who might labour to gain the good-will of the
Indian tribes, and by fair dealing and a generous
communication wean them from a state of barbarism
to civility and industry. It seems, I think, probable,
that they might soon become reconciled to much of
the English manners in their dress and habitations,
and gradually induced to take large imports of
clothing, furniture, implements, and food, from us. In
order to purchase these, they would necessarily apply
themselves to procure such commodities of value, for
the exchange, as they might find to be most in request.
Thus, by a discreet management, it is reasonable to
believe, that our British wares and manufactures
might be dispersed to many thousands of people on
this continent, and so many solid emoluments reaped
from the intercourse, as would amply overpay our
utmost affiduities in the prosecution of it.

—Edward Long, *The History of Jamaica*
(Long 1774, 324)

THE ABOVE OBSERVATIONS, written in the mid-
eighteenth century by the British historian of the Caribbean Edward
Long, speak to the historical depth of the interpenetration of racial ideologies and political economy in the Mosquito Coast. Long's words also
dramatize the profound paradox of being a native of a New World that
has for five hundred years been in the process of being conquered and
"civilized." The conquest of the Americas produced an ideological system that, in order to justify European domination, posed Indians as

savage, premodern foils to European progress, civilization, and modernity. Europeans placed Indians in the primitive half of an ontological dichotomy between civilization and savagery, man and nature. In the other half of the dichotomy, Europeans and their North and South American standard-bearers have simultaneously been engaged in introducing a mercantilist-cum-capitalist economic system into the farthest reaches of the Americas. Given that within this ideological system a benchmark of civilization and progress is the degree of involvement with the world economy, a dramatic and often tragic conflict arises between the opposed forces of identity and economy. In this book I have traced the ways in which this conflict has played itself out in the history and social science of the Mosquito Coast, as well as in the Mosquito Coast itself.

The contradictions of this Euro-American drama make themselves particularly manifest in the Mosquito Coast of Central America. The Mosquito Coast lies on the boundary between Mesoamerica and the Caribbean. Caribbeanists commonly refer to the Caribbean as an economically precocious region that at an early date was forged "from scratch" into a center of export production in the wake of the devastation of its indigenous inhabitants. The role of the Caribbean as an exploited peripheral region within an expanding European world system foretold the role that would be forced on the rest of the Third World. The Mosquito Coast unmistakably represents a Caribbean society. The region became an active participant in the growing contraband trade in the western Caribbean from the time of the establishment of the Providence Colony in the early 1600s. Although, as a result of complex historical twists of fate, the region did not become a formal British colony nor did it witness the rise of a typical Caribbean plantation complex, the economy of the region became inextricably linked to a growing world economy. As a result, the inhabitants of the region became increasingly dependent on goods of foreign manufacture, and they adapted their productive strategies accordingly. In Long's prophetic words, they became civilized.

This process intensified in the twentieth century when a series of US and Canadian lumber, mining, and banana companies began operations, making Puerto Cabezas the most modern and international city of the Mosquito Coast. Porteños looked positively on their own cosmopolitanism, as well as on their reliance on, and access to, high-status international sources of goods and money. This positive self-image was in part rooted to the strategic alliance made between natives of the Mosquito Coast and the English against the Spanish and Nicaraguans of the Pacific Coast. Costeños valued their contact with the English as a civilizing influence, and they adamantly resisted Nicaraguan "reincorporation" on the grounds that the Nicaraguan rule would place a barrier to their economic progress. In this sense, the inhabitants of the Mosquito Coast region have over time actively and consciously maximized their interaction with the Caribbean and its particular nexus in the world economy. In fact, a number of my Porteño informants, when asked to comment on the ways in which Pacific Nicaraguans perceived them during "company time" when they traveled to Managua, described themselves as "dollar men" because Spaniards, in their opinion, perceived Costeños as having greater access to cash, specifically US dollars. In the continuing climate of economic depression and "abandonment" in which the region has found itself in the years after the revolution, Porteños have a harder time living up to their billing as "dollar men," particularly in light of the wave of relatively wealthy Pacific Nicaraguans who returned to Managua from Miami after the Sandinista electoral defeat, speaking Standard American English (SAE) and carrying US passports. In complicated and regionally specific ways, these expressions of cosmopolitanism dovetail with Caribbean constructions of Blackness and Englishness—discourses to which insiders and outsiders in the Mosquito Coast have appealed for hundreds of years.

On the other hand, the Mosquito Coast is part of Mesoamerica, a Mesoamerica that is renowned, in the scholarly literature, for its Indian survivals. Again as a result of a number of highly contextual historical twists of fate, the Mosquito Coast is known, both by insiders and outsiders, as a place inhabited by Indians. In this regard, the region stands in contrast to the majority of Nicaragua, Central America, and Latin America, where the great majority of the population is referred to in a wide variety of terms such as Ladino, Mestizo, *el pueblo* (the people), campesino (peasant), *gente humilde* (common folk), and *del campo* (country folk)—all terms that are used in contrast to "real" Indians. As Indians, Costeños have been associated with a series of stereotypical traits, some more insidious than others, that place them on par with a static and unchanging natural world that stands in contrast to a dynamic modern world. David Frye identified this tendency to view Indians as inherently unchanging as a "colonial ideology" (Frye 1996, 10).

The complex and dynamic history of ethnic, tribal, and racial identification of the inhabitants of the Mosquito Coast is not merely a philosophical problem that Euro-American scholars have considered over the centuries. Rather, the contestation and use of these categories has been a highly charged and integral part of the social and political practice of the region. In this book I carefully trace the expressions of these ideologies, and in the process I interrogate both the standard anthropological "other" (in this case the diverse historical actors who have operated in the Mosquito Coast) and our own selves as historians and social scientists. In this respect I am following Andrew Lass's call to "treat [anthropological] theory . . . as an ethnographic object" (Lass 1997, 722). Literature review, of course, is a standard part of any scholarly work. However, I do not intend the discussion of previous scholarship to simply represent my attempt to situate my argument vis-à-vis that of scholars who have worked on similar issues. Rather, I trace the complicated ways in which social scientists and their concepts have mingled with and influenced and been influenced by their subjects. In the Mosquito Coast, where activist scholars of both the right and left have played significant roles as advisors and policy-makers, this mutual influence warrants such scrutiny.

In some extreme cases the line between scholars and actors has been impossible to draw. One particularly notable example of this phenomena is E. G. Squier, a nineteenth-century US scholar and diplomat, who wrote a highly polemical attack on the Mosquito Government as being composed of "drunken negroes," while simultaneously encouraging the US State Department to intervene in favor of Nicaragua in the dispute between Nicaragua and Great Britain over the status of the country of Mosquito (see Olien 1985 for a fascinating analysis of "anthropological scholarship and political propaganda").

Another, more recent, example is the case of the late Bernard Nietschmann, who served as a hawkish adviser to insurgent Miskito groups during the Contra War while publishing, with the help of the arch-conservative press "The Freedom House," a rabidly anticommunist "scholarly" treatment of Miskito identity. These two examples represent clear cases of what anthropologist Richard Handler condemned in his work on Quebecois nationalism as the "close congruence between actors' ideologies and observers' theories" (Handler 1988, 8). In many cases, as scholarly writing attempts to objectify and rationalize "native" ideology, local social movements incorporate these rationalized interpretations of their culture into their own rationalizations of their culture. This situation creates "two discourses that feed off of each other" (Handler 1988, 9). This process became increasingly charged during the Contra War as cold-war polarization deeply divided the scholarly approaches to the Costeño-Sandinista crisis.

I argue for the importance of consciously resisting the tendency to, in the words of Raymond Smith, "biologize social relations." I have demonstrated at length the ways in which identification as Miskito Indian and Creole, although undeniably an important matter among Costeños, has been overdrawn in the scholarly literature on the region. In the contemporary period, developments linked to the cold-war struggle between Contras and Sandinistas, the globalization of indigenous activism, the regional autonomy process, and official ethnicity have provided a strong impetus to force an otherwise highly fluid social situation with regard to socio-racial identifications into a standardized and objectivized system that operates on certain anthropologically-derived presuppositions about the relationship between race and culture.

The struggle for regional autonomy in eastern Nicaragua, in addition to representing a struggle for increased political and economic control vis-à-vis the Nicaraguan state, represents also a struggle over the meanings of being Black or Indian. This struggle takes place, not only in formal political contexts, but also in everyday social interaction. Costeños are actively engaged in the process of reworking and creating ideologies of racial difference, which are enacted and transformed in practice. They are trying to sort out what it means to be a Miskito, Creole, or Mestizo in the Mosquito Coast. As Brackette Williams has shown in the case of Guyana, the ethnic stereotypes and syncretic cultural forms that emerge from this process are forged in individuals' everyday practice. However, this process does not occur in an ideological vacuum where any cultural creation is possible. Rather, it occurs within an ideological arena heavy with the weight of the past's ideological, which is to say categorical, baggage (Williams 1991).

Apart from a providing a fruitful approach to understanding the roots of the Costeño-Sandinista conflict of the 1980s, the analysis that I develop in this book helps us to assess the future prospects for the Mosquito Coast. Allow me to introduce a final anecdote. In 1992 I attended the "Indigenous Assembly" of Miskito Indian communities that had been called by Stedman Fagoth, the controversial ex-leader of the largest Miskito faction of the Contras. Representatives from most Miskito villages and neighborhoods had walked, paddled, and driven for days in order to crowd into the large auditorium in the river city of Waspám. Fagoth drew the following two lists on the chalkboard:

1. Texas
2. California
3. Ukraine
4. South Africa
5. RAAN [the North Atlantic Autonomous Region]

Oil	180 million
Pesca [fish]	150 million
gold	150 million
lumber	100 million
total	580 million

He proceeded to explain, in Miskitu, to his audience that the first list was of the five wealthiest regions in the world in terms of natural resources. The second list represented the monetary value of these resources that would soon be enjoyed by Costeños once the US companies would accept their invitations to return.

For better or for worse, Costeños are searching for viable ways to cash in on the natural resources that exist within the Mosquito Coast. Their cosmopolitan ethos and their experience of environmental dissonance—the nagging sense that they should not be so poor while living in such a naturally abundant region—give them a strong ideological predisposition to attempt to rectify their current situation through recourse to foreign extractive industries. Just like the mythical Indian of Mosquito Coast folklore who could turn the leaves of oranges trees into bills of cash, the modern inhabitants of the Atlantic Coast and their leaders are working on the same magic. The trick will be to benefit from this conversion within a global economic system that rarely rewards the custodians of raw materials.

Notes

Chapter 1   The Setting

1. I conducted the majority of my ethnographic fieldwork in Nicaragua, most of the time in Puerto Cabezas, from April 1992 until September 1993. Although I was born and raised in Los Angeles, California, my family is from the Pacific side of Nicaragua and I make regular visits to the country. I employed both participant-observation and formal and informal interviews with a wide variety of informants, including foreigners, Costeños, and Pacific Nicaraguans. Except for widely known political leaders, I employ pseudonyms for all of the people that I refer to in this book.

2. The flight of these companies at the time of the triumph of the Sandinista Revolution punctuated the end of company time.

3. Nicaraguans use the term *Costeño* as a generic way of referring to the inhabitants of the Mosquito Coast. In Spanish the region is most commonly referred to as the *Costa Atlántica*. In the chapters that follow, I use the term *Costeño* as a key analytical and descriptive category. In the languages of the Mosquito Coast, the category of Costeño closely parallels the term *cus uplika* in Miskitu and "coast people" in English.

4. Edmund Gordon and Mark Anderson identify "two competing notions of blackness" among the Garifuna of the southern Mosquito Coast—one traditional and the other modern (Gordon and Anderson 1999, 292). It is precisely this association of modernity and blackness among Costeños that I am identifying here.

5. Inhabitants of the city of Puerto Cabezas refer to themselves in Spanish as *Porteños*. In English and Miskitu the corresponding terms are "port people" and *Bilwi Uplika*.

6. Miskitu, Miskito, and Mosquito are used variably to refer to a language, region, and people. In this book I use "Miskitu" to refer to the indigenous language of Nicaragua and Honduras, "Miskito" to refer to the socio-racial category, and "Mosquito" to refer to the region. This is a distinction that I make for the purposes of analytic clarity. According to some linguists, missionaries, and educators, the Miskitu language does not have an *o*. As a result, over the last twenty years the *u* has been increasingly used to refer to the language and the people. Although this change has been accepted by some Nicaraguan, North American, and European academics and journalists, most Costeños, with the exception of some educators and political leaders, have not replaced the *o* with a *u* in their writing. A recent linguistic analysis of Miskitu phonetics by Margaret Badlato was inconclusive as to whether the Miskitu phonetics has the letter *o* (Badlato 2001, 47). However the phonetic bottom line is ultimately adjudicated, it is reasonable to claim that Miskitu has an *o* by virtue of the fact that Miskitu speakers often believe that their language has an *o*. The case of the Miskitu *o* provides an example of modern

cultural politics in the region in which some Costeños and others are attempting to conceptually purify socio-racial categories that in practice are flexible.

7. The Contra War starting in 1980 pitted the newly formed armed forces of the Sandinista government, which came to power by overthrowing Nicaraguan dictator Anastasio Somozo in 1979, against the US-backed Contras whose ranks included former National Guard troops and leaders. The Contras attacked Nicaraguan targets primarily from bases in Honduras along the border with Nicaragua. In the Mosquito Coast, many Costeños joined the Contras and operated under their own leadership and in their own region (on the eastern part of the Honduras border) under the larger Contra organizational structure that was led by Nicaraguans from the Pacific. Although most of the units of Costeños had demobilized before the late 1980s, some retained their arms well after the elections of 1990 that removed the Sandinista administration from office.

8. Costeños use the term "community" (*comunidades* in Spanish, and *comunidad nani* or *tawan nani* in Miskitu) to refer to the region's settlements. It is a very important concept and I will return to it at length in chapters 4 and 6.

9. The distinction that I make between primitivism and cosmopolitanism recapitulates the civilization vs. nature dichotomy that Fredrick Pike fruitfully explored in his historical analysis of United States-Latin American relations in the Americas, titled *The United States and Latin America: Myths and Stereotypes of Civilization and Nature* (Pike 1992). However, in contrast to Pike, who focuses on the ways in which North Americans applied this flawed worldview to Latin Americans, I recognize that within Nicaragua (and the Americas generally) this framework is adopted in varying degrees by those very individuals who North Americans have viewed as primitive. Hence a primitivist ideology does not easily index a defined group of people (e.g., North Americans, Latin Americans, Pacific Nicaraguans, Costeños). Rather, it is part of a complex of ideas that are expressed in a contextual way across a broad spectrum of regions and social groups.

10. Concepts such as culture, race, identity, and ethnicity have become highly politically charged and often appear at the center of contentious political struggles and social movements in the modern world. The studied articulation and internalization of these concepts within modern Latin American social movements represents a principal distinguishing feature of what Sonia Alvarez and Arturo Escobar define as new social movements, which they contrast to old class-based movements (Alvarez, Dagnino, and Escobar 1998, 6; Alvarez and Escobar 1992, 3; Wade 1997, 95) such as the crushed national-popular projects (Hale 1997, 573) of Latin America. With regard to the current wave of indigenous activism in the Americas, Michael Kearney identifies a modern process of new ethnicity in which the construction of ethnicity by contemporary indigenous people has become and is becoming, more of a conscious, intentional activity than before (Kearney 1996, 10; also see Brysk 1996, 2000; Messer 1995; Wright 1988).

11. In an article that reviews the rise of the cultural politics of identity, Charles Hale identifies this problematic entanglement of analyst's lens and topic of study in Latin American anthropology (Hale 1997, 569; see Jackson 1995, 16, and Handler 1988 for a similar observation). This phenomenon represents an element of a larger crisis of representation (Marcus and Fischer 1986) and a related crisis in confidence (Watanabe 1994, 25) that has left anthropologists calling into question not only the value of their traditional methods and

rhetorics but also the virtue of the anthropological enterprise in light of the structures of inequality in which they operate.

12. I put the word "debate" in quotation marks here because, to quote Johannes Fabian, "I don't know of any essentialists calling themselves essentialist." Fabian recognizes that these two labels are currently employed to mark positions, but he disputes the way that this debate is framed on the grounds that "essentialism is essentially an ontological position; it asserts a reality, in this case Maya identity. Constructivism (at least in the understanding of someone who has been put in that corner) marks an epistemological position. It regards the conditions of possibility of, in this case, knowing what Maya identity might be. Put somewhat differently, essentialism is one of the things constructivists try to understand" (Fabian 1999, 490).

13. This theoretical move closely corresponds to a similar moment in the 1960s and 1970s when social scientists, sparked to some degree by the controversy surrounding Clifford Geertz's essay on primordial identity (Geertz 1963), proposed boundary maintenance (Barth 1969) and interest group models as a foil to static trait-oriented or culture-as-things (Jackson 1994, 385) approaches to politicized cultural, racial, and ethnic groups.

14. See the recent work of Kay Warren (1998, 1999) for a provocative example from Guatemala. Also see Christopher Brumann's appeal (1999) to retain the concept of culture, as well as Abu-Lughod responses in a 1999 issue of *Current Anthropology* dedicated to this topic.

15. Here Fernandez adds to Jean Jackson's provocatively titled article, "Is There A Way to Talk about Making Culture without Making Enemies?"

16. Hobsbawm and Ranger's provocative volume, *The Invention of Tradition*, would have to be considered the prime example of this approach (Hobsbawm and Ranger 1983). The following work also stands out in my mind: Bourricaud 1975; Diskin 1991; Hahn 1996; Handler 1988; Handler and Linnekin 1984; Herzfeld 1982; Jackson 1994, 1995; Vail 1989; Williams 1991. I would also include Friedlander's passionately written polemic on forced identity in Mexico in which she decries the elite Mexican glorification of the Mexican Indian while simultaneously using Indian identification as a strategy of marginalization (Friedlander 1975, 1976). Kay Warren's earlier work in Guatemala dealt with this theme (Warren 1989, 1993).

17. This is not to say that this approach is inherently antagonistic or that those that I identify as falling into this camp literally make enemies in the fieldwork setting, but rather that the analyses that they make of the cultural production of the group or groups that they study calls into question or potentially undermines at some level the premises of this cultural production that is practiced by one or more of the groups with whom they are involved.

18. In this group I include anthropologists who explicitly recognize that the appeals to culture and identity of the people they study have emerged as strategies of resistance that are forged in a highly politicized context. They, however, are hopeful and optimistic about the unifying potential of these strategies. In the Latin American context I include the following authors: Brysk 2000; Gandin 1997; Gossen 1996; Kearney and Nagengast 1990; Kearney 1996; Kidd 1995; Nash 1995; C. Smith 1991; Ströbele-Gregor 1996; Varese 1996; Warren 1999; Watanabe 1994; Whitten 1996; R. Wilson 1995.

19. In doing so I follow the lead of anthropologists, historians, and social scientists who have innovatively responded to the challenge of practicing

anthropology in the crucible of the political and social upheaval of twentieth-century Central America. Recent works by Les Field and Jeffrey Gould on the Pacific half of Nicaragua have effectively dealt with the issue of identity politics in this part of the country, where a "myth of mestizaje" exists that perpetuates the construction of the Pacific as a place that lacks indigenous influence (Gould 1998; Field 1999). Gould's work is part of a set of innovative treatments of the politics of mestizaje in Latin America. See the special volume of the *Journal of Latin American Anthropology*, edited by Charles Hale (1996), that is devoted to this issue, as well as Marisol de la Cadena's book on mestizaje in the Peruvian context (de la Cadena 2000). All of these works implicitly or explicitly take up the call to write against culture because they take up a history-of-identity approach to a distinctively "halfie" social category (Mestizo), thereby resisting the temptation to take the prevailing identity categories on face value—as bounded, unchanging entities.

CHAPTER 2   NICARAGUA'S TWO COASTS

1. The Spanish took advantage of this feature to build a Pacific fleet using native labor, which in its first years primarily transported Nicaraguan Indian slaves to the mines of Peru (Sherman 1979, 237).

2. Newson, whose numbers correspond generally with other estimates of the pre-Conquest population, puts the Nicaraguan population level at about 1.6 million, of which over 1 million lived in the Pacific lowlands and about 350,000 lived in the Central Highlands. The Caribbean Coastal Plain had by far the lowest population density, with 60 percent of the land area but only 5 percent of the total population. According to Newson the population density of the region (one person per square kilometer), was dramatically lower than that of the Pacific Lowlands (sixty people per square kilometer) and the Central Highlands (fifteen people per square kilometer) (Newson 1987, 88).

3. Lateric soils (acidic, bright red in color with a high content of iron oxide and aluminum hydroxide) predominate in and around Puerto Cabezas as well as the Atlantic coast in general. During my stays in Managua, I noted that the red soils of the Atlantic often stood out in the minds of Pacific Nicaraguans who had spent time in Puerto Cabezas as an unforgettable distinguishing feature of the region.

4. *Cacique* was an Arawak-derived Taíno Indian word meaning "leader," which the Spanish applied to New World Indians in general (Moscoso 1991, 38). This represented a typical case of the Spanish imposing native terminology in an over-generalizing way on a complex American social reality.

5. Strong noted that as of the late 1940s, the region was almost completely archaeologically unexplored (Strong 1948, 121, 138).

6. Julian Steward viewed this decrease in productive skill as an example of the high degree of post-Conquest "deculturation" of Caribbean tribes. According to Steward, the pre-Columbian populations of the Eastern Coastal Plain of Nicaragua and Honduras conformed to what he labeled the "Circum-Caribbean Culture," which represented a middle stage between the "civilized peoples" (Steward 1948, 7) of Central Mexico and the Peruvian Andes, and the less-developed "Marginal" and "Tropical Forest" tribes (27). As a result of the Conquest, the cultural level of these Circum-Caribbean tribes composed of semi-civilized people "stepped down to the Tropical Forest level" (15).

7. This history helps to explain the overwhelming preponderance of Nahuatl toponyms and ethnonyms in Central America, many of which, counterintuitively, emerged during the colonial period (Newson 1987, 30; also see Guerrero and Guerrero 1982 and Incer 1985).

8. The use of Nahuatl as a lingua franca in lower Central American continued into the seventeenth century (Stone 1964, 214; also see Wolf 1959, 41).

9. Nahua is a language grouping that includes a wide variety of historical and modern dialects. Nahuat refers to dialects that branched off at an earlier date and were spoken in the periphery of Middle America. Nahuatl refers to the dominant language of the Mexica State (arising in the fourteenth and fifteenth centuries) that had its "intellectual capital" in Texcoco. This "polished and sophisticated" dialect came to be the court language of the non-Aztecan ruling groups throughout the Aztec Empire (Wolf 1959, 42).

10. The name of the modern Nicaragua department that occupies the eastern border of Lake Nicaragua bears this same name—Chontales. Daniel Ortega, the beleaguered ex-president of Nicaragua, who from the moment of his rise to power was regarded with disdain as something of a "rustic" country bumpkin by many of the Nicaraguan elite centered in Managua, Leon, and Granada (Nicaragua's three major cities and not coincidentally the areas of highest Mexican-derived pre-Columbian population) is the most prominent recent native *Chontaleño*.

11. *Caribe* was a generic (non-Nahua) term used by the Spanish to label tribes from the Lower Antilles and the northern coast of South America who allegedly practiced cannibalism (Incer 1990, 248).

12. It is difficult to determine whether or not this alleged nomadism was a feature of pre-contact Mosquito Coast groups or whether, if it existed at all, it was a defensive response to the pressures of European (and pre-Columbian central Mexican) contact. Offen argues that the belief in Mosquito Coast nomadism is part of a "mythical landscape" that plagues the historiography of the region (Offen 1999, 222).

13. A number of historians have described seventeenth-century Spanish attempts to conquer the region (Gamez 1939, 45–53; Potthast 1988, 18–29; Houwald 1990, 11–140).

14. *Lenca* usually referred to highland groups that occupied the Segovias of northern Nicaragua and central Honduras, while *Jicaque* usually came to refer to lowland groups in the Caribbean watershed of the Segovias. These eventually became officially recognized Indian group names in Honduras. The modern ethnological literature also maintains the use of these terms (Steward 1948, 30; Johnson 1948, 60). The modern Jicaque occupy the Yoro region of northern Honduras at the source of the Aguan River (Incer 1990, 251).

15. See Moscoso (1991) and Romero Vargas (1993a) for detailed descriptions of the institutions through which the Spanish exploited communally organized Indian labor in Nicaragua.

16. Jeffrey Gould described in detail the process by which Nicaraguan Indians finally became formally redefined as *Ladinos* in the early twentieth century (Gould 1993b, 201). He calls into question the common (Nicaraguan nationalist) portrayal of this process as being a simple "one-way road to assimilation with the Indian at the beginning and the ladino citizen at the destination." Although he critiques the economic determinism of Jaime Wheelock's perspective that underscores "the loss of land and consequent proletarianization

as the principal cause of Ladinoization," he concedes that the "acceptance of a mestizo Nicaraguan identity usually involved the withdrawal of indigenous claims to communal land and the loss of communal autonomy" (Gould 1993a, 395). Gould concedes that after hundreds of years of struggle central Nicaraguan Indians finally became defined as Ladinos.

17. Rights did correspond with the labor and tributary obligations imposed on formally recognized indigenous communities. The most prominent of these rights was the possession and use of communal lands that throughout the colonial period were selectively recognized by Spain (Romero Vargas 1993a, 11).

18. In the last fifteen years there has been a renewed interest within Nicaragua in the traditionally "denied existence" and "obstinate persistence" (Membreño 1994, 181) of Pacific indigenous communities. This research, falling within the Latin American indigenist tradition, has attempted to address what is perceived as an anomalous feature of Nicaraguan society, that despite the widespread belief that Indian communities in the Pacific ceased to exist, certain Pacific Nicaraguans continue to have an "Indian identity" although they do not retain indigenous language or dress. A major goal of this research, then, is to positively demonstrate that in fact these people indeed are Indians. For examples see García Breso (1992), Rizo (1993), Membreño (1994), and C. Sánchez (1994).

19. Although the Spanish colonial rulers and later the Nicaraguan elite used Indian communal affiliation to their own advantage, this does not mean that indigenous communities were not at times able to use their "communal solidarity" to resist their exploitation (Gould 1993b, 199). Gould provides a fascinating example of a Pacific indigenous community's (Subtiava) resistance to the pressures of "Ladinoization" and capitalist expansion (ibid.).

20. For particularly illustrative examples, see Gamez (1939, 59); Floyd (1967, 22); Smutko (1985, 72); Dunbar Ortiz (1986, 59); Incer (1990, 291, 294); Solórzano (1992, 38).

21. Geographer Karl Offen convincingly refutes the often repeated claim to the effect that the shipwrecked African slaves joined Sumu communities, which together subsequently became the Miskito Indians. This claim views the Miskito as "transformed Sumus" and in general downplays the cultural continuity between the pre- and post-shipwreck populations. He argues that a sizable "proto-Miskitu" population, which is sometimes referred to in the early colonial literature as "Guaba" Indians, inhabited the Cape Gracias a Dios section of the Mosquito Coast well before the shipwreck (Offen 2002).

22. Much of the scholarship that views the emergence of the Miskito Indians as primarily a biological phenomenon relies in part on the work of Eduard Conzemius, the first professional ethnographer of the Mosquito Coast, who published a full-length monograph in 1932. In this monograph Conzemius wrote, "The hybrid tribe of the Miskito owes its origin to the intermarriage of the Bawihka with the Negroes escaped from the slave ship which was wrecked to the south of Cabo Gracias a Dios in 1641" (Conzemius 1932, 17).

23. Modern histories have consistently cited the following four sources in their historical reconstruction of Miskito Coast history. These easily accessible accounts written by English and French buccaneers who visited the region in the last quarter of the seventeenth century make the first reference to the inhabitants of the region as "Miskito Indians": William Dampier's *A New*

Voyage Around the World (1698), Raveneau de Lussan's *Raveneau de Lussan, Buccaneer of the Spanish Main and Early French Filibuster of the Pacific* (1930) [1689], Alexandre Exquemelin's *The Buccaneers of America or, A true account of the most remarkable assaults committed of later years upon the coasts of the West Indies by the bucaniers of Jamaica and Tortuga* (1684) [1678], and the mysterious M.W.'s *The Mosquito Indian and his Golden River* (1728).

24. In the early descriptions of the area, a wide variety of spellings are used for "Miskito," such as Mosqueto, Mosquito, Moskito, Mosco, Moustique, Musketo and Musquito (Helms 1971, 15).

25. Parsons noted how the instructions of the directors of the Providence Company regarding their conduct with the Indians of the Coast had been explicit: "You are to endear yourselves with the Indians and their commanders and we conjure you to be friendly and to cause no jealousy" (Parson 1956, 13).

26. In Colonial Spanish America a complicated system of categories emerged (known as *castas*) that attempted to order and name the varying levels of racial mixing between Whites, Blacks, and Indians. The most essential terms were *Mestizo* ("Spaniard and Indian woman beget mestizo"), *Mulatto* ("Spaniard and Negress beget mulatto"), and *Zambo* ("Negro and Indian woman beget sambo de Indio") (Mörner 1967, 58). A host of other terms emerged to mark the complicated combinations that resulted. These categories became part of a colonial society that was stratified on the basis of "blood" and "birth." As Helms has pointed out, the absence of Spanish control in the Mosquito Coast sheltered the inhabitants from the legal and social consequences in Spanish society of inclusion into the Zambo or Indian caste (Helms 1977, 63). It is important also to point out that these terms putatively made reference to varying levels of European, African, and Indian "blood" but did not refer to legally, or socially, constituted collective entities. In this sense they were descriptions rather than ethnonyms.

27. See Conzemius for a description of the different versions of the shipwreck account among the colonial sources (Conzemius 1932, 16).

28. William Dampier, an English pirate who visited the region in 1681, described the "Moskito Indians" in the following manner: "They are but a small Nation or Family, and not 100 men of them in number, inhabiting on the Main, on the North side, near Cape *Gratia Dios*; between Cape *Honduras* and *Nicaragua*" (Dampier 1698, 7).

29. After the British occupation of Jamaica in 1655 (in partial fulfillment of Oliver Cromwell's "Western Design" to divide the Spanish Main) (Parsons 1956, 9), buccaneers incessantly raided Spanish settlements from Campeche to Venezuela. Mosquito Coast inhabitants (regardless of whether they were labeled Indians, Zambos, or Mulattoes) formed an integral part of the legendary and infamous English expeditionary forces that sacked Pacific Nicaraguan cities, establishing a pattern of Mosquito Coast-based raids on the Pacific that were continued well after the passing of the heyday (1640–1685) of European state-sponsored buccaneering (Floyd 1967, 28; Naylor 1989, 34).

30. In 1688 the governor of Jamaica, in a letter to the Lords of Trade and Plantations in London, wrote: "Some Indians known by the name of 'Musketa' Indians (whose country is called Cape Gratias de Dios, in latitude 15° 20′ or thereabouts) have been here with me and have told me that they became subjects of King Charles I, and they earnestly desired the King's protection or they must fall under the French or Dutch" (Olien 1983, 204).

31. See Romero Vargas and Gabbert for thorough historical accounts of slavery, both Indian and African, in the Mosquito Coast (Romero Vargas 1995, 273–296; Gabbert 1992, 38–70).

32. Although Exquemelin's account has been cited in the historical literature as one of the first to employ the term "Mosquito Indian," he uses the term only once (Exquemelin 1685, 158). He most commonly uses the phrase "*Indians* of the Cape" and "*Indians* of those parts."

33. In the mid-1980s, US anthropologists Michael Olien, Phillip Dennis, and Mary Helms filled the pages of the *American Ethnologist* with a lively debate about political authority in the Mosquito Kingdom (Dennis and Olien 1984; Helms 1986). Dennis and Olien argued that, contrary to Nicaraguan and US nineteenth-century claims as to its falsity, the Mosquito Kingdom and the Mosquito king represented very real and durable institutions that had deep roots in Miskito culture. Helms argued that Dennis and Olien had overstated their case and that in actuality the historical truth lay somewhere in between the US and Nicaraguan critics' of the Mosquito Kingdom as a "British puppet" and Dennis and Olien's Mosquito Kingdom as a "centralized political structure" that endured for 240 years (Helms 1986, 506).

34. For example, Gabbert estimates that in 1757, African slaves numbered 500 and Indian slaves 300 of the total regional population of 8,124. The number of whites, 154, paled in comparison to the number of free Indians, 7,000 (Gabbert 1992, 55).

35. According to Helms, in Jamaica before the stabilization of an economy based on African slave labor, Indians slaves helped to fill, at least in part, the economic gap created by the curtailing of buccaneering in 1685 and the ceasing of the flow of white indentured labor in 1700. She claims that the lack of documentation of the use of mainland Indian labor in Jamaica owes to the fact that primarily "struggling small farmers" used Indian labor, which was significantly cheaper than African slave labor (Helms 1983, 185).

36. In 1832 Mosquito King Robert Charles Frederic passed a law that forbade the taking of Indian slaves (Olien 1983, 222).

37. The newly independent Central American Republic outlawed slavery in 1824 (Naylor 1989, 256).

38. Bartolomé de Las Casas, famous Spanish witness to the "devastation of the Indies," estimated that the Spanish sent a half-million Indian slaves to Panama and Peru (Las Casas 1992 [1552], 56). Newson has confirmed this figure (Newson 1987, 105). See William L. Sherman's *Forced Native Labor in Sixteenth-Century Central America* for an exhaustive treatment of the slave trade in Nicaragua (Sherman 1979).

39. During the eighteenth and nineteenth centuries, the English typically referred to the region as the Mosquito Shore or simply Mosquito.

40. Robert Hodgson, the first British superintendent of the Mosquito Shore, firmly believed in the tremendous strategic importance of the Mosquito Indians in the British struggle against Spain. In 1741 he wrote to Governor Trelawny of Jamaica, "By the help of our friends the Mosquito Indians I should imagine we might induce, by the offer of liberty, the neighboring Indians to revolt. Indeed I do not think it romantick in the least to expect that we might, by supporting the Indians a little, spread the revolt from one part to another, till it should be general over the Indies, & drive the Spaniards entirely out" (Potthast 1988, 123).

41. See Karl Offen's PhD dissertation for an extended discussion of the role of English symbols of prestige for the Miskito Indians (Offen 1999, 352–395).

42. Many Miskito villages did not fall within the geographical boundaries set by the Treaty of Managua for the Mosquito Reservation. The entire Coco River was not subject to the Treaty of Managua and instead became part of Nicaraguan territory that was named the Comarca Cabo Gracias a Dios. Karl Offen argues that the boundary of the Mosquito Reserve neatly corresponds to the boundary between the Tawira Miskito and the Sambo Miskito (Offen 2002).

43. The "Great Awakening" is the term given by the Moravian Missionary Church, which started to evangelize in the region in the early 1800s, to the mass conversion of Miskito Indians to Christianity in the 1880s. See Lioba Rossbach for a description of Moravian-Miskito relations in the nineteenth century (Oertzen, Rossbach, and Wunderich, 1990).

44. The full text of the Harrison-Altamirano Treaty is reprinted in Oertzen, Rossbach, and Wunderich (1990, 436–437.)

45. The formalization of Indian and Creole lands stood in the way of this process of heightened penetration of capital by which the Mosquito Coast was becoming more and more an "enclave economy." The government granted monstrous parcels of land to foreign companies, ignoring the claims of Indian villages. For example, the Emery Company of Massachusetts was granted a parcel one-tenth the size of the region. In 1903 one grant, which was later annulled, gave the Dietrick Company the rights to the exploitation of an area one-fourth the size of Nicaragua (Vilas 1989, 43). The work of surveying and giving titles was not seriously begun until 1915, when the land commission began to function. Between 1915 and 1920, 121,179 acres were set aside for forty-five Sumu and Miskito villages. One way the government avoided its responsibility was to require that the Indian villages pay for the surveys of the land they claimed, or pay for a new survey when this land came into dispute.

CHAPTER 3   FROM BILWI TO PUERTO CABEZAS

1. Centuries before, English pirates and mahogany traders had given the name Bragman's Bluff to the area's most distinguishing feature, a broad twenty-foot-high mesa that dropped abruptly at the sea.

2. The village that today is known by Miskitu speakers as Sawmill, located along the banks of the Wawa River, was one such early lumber village, composed of mostly Costeño workers and foreign overseers. This village exists to this day, although the sawmill to which it owes its name was long ago dismantled. German Moravian missionary and linguist George Heath claimed that the original indigenous name of Sawmill was *Iniwaska* and that the sawmill was dismantled at the turn of the century (Heath 1927, 88).

3. A variety of spellings appear in the historical record, including "Brancman's" and "Brangman's." These English names were most commonly used in the eighteenth century. Spanish sources referred to the place in Spanish as "Caleta Barrancas" and "Monte Gordo" (Incer 1990, 497, 539).

4. Bilwi is a Sumu word that means "snake eye" (Valle 1944, 22). The fact that Bilwi is a Sumu word has led Mosquito Coast historians to conclude that a Sumu group originally inhabited the site and later was driven inland by Miskito Indians.

5. Geographer Karl Offen, in an article about racial distinctions among Miskito Indians, claims that Bilwi was settled by Tawira Indians, while Karatá, to the south, was settled by Sambo Indians. Offen claims that the Tawira-Sambo distinction among Miskito Indians was based on the recognition of phenotypic distinctions between the Tawira (straight-haired) "pure" Indians and Sambo mixed Indians (Offen 2002, 328).

6. The 1860 Treaty of Managua, which abolished the country of Mosquito and established the Mosquito Reservation in its place, also replaced the title of Mosquito King with the Mosquito "Hereditary Chief."

7. The use of last names directly corresponds to the adoption of Christianity by Costeños, which did not occur on a large scale until the so-called "Great Awakening" of the 1880s and 1890s.

8. In Miskitu, *Wita* means headman or leader and it is unlikely that "Andrew" actually used this term as his last name. Rather, it appears that the Nicaraguan officials who prepared the "Decrees of Incorporation" were not able to effectively communicate with the Miskito representatives. This conclusion is further confirmed by the fact that the names of many Miskito villages are misspelled in the document. This and other evidence supports the claim that the 1894 Miskito convention was illegitimately staged by the Nicaraguan government.

9. In his book, *Tropical Enterprise: The Standard Fruit and Steamship Company in Latin America* (1978), Karnes described the decision to enter into agribusiness in Nicaragua as a "costly mistake." In chapter 8 ("Anarchy and Losses in Nicaragua") he described in detail from a corporate historian's perspective the rise and fall of the Bragman's Bluff Lumber Company in Puerto Cabezas. Karnes used primary sources from the company archives, as well as interviews with surviving company employees.

10. This is an anglicized form of the Spanish *síndico*, which is the Nicaraguan administrative title that replaced the Mosquito position of "headman." The office of síndico was created by the Nicaraguan government in the Atlantic Coast on February 18 of 1919 (Ruiz y Ruiz 1925, 12). This change of terminology, of course, represented part of the overall Nicaraguan project of Hispanicization of the former country of Mosquito.

11. After the "Reincorporation" of 1894, the Mosquito Reservation became the Nicaraguan "*Departamento*" of Bluefields (later renamed Zelaya), and the city of Bluefields, which already hosted British and US consulates, became the seat of the national government.

12. Apart from administrative workers, both banana and lumber companies required laborers with special training (which these companies did not provide) to complete particular tasks essential to their operation, such as carpentry, tie-rod fabrication, and mule husbandry. Companies used policies, such as higher pay scales and subsidized company housing, to recruit and retain these laborers who were valued more than laborers who were considered interchangeable because of the lower skill level required to complete their respective tasks. Hence the companies specifically used the distinction between skilled and unskilled labor. See Chomsky (1996) for a thorough discussion of labor and management in the banana industry of the Caribbean coast of Central America.

13. To this day Costeños refer to Pacific Nicaraguans as the "Spanish" in English, "*españoles*" in Spanish, and "*ispail nani*" in Miskito.

14. The Fortress of the Conception, El Castillo de la Concepción, was a Spanish fort along the eastern frontier of Spanish influence in Nicaragua. It lies along

the San Juan River, which flows from the Lake of Nicaragua, in the heart of the Spanish-controlled half of Nicaragua, to the Caribbean Sea. English and Miskito raiders continually used this route to sack Nicaraguan cities. From early colonial times to the time of construction of the Panama Canal, the route was regarded as ideal for a canal between the oceans.

15. According to the 1920 Nicaraguan census, the three Atlantic Coast counties which composed about half of the national territory contained only 43,698 inhabitants, 7 percent of the national population (República de Nicaragua 1920). Indeed, Nicaragua's Atlantic Coast continues to be one of the most sparsely populated regions in all of Central America.

16. In present day Nicaragua it is the common perception that Costeños have darker skin than Pacific Nicaraguans because of their African and Indian heritage—a heritage that has historically been denied in the Pacific Coast. Although there does exist a very dark-skinned minority in the Atlantic Coast and a very light-skinned minority in the Pacific Coast, it has not been my perception that (apart from these minorities) the majority of Costeños have darker skin than the majority of Pacific Nicaraguans. This observation is, of course, very subjective and ultimately irrelevant.

17. Jeffrey Gould demonstrates that in the Pacific region at the turn of the century, many communities that identified themselves as Indians began to identify themselves as Ladinos and Mestizos as their lands were expropriated by coffee growers. Gould contrasts this relatively recent shift to the widespread Nicaraguan belief that Nicaragua possesses a racially homogenous population—a belief he labels the "myth of Nicaragua mestiza" (Gould 1993a).

18. Puerto Cabezas was named after General Rigoberto Cabezas, the Nicaraguan officer who in 1894 militarily occupied Bluefields, effectively overthrowing the Mosquito government.

19. It is important to note that these figures are of highly questionable accuracy considering Ruiz's attempt to discredit Miskito land claims in Puerto Cabezas by claiming that the city is not a legitimate Miskito community and is rather a recently inhabited Mestizo city.

20. Modern inhabitants of the city recall that until the cessation of US lumber operations in the area (1979), this area of town was known as the "zone" or "American zone." In chapter 4, I explore Porteño memories of "company time" in the zone.

21. By the beginning of the twentieth century, rural Nicaraguans in the Pacific region who in the past had been labeled as Indians came to be identified according to the non-racially-marked term *campesino*. The indigenous communities in urban neighborhoods of Sutiava and Monimbó, located respectively in the major Pacific Nicaraguan cities of León and Masaya, represent a notable exception to this rule. These neighborhoods have throughout the twentieth century been identified in many contexts as Indian communities, and they manifest some of the typical Latin American "closed corporate community" institutional features, such as communal land holdings, "*cargo*" arrangements, and "*cofradías.*" These institutions continue to exist in other Pacific Nicaraguan communities, but what is distinct about Sutiava and Monimbó is that they are communities that regard themselves as Indians. See García Breso (1992) and Gould (1993b) for a description of Indian identity in the Pacific.

22. After the "Reincorporation" of 1894, Costeño leaders vehemently condemned this practice on the part of the national government in Managua.

Even US diplomats, who generally favored a Nicaraguan takeover of the Mosquito Coast, recognized the parasitism of the central government's fiscal policies in the Atlantic Coast—a parasitism that directly contradicted the commonly held opinion in the Pacific Coast that the "Coast" and the Costeños were economically unproductive. Take, for example, the following report sent by William Heard, US consul in Bluefields, to the US secretary of state in 1923:

> I have observed from the reports of the Collector General of Customs that an average of $15,000 is collected annually as a Municipal tax on goods imported into Bluefields. This sum, however, is taken by the Central Government towards liquidating its indebtedness. The Municipal licenses or taxes of Bluefields average $3,000 per month, but as previously pointed out all of this is embargoed. The total collections at El Bluff Custom House was $418,611 for 1922, this includes duties on imports and exports, storage charges, fines, 12½% surtax, hospital dues, tonnage and lighthouse, forestal tax, municipality tax, wharfage, consular fees and overtime payments. It will thus be seen that the people of this coast are contributing nearly half a million dollars to the general revenues of the country for which they receive practically nothing. (Department of State Records 817 08/21, Heard to Secretary of State, Bluefields, Dec. 19, 1923)

CHAPTER 4   COMPANY TIME

1. Harold Denny was a New York Times journalist who traveled to Puerto Cabezas in 1929.

2. For examples of approaches that focus on the effects of the "class-ethnic" hierarchy in the region, see Bourgois 1981, 1985, 1992; Hale 1987b, 103; Jenkins Molieri 1986; R. Adams 1981; Buvollen 1987; Diskin 1987, 1989; García 1996; CIDCA 1984; Dunbar Ortiz 1988; Schneider 1996; Vilas 1989.

3. Puerto Cabezas during company time contained social and institutional configurations that were remarkably similar to those of lumber towns of the American South and West (see Allen 1966; Brown 1923; Kellogg 1914; Maxwell and Baker 1983; Robbins 1982). In many ways it makes sense to view Puerto Cabezas during company time as an extension of the North American frontier.

4. Bourgois noted the use of this term by Creoles, who he claimed used it to refer to Mestizos (Bourgois 1992, 28). I found in my interviews with Porteños that the term was not directly linked with a particular socio-racial group; rather, it was used to describe rural agriculturalists regardless of any socio-racial identification.

5. I will briefly return in this chapter to the issue of gender and the central "Where are the women?" question that Cynthia Enloe convincingly argues has received inadequate attention in the study of labor and globalization.

6. As I will describe in greater detail later, in the modern usage of the Atlantic Coast, to refer to a Miskito Indian as being from "the communities" (*cómunidad nani ra* or *tawan nani ra* in Miskitu, and *de las comunidades* in Spanish) is a way of saying that person is a rural person from a small village. The implication is often that such a person is from a small inland village and not from the outside-oriented cities and villages.

7. "Los gringos ni estan aqui pero nos siguen cagando."

8. "Las empresas norteamericanas debieran de pagar a los Costeños y al pueblo Nicaraguense por todo el daño que causaron y no al reves."

9. The log pond was an essential element of logging cities throughout the American West in this period. Industrial historians Maxwell and Baker wrote: "Any description of the operation of a major sawmill must begin at the millpond. Most companies . . . considered the log pond an essential part of their operations, and when none already existed, they built one" (Maxwell and Baker 1983, 73).

10. "En esa época las lagunas esas estaban llenas de madera. Uno podría caminar de un lado para el otro sin mojarse pisando puros trozos de pino, buen pino. Despues metieron caoba y cedro. Y alli mismo al lado estaban los aserríos que en tiempo de madera trabajaban todo el día con aquella gran bulla. En esa época siempre había bulla por todos lados, aquellos camionazos gringos, no como los sovieticos que hay ahora que no sirven. Puerto Cabezas parecía panal de abejas."

11. In the Mosquito Coast and more generally in Nicaragua, a set of three terms are used to identify people of Asian and Middle Easterner descent or birth who live in Nicaragua. Nicaraguans refer to Middle Easterners, often Palestinians or Lebanese, as "Turcos." East Asian immigrants from mainland China and Hong Kong, most of whom came to the Atlantic Coast region in the first half of the century during company boom periods, are referred to as "Chinos." Both "Turcos" and "Chinos" are known for their success in small- and medium-scale retail. "Hindu" is the term used to refer to South Asians regardless of their religion or nationality.

12. After the last of the companies fled the region in 1979, the Sandinista government confiscated unoccupied and unclaimed properties in Puerto Cabezas and throughout Nicaragua. The properties were then distributed to governmental and private institutions that were linked to the revolution. The Sandinista administration formed CIDCA (Centro de Documentacion e Investigaciones de la Costa Atlantica), a social science research group, to study the growing problems that were arising on the Atlantic Coast.

13. The role of women as workers in Puerto Cabezas during "company time" was in many ways similar to the role that Cynthia Enloe attributed to women in Central and South American banana plantations in her *Bananas, Beaches, and Bases* (1989). She wrote: "Notions of masculinity and femininity have been used to shape the international political economy of the banana. Banana plantations were developed in Central America, Latin America, the Caribbean . . . as a result of alliances between men of different but complementary interests. . . . To clear the land and harvest the bananas they decided they needed a male workforce, sustained at a distance by women as prostitutes, mothers and wives" (Enloe 1989, 129).

14. Bluefields is the Atlantic port that offers the greatest accessibility from the Pacific region of Nicaragua. The Managua-Bluefields trip requires a two-pronged voyage. From Managua, passengers and cargo are transported along an all-weather road to the river port of Rama (about fifty kilometers from the Atlantic coast). This is the only all-weather road that exists in the Atlantic Coast. At Rama, passengers and cargo are loaded on riverboats that make the meandering voyage down the Rio Escondido to Bluefields. The two hundred-kilometer trip lasts at least twelve hours. Owing to the difficulty of

this trip and the low quality of the Bluefields area port facilities, goods and materials of Pacific origin destined for international markets are most frequently transported from Pacific Nicaraguan ports to the Atlantic Ocean via the Panama Canal. The Bluefields-Managua land route is primarily used to transport goods and materials of domestic production and consumption. As a result of Bluefields's accessibility, albeit limited, vis-à-vis Pacific Nicaragua, it has in the twentieth century captured the majority of the domestic Pacific-Atlantic commerce. Puerto Cabezas, on the other hand, has since its abrupt birth in the 1920s been primarily an international port that links the northern Mosquito Coast "enclave" to North America and the Caribbean.

15. As the Standard Fruit Company expanded its operations in Nicaragua, it bought majority shares in two US commercial companies that operated stores in the Atlantic Coast: the Wawa Boom Company and the Bluefields Mercantile Company (Karnes 1978, 115–117). These takeovers speak to the importance to the company of adding retail commerce to their resource-based business.

16. "Aqui en Puerto uno tenía, pues, del todo. Si no lo encontrabas donde los gringos lo encontrabas donde los chinos aqui en la calle commercial. Llegaban todas las semanas barcos llenos de productos que venían directo de los Estados Unidos y eran productos buenos, los mismos que los gringos usaban—botas de hule, jabones, camisas, lo que fuera. Y repuestos para motores? De toda clase. Aqui la vida era muy buena."

17. I discuss the Chinese community of Puerto Cabezas in a 2001 article titled "The Chinese Creoles of Nicaragua: Identity, Economy and Revolution in a Caribbean Port City" (Pineda 2001a).

18. During the Constitutionalist War of the late 1920s, Bragman's Bluff Lumber Company charged the Liberal Forces in Puerto Cabezas for use of the company radio that was used to communicate with the Pacific Coast. When the Liberals could not pay their radio bill, the company refused service—thereby leaving the Liberal "provisional government" without communications. This case illustrates the degree to which US companies possessed resources and infrastructure in the Atlantic Coast greater than that of the Nicaraguan governmental, or quasi-governmental, factions.

19. In Asang, Helms identified an "ethic of poverty" among Miskito Indians who, despite the "soundness of the subsistence economy," suffered the absence of cash and foreign products in the depressed coastal economy of the 1960s (Helms 1971, 156).

20. See T. M. Scruggs for a thorough discussion of the role of music in the construction of Nicaraguan nationalism (Scruggs 1999).

21. Census data from Nicaragua confirm this perception for the Mosquito Coast as a whole. Using the 1920 census, if we calculate the percentage of non-Central American foreigners within the total population, we find that the three Atlantic departments, Comarca San Juan del Norte, Bluefields, and Comarca Cabo Gracias a Dios, contain the three highest values, 10.9 percent, 6.3 percent, and 1.4 percent, respectively. Managua, the capital city of the republic, comes in a distant fourth at 0.84 percent, while the populous departments of Chontales and Nueva Segovia contained only 0.06 percent non-Central American foreigners (República de Nicaragua 1920, 4).

22. "Kampani time ra upla manas nara iwi kan . . . States wina, Jámaica wina, Germany wina, Cayman wina, Pánama wina, diara sut. Nation bani ba Bilwi ra balan wark daukaia dukiara. Bilwi tawan tara kan."

23. Helms noted a similar use of "nation" in the Coco River Miskito village in which she worked in the late 1960s (Helms 1971, 158, 218).

24. The use of Puerto Cabezas for military purposes by the US armed forces arose almost immediately after its creation by Bragman's Bluff Lumber Company. Karl Mueller, a Moravian Missionary who visited Puerto Cabezas in 1927, described the city in the following manner: "Bragman's Bluff is the name of the elevation (ca. 90 ft.) on the coast, on which the industrial and administrative town of Puerto Cabezas (ca. 2,500 inhabitants, mostly British and American) is built. The town has a well-built dock, an ice plant, a large Department Store (The Commissary Department of the Company), railroad yards, round house, and repair shops, and above all a sawmill, capable of cutting 55,000 feet of lumber per day. It has a fine hospital, a creditable club house, ball grounds and tennis courts, and at present is the headquarters of the American Marines for the upper coast, with a considerable garrison, a US war vessel stationed in its harbor and 2 US aeroplanes regularly stationed in the flying-field" (Mueller 1931, 67).

25. See LeGrand (1984) for a treatment of agrarian politics in a United Fruit Company banana region on the Caribbean coast of Colombia; see May and Plaza (1958) for a pro-company perspective on the role the United Fruit Company in the Caribbean; also see Chomsky (1996) for an excellent treatment of labor and race relations in a banana-exporting region of Costa Rica that has many of the same Anglo vs. Spanish and West Indian vs. Central American dynamics as the Mosquito Coast.

26. Helms' definition of peasantry, which she derived from the Mesoamerican anthropology of Redfield (1956), Wolf (1966), and Foster (1967), is as good as any for my purposes: "Rural cultivators who carry on agriculture as a traditional way of life, rather than for profit in a capitalistic sense, and part of whose is tapped by the state in order to support is own structure and activities" (Helms 1971, 4).

27. North American anthropologist Eduard Conzemius, who conducted fieldwork in the Mosquito Coast in the 1920s, made the following observations: "Rice is rarely cultivated and has been introduced recently; it is known by its English or Spanish name . . . it differs considerably from the native wild rice of tropical America." He also noted that beans "are grown to a very small extent by either Miskito or Sumu . . . it is very probable that beans have been introduced only in recent times" (Conzemius 1932, 63).

28. Using official Nicaraguan agricultural census data from 1963 and 1971, Vilas determined that the total acreage dedicated to farming in the Department of Zelaya (the pre-revolution name of the region) increased by 60 percent, from 468,000 acres to 774,000 acres (Vilas 1989, 73). Also, the number of cattle doubled. Vilas also noted a marked rise in the number of agricultural workers: "The number of self-employed agricultural workers grew 40 percent between 1963 and 1971, and the number of unpaid family members grew 38 percent; the two occupational categories, which together in 1963 constituted 66 percent of the economically active agricultural population in Zelaya, grew to 90 percent in 1971, possibly as result of the expansion of the agricultural frontier through immigration both spontaneous and planned" (Vilas 1989, 72).

29. It seems that Rio Coco rice and bean production filled the gap left by the bust of Standard Fruit banana operations, which had been particularly aggressive in their attempts to keep Costeño workers dependent on foreign products,

including food. Helms's observations confirm this conclusion: "Only after the decline of Standard Fruit's banana operations in the early 1940s did rice cultivation, along with bean production, become commercially important to the Miskito, who found a regional market for their crops at the gold mines, lumber camps, and administrative centers of the coast" (Helms 1971, 135).

30. Starting in the twentieth century, Waspám became a central orienting point on the Coco River. Coco River villages came to be popularly identified as "*rio arriba*" (upriver) or "*rio abajo*" (downriver), based on their position relative to Waspám. In the present, the distinction between "*rio arriba*" and "*rio abajo*" is a deeply entrenched native category, which demonstrates the continued importance of Waspám as a riverine port.

31. In 1960 the World Court adjudicated a long-standing border dispute between Nicaragua and Honduras. Owing to the historical absence of Spanish colonial and Central American governmental presence on the Mosquito Coast, the exact boundary between Honduras and Nicaragua had never been decided. The World Court in 1960, judging in favor of Honduras, designated the Rio Coco as the official border, dividing the northern sector of the Mosquito Coast in two. Coco River villagers had historically used both sides of the river for hunting and agriculture, maintaining residences on one side and "*insla nani*" (Miskitu for swidden plots) on the other. Although these villagers had limited interactions with Central American governments, they generally regarded themselves as Nicaraguan citizens. After the World Court decision they found themselves in the difficult situation of having to choose between Nicaraguan and Honduran citizenship, and abandon their plots or residences on the opposite side of the river. Thousands of villagers who had been living along the northern shore of the river crossed the river and established residence in Nicaragua, some of them relocating to special inland settlements along the Puerto Cabezas-Waspám road, such as Santa Marta and Tasba Raya (Vilas 1989, 67). This forced relocation of Coco River villagers toward Puerto Cabezas represented the first of a series of similar forced resettlements that culminated in the massive evacuation of the Coco River region toward Puerto Cabezas and inland camps (Tasba Pri) ordered by the Sandinista Government in the early 1980s (Ortega 1991). Miskito villagers bitterly resented this imposition by the "Spanish" governments but were powerless to resist it. In the 1980s the Rio Coco was to become the principal zone of combat between the Miskito/Contra insurgency and the Nicaraguan government. Nicaraguan anthropologist Galio Gurdián, who had received his master's degree from the University of Chicago in 1979 and worked closely with the Sandinista government during the 1980s, served a brief stint as the director of Tasba Pri at the end of 1983 (Gurdián 2001, 80). Gurdián was a founding member of the Sandinista-sponsored research group CIDCA that included current University of Texas anthropologists Charles Hale and Edmund Gordon. All three of these researchers have acknowledged the contradictions that went along with CIDCA's connection to the Sandinista administration, particularly its policy of forced relocation of people in the Coco River region. In his 2001 PhD dissertation at the University of Texas, Gurdián claims that he was deeply troubled about the errors in Sandinista policy regarding the Atlantic Coast, but he chose to inhabit the role of dissident voice within the Sandinista administration. Gurdián discusses at length the hazards of establishing a legitimate role for CIDCA as an engaged social science

research institute during this time of armed conflict and intense international scrutiny (ibid.).

32. Tuno is a rubber-like raw material used in the production of chewing gum.

33. Such was the level of deforestation in the northern Atlantic region that when NIPCO closed in 1963, Nicaragua for the first time became a net importer of wood (Jenkins Molieri 1986, 206).

34. For example, ATCHEMCO fenced in the offices and industrial installations of the company in an area known as "*la zona.*" Nicaraguans were not allowed to enter the zone without permission. According to a study carried out by Nicaraguan sociologist Sandra Gómez, a rigid ethnic hierarchy operated in La Tronquera in which North Americans occupied the highest rung, followed by Creoles and then Miskito Indians (Gomez 1991, 51–57).

35. Mining companies, discouraged by the difficulty of building and maintaining the roads between the mines and Puerto Cabezas, commonly transported materials to and from Puerto Cabezas by plane. In the 1940s the mining city of Siuna, run by the Neptune Gold Mining Company of the United States, which had seven hundred employees and "the best hospital in the country," was essentially unapproachable by land (Talleres Gráficos Pérez 1941, 12).

36. The parallels between prewar Puerto Cabezas and the postwar mining cities are striking. In the absence of Nicaraguan governmental structures, there came to exist a "de facto government-citizen relationship between the company and local workers" (T. Adams 1981, 64). Companies paid the salaries of the police. Taxes on the minerals, mostly gold, that they extracted were avoided by paying kickback money to the Somoza dictatorship.

37. The majority of Sumu speakers, particularly men, also speak Miskito (Salamanca 1993; Áviles Campo 1993).

38. During the 1950s the government began its first concerted effort to take charge of the educational system in the region and enforce its policy of Spanish-only instruction. Before this, the Moravian Church was almost exclusively responsible for education, instructing in English and Miskitu. Public schools were set up all along the coast and the Rio Coco. Spanish slowly began to replace English as the second language of the Miskito. Creoles also began to take on Spanish as a second language. In the 1970s the government began to offer scholarships to Miskito and Creole youths to study in Nicaraguan universities. The majority of the Miskito leaders who emerged after the Revolution were educated in Managua.

39. Notable exceptions to this generalization were the Moravian schools at Waspám and Bilwaskarma, which were top-of-the-line Miskito schools.

40. At the recommendation of a 1953 World Bank delegation, these forest reserves began to be established in 1959 as part of the Proyecto Forestal del Norte that was spearheaded by INFONAC (Instituto de Fomento Nacional). The purpose of this project was to reforest pine savannas devastated by North American lumber companies, combat forest fires, and establish in the future wood-pulp and paper-processing complexes (Vilas 1989, 63).

41. The Catholic Church has been the second-strongest church in the region since the turn of the century. However, Catholic activities in the region have been primarily instigated by the North American-run Capuchin Mission, which has operated independently of the Nicaraguan Catholic Bishopric in the Pacific region. In 1970 the Moravian Church estimated its membership at 30,000 out of a total regional population of 75,000. During the same time,

the Catholic Church claimed about 35–40 percent of Miskitos as Catholics (Hawley 1997, 121). For a brief history of the Moravian Church in Puerto Cabezas, see Coleman and Green (1976).

42. Moravian Synod meetings occurred in 1968 and 1971 in Puerto Cabezas, and in 1974 in Bluefields (Wilson 1983, 52).

43. It is interesting to note that the Moravians refrained from evangelizing in the Rama language because this language was viewed to have too few speakers to warrant preservation. University of Oregon linguist Collette Craig has argued that the decision by the Moravians not to evangelize in Rama was a key factor in the decline of the Rama language, which today has less than fifty speakers (Craig 1992, 12–15).

44. Given that ALPROMISU was the immediate predecessor to MISURASATA (the indigenous organization that eventually came into direct conflict with the Sandinista government), it was often referred to in the extensive literature produced by journalists and social scientists about the Costeño-Sandinista conflict. The most thorough account of the formation of this organization comes from German scholar Ernesto Richter (Richter 1987). Also see Jenkins Molieri 1986, Hale 1994b, R. Adams 1981, Vilas 1989, CAPRI 1992 (60–63), C. García 1996, Hawley 1997, and Sanders 1985.

45. ACARIC received funding from USAID that was filtered through the Nicaraguan development project INFONAC. It also received funding from Catholic Relief Services and the American Institute of Free Labor Development. In general, funding for organizations such as ACARIC and ALPROMISU was part of a larger US "Alliance for Progress" fight against socialism and communism through "development" (Hale 1994b, 125; Jenkins Molieri 1986, 243).

46. Tuno is a raw material used in making chewing gum. From 1955 to 1979 the Wrigley Company was the main international buyer of tuno in Nicaragua. Throughout the twentieth century the collection of rubber and tuno represented one of the main sources of cash and foreign products for villagers who lived along the Rio Coco and its tributaries where these plants were found (Jenkins Molieri 1986, 214–218).

47. In the late 1960s CASIM (Comité de Acción Social de la Iglesia Morava) was established by the Moravian Church to promote economic development in the region (Vilas 1989, 87).

48. The organization held annual meetings in 1975, 1976, and 1977.

49. Sisín was one of the *Diez Comunidades* (of which Bilwi was a part) that filed collectively for land titles at the turn of the century. The *Diez Comunidades* also received a land grant from the IAN (Instituto Agrario Nicaraguense) in 1976 (Jenkins Molieri 1986, 300).

50. In these paragraphs I am referring to Rev. Alfred Higgins, retired pastor of the "Beach" Moravian Church in Puerto Cabezas, and Rev. Borley Taylor, current pastor of the San Luis Moravian Church, also in Puerto Cabezas. Given that I had already established friendships with their adult children, I had the opportunity to speak with them informally at their homes in a relaxed familial setting. The conversations that I refer to in this paragraph took place during the first few months of my fieldwork when my Miskitu speaking ability was very limited. Like many of my informants in Puerto Cabezas who had had extended dealings with North American and West Indian English speakers at some point in their lives, they were eager to demonstrate to me their ability to speak "good" English as well as Mosquito

Coast Creole English. Our conversations were primarily in English and Spanish, although we did "practice" Miskitu. I did not tape-record our conversations, nor did I take notes as we spoke; rather, at a later time I wrote narrative accounts of our conversations that included brief quotations and key words. In these paragraphs I use quotation marks to bring attention to the key words that they used in our conversations.

51. Pope Paul VI had lamented the "division between Gospel and culture" as "the drama of our time" (Smutko 1992, 65).

52. Susan Hawley has argued convincingly that these pastoral innovations "led to the articulation of a more self-conscious and politicized ethnic identity among the Miskitu" (Hawley 1997, 119).

53. "Evangelizadores Laicos Miskitos" (Smutko 1983, 45).

54. In the oral traditions (*sturka* in Miskitu) of the region, Moris Davis and Awas Tara are figures associated with the mythical past, *pas taim* in Miskitu and "first time" in English.

55. Miskut is also a figure in the *sturka* of the region. He is a heroic character who brought the Miskito to their present home along the Rio Coco.

56. Owing to the fact that to this day, Christian missionaries continue to be the source of almost all written material in Miskitu, Miskitu speakers very rarely have the opportunity to read non-religious material in Miskitu—much less nonreligious material that directly pertains to them (see Helms 1971, 177).

57. In his book-length study *Between Land and Water: The Subsistence Ecology of the Miskito Indians, Eastern Nicaragua* (1973) Nietschmann, a cultural geographer, relied heavily on Marshall Sahlins's pre-1980s work on "primitive exchange" and noncapitalist economies (Sahlins 1965, 1968, and 1972).

58. See Jamieson (1998, 2003) for a more recent ethnographic perspective on shifting racial identification in the Pearl Lagoon basin.

59. Nietschmann echoed Helms's conclusions with regard to the role of women in maintaining Miskito "traditional" culture. He wrote: "Traditional Miskito culture, kinship patterns, and food distribution are largely precipitated and maintained by Miskito women. Women form a consanguineal core which has kept Miskito cultural patterns intact" (Nietschmann 1973, 58).

60. Here I agree with Raymond Smith's approach that he articulates in an article on race, class, and political violence in Guyana: "The question is not whether cultural constructions of race continue to exist in the modern world—they do—but under what conditions does 'race' or 'ethnicity' come to be a major fault line in the society, making for violence of the kind that was seen in British Guiana in the 1960s" (Smith 1996, 175). At this point in the analysis, I am setting the stage for an analysis of the role of race in the 1980s, when socio-racial identifications in many ways did become fault lines.

61. According to data from a CIERA-MIDINRA report (1985), the Creole population of the city of Puerto Cabezas dropped drastically after the Sandinista Revolution, falling from 63 percent of the population in 1963 to 40 percent in 1980 to only 5 percent in 1984.

CHAPTER 5   NEIGHBORHOODS AND OFFICIAL ETHNICITY

1. Although Costeños recognize that they are Nicaraguan citizens and in many contexts are quite receptive to Nicaraguan nationalism, they most frequently refer to Pacific Nicaraguans as simply Nicaraguans.

2. Although I had a respectable batting average during the regular season, my lack of home-run power at the plate, as well as the early elimination of my team (sponsored by Marta's Videos) from the city playoffs, put me far out of contention for the Puerto Cabezas all-star team. Thus, my inadequacies as a player prevented my true participation as participant/observer in the intra-regional series.

3. In 1987 the Sandinista Government divided the Atlantic Coast region into one northern and one southern "autonomous region," called the RAAN (*Región Autónomo del Atlántico Norte*) and the RAAS (*Región Autonomo del Atlántico Sur*). This official territorial demarcation coincided roughly with the preexisting Costeño folk division of the region into North and South. The North is bordered by Honduras and has Puerto Cabezas as the principal port. The South is bordered by Costa Rica and is connected from Bluefields to the Pearl Lagoon/Rio Grande area by a series of navigable canals and rivers. The Rio Grande of Matagalpa marks the boundary between the two autonomous regions.

4. Two Costeños from Pearl Lagoon and Bluefields played Major League Base-ball in the United States in the 1970s and 1980s. They were Al Williams from Pearl Lagoon, a 6′4′′ pitcher for the Minnesota Twins who had limited success over a brief career, and the highly heralded outfielder David Green from Bluefields, who had a number of disappointing seasons for the San Francisco Giants and St. Louis Cardinals. Costeños relish in recounting the successes of these native sons, even more that of the more-accomplished Nicaraguan pitcher Dennis Martinez, who played in the major leagues until well into his 40s and was one of the winningest Latin American pitchers in major league history. Martinez is highly regarded by Costeños, but as a Spaniard he is more socially distant. Marvin Benard, born in Rosita, is the most recent Costeño to have success in the major leagues, with a respectable career as an outfielder playing for the San Francisco Giants from 1995 to 2003.

5. Philip Dennis, in a recent ethnography of Awastara, a Miskito village up the coast from Puerto Cabezas, notes that the villagers view Puerto Cabezas as an exciting place where people can spend money and have a wild time—away from the eyes of judgmental fellow villagers (Dennis 2004, 70).

6. The following text is a paraphrased version of these jokes that I reconstructed from my field notes. In the text I attempt to retain some of the flavor of the Creole English in which it was originally told.

7. Creole English speakers of the Atlantic Coast use the term "meager" in con-texts in which a North American English speaker would be more likely to use "skinny" or "thin." In the Mosquito Coast, the term strongly implies poor health and unattractiveness. In Nicaragua, and indeed most of Latin America, the ideal body type for both men and women is much heavier than the ideal body type in the United States. My Porteño informants, both male and female, frequently scoffed at the US women that they saw on television as "meager."

8. I use the word "myth" here not to imply falsity but rather to emphasize that these stories constitute a group of narratives, or folklore (or "tale types" in the language of folklore studies), that form part of an oral tradition that thrives in the city.

9. "Antes de que viniera la empresa norteamericana vivía una familia aquí. Era un Miskito que se llamaba Noah Columbus. El vivía allá por los tanques donde está el Hospital Moravo. Hoy día ese lugar se llama "El Cocal." Pero

en aquel entonces ellos eran los únicos que vivían en Bilwi. ¿Vos sabés que este pueblo se llama Bilwi en Miskito? Todo esto donde estamos nosotros era puro monte. Allí en El Cocal es donde empezó Bilwi."

10. According to a survey made by the Ministry of Housing in 1983, El Cocal's population was 88 percent Miskito, 12 percent Mestizo, and 0 percent Creole. Out of the twenty neighborhoods identified by the survey, only "Barrio Sandino" and "Barrio Germán Pomares" had higher percentages of Miskito residents. It is significant to note that both of these neighborhoods represent new settlements that were populated primarily by Miskito refugees fleeing the war and evacuation suffered along the Coco River in the early 1980s. According to a Ministry of Health survey conducted in 1981 in the midst of the refugee crisis, El Cocal already represented the most populous neighborhood of Puerto Cabezas, with 1,596 residents and 166 houses. More recent estimates put the population at 2,900, with 90 percent identified as Miskito (Muñoz 1992, 265).

11. "Antes la gente se agarraba a vergazos . . . a veces a puñalazos si era cosa seria. Pero ahora con estos Miskitos si peleás con uno de ellos vuelven a su casa y luego te matan el la calle con un AKA."

12. "Naku sika. Pas taim Noah Columbus witin kiamka wal nara iwi kan. Witin Bilwi tah kan . . . título bri kan. Diara sut pain kan, plun manas, lih manas, ispail apu Sakuna witin guaro laik kan. Yu kum Karatá baska nara balan. Naipe pulan bara un bottle kum kum saki munan. Noah Columbus uba blah takan—*blocked up, man.* Lus baman . . . lalah manas lus takan. Baku witin bui Bilwi titleka lus takan. Karata baska ba lilia mahka wan. Titan buan taim, Noah bila: 'Oh shit.'"

13. I discussed this case in a previously published article, as well as my PhD dissertation at the University of Chicago (Pineda 1998, 2001b).

14. According to a language survey of Puerto Cabezas conducted by a team of German and North American researchers in the mid 1980s, 35 percent of Miskito respondents and 51 percent of Creole respondents claimed to be trilingual. Four hundred and fifty Porteños in different neighborhoods were surveyed, 52 percent of whom were labeled by the researchers as Miskito, 22 percent as Mestizo, and 10 percent as Creole. The Beach was specifically included because researchers regarded it as a Creole English-speaking neighborhood. I observed that very few Beach People used the term "Creole" in any social context, although they did emphasize the fact that they spoke English (Meschkat 1987).

15. In general, my research strategy with regard to matters of identity was to recognize and use the categories of identification that my informants offered, rather than to compel them conform to my own categories or official categories. Not a single resident of The Beach I interviewed would naturally respond to a question using the term "ethnic group" or "*étnia*" because this type of language simply did not enter into common usage. Therefore, on those occasions where I did want to probe the self-identification of informants with regard to official ethnic categories, I would simply list these official ethnic groups and ask them to identify themselves with one or more of them. For example, "What are you then—Miskito, Creole, or Mestizo?" I do not presume that solely because an informant, in response to my query, should identify themselves in a particular way that they therefore were, to use the problematic phrasing of a certain kind of misguided multiculturalism, a

"member" of that group. It has been my experience that Porteños use ethnic terminology in a very fluid and context-bound manner. Therefore, any instance of ethnic identification or labeling must be understood in the context in which it was produced. See Gabbert (2001) for a fruitful approach to ethnic categories in the case of the Yucatan.

16. In contrast to the rest of Nicaragua, houses in the Atlantic Coast are typically built entirely of wood and are elevated off the ground from about two to as much as eight feet by large circular posts that are inserted into the ground. Pacific houses are typically made of concrete or adobe on top of a concrete foundation.

17. In the last thirty years as Nicaraguan government presence has increased, especially after the Sandinista Revolution of 1979, Spanish has been increasingly used by Porteños in official contexts, particularly those that require dealing with local and national governmental institutions.

18. After overthrowing the Somoza dictatorship in 1979, the Sandinista Directorate created an entirely new police force and army known as the EPS, Sandinista Popular Army.

19. "Este es un problema muy difícil . . . muy difícil porque han pasado muchos años y han pasado muchos gobiernos y no se ha dado una solución completa a este problema. Esperamos aqui con nuestra presencia [the national directorate of the Port Authority] . . . estamos seguros que no vamos a solucionar todo el problema pero por lo menos con nuestra presencia iniciar un diálogo regional para que tanto como el gobierno central como las autoridades locales y la ley misma de autonomía y las comunidades lleguen a una solución integral de este problema . . . el problema de la tenencia de tierra. . . . La gran parte de lo que indicaba el amigo Carpentier acerca de la historia de estos terrenos ya la habíamos manejado, inclusive nosotros hemos estudiado el Tratado Harrison-Altamirano y nos hemos metido en la historia para comprender más el problema. Hemos hecho una seria de entrevistas, hemos buscado documentación etcétera para darle solución a este problema. No es necesario mirar ni a la historia de la propiedad ni al mismo Tratado Harrison, sino un poco mas contemporaneo nosotros como empresa indicamos ser propietarios de estos terrenos. Esto que está aqui conmigo es un mapa, un plano . . . donde indica de acuerdo a los documentos de propiedad que estan debidamente registrados en Bluefields, que es donde se registra este caracter de propiedad, que hay una polygonal aqui [pointing to the map] que claramente pertenece a la Portuaria. . . . Por la gente que nos hemos entrevistado todo indican que han hecho negociaciones directas con la comunidad de Karawala [sic] concretamente con el Señor Chico Francis. . . . ¿Entonces cual el la realidad en si de todos estos terrenos? Mas de la noventa por ciento en la practica han sido tomados. Hemos hecho nosotros entrevistas con las personas. Unos han argumentado que han sido dados directamente por la Alcaldía, otros nos indican que han sido dados directamente por la Portuaria, pero la gran mayoría indican que han sido dadosen calidad de venta o arrienda de parte de la comunidad de Karatá. Entonces en este sentido yo corregiria un poco a lo que decía Carpentier con respecto a lo de Karatá . . . hasta hoy surge en el conflicto el barrio El Muelle. Con quien hemos estado en diferentes momentos vinculados ha sido con la gente de la comunidad de Karatá. . . . Pero si Uds. hablan con la gente alrededor del Cayuco enseñan documentos dados por la comunidad de Karatá."

20. In Nicaragua the departamento represents an administrative and territorial division corresponding to counties in the United States. As a result of the regional autonomy process, the Nicaraguan government divided the former department of Zelaya (previously one of eleven departments in Nicaragua) into two autonomous regions called the "North Atlantic Autonomous Region" and the "South Atlantic Autonomous Region," popularly known as RAAN and RAAS, respectively. The government empowered each of these regions to create a legislative body. Nicaraguan departments do not have separate legislative bodies.

21. "multiétnica, pluricultural y multilingue" (CAPRI 1992, 230).

22. The distinction between language and tongue in English is parallel to that between *idioma* and *lengua* in Spanish. *Lengua* carries connotations of intimacy and informality, as opposed to the more formal and neutral term *idioma*. Given that within the Pacific Nicaraguan imagination indigenous languages are perceived to be closer to nature, it is significant that the text chooses to call indigenous languages *lenguas*.

23. Anthropologist Roger Lancaster discussed the nature of Nicaraguan racial prejudice, focusing primarily on the Pacific Coast (Lancaster 1991). In his subsequent book, which is primarily on sexuality and gender in Managua, he includes interesting material on the perception of Pacific Nicaraguans of Costeños as primitive "*Negros*." He labeled this ideological connection of dark-skinned Costeños and savagery as "Atlanticity" (Lancaster 1992, 213).

24. "cultura," "tradiciones," "valores," "arte," "organizaciones sociales," and "formas comunales, colectivo o individual de propiedad" (CAPRI 1992, 229–237).

CHAPTER 6   COSTEÑO WARRIORS AND CONTRA REBELS

1. The chronology of the Costeño-Sandinista conflict has been traced in painstaking detail by a host of national and international analysts. My intention here is not to reproduce any of this work, but rather to illustrate the ways in which the analyses of the conflict themselves reproduced and reflected prejudices and stereotypes that were active in Nicaragua and that should be given interpretive attention.

2. Many Costeños, primarily merchants (many of whom were Chinese) in addition to businessmen and soldiers associated with the Somoza regime, fled the region in the months leading to the Sandinista takeover in July of 1979 (Pineda 2001a). In contrast to later refugees, these people possessed significant assets, which allowed them to establish themselves in Central American cities and the United States.

3. Americas Watch, a non-government human rights watchdog group, has documented the Reagan administration's consistent exaggeration and fabrication of evidence of Sandinista atrocities (Americas Watch Committee 1984 and 1986). The Inter-American Commission on Human Rights, without specifically mentioning accusations made by the Reagan administration, published a report that, although highly critical of Sandinista policies in the region, failed to confirm the most serious of atrocities allegedly committed by the Sandinista army—specifically the mass killings of Miskitos. The IACHR report did confirm arbitrary detentions and some cases of torture, abuse, and murder during the period of 1981 to 1983 (IACHR 1984). Also see Diskin

(1987) for documentation of the distortions and misinformation produced by the Reagan administration.

4. For the official view of the United States government, see US Department of State 1984, 1986a, 1986b.

5. In my master's thesis at the University of Chicago, I compared the demands made by Costeños at the turn of the century with their postrevolutionary demands in the 1980s. I illustrated how at the turn of the century Costeños justified their resistance to incorporation into the Nicaraguan state on the basis of their relationships and affinities to England. This practice stands in contrast to the modern postrevolutionary period in which Costeños have made claims that ground their distinctiveness in their status as indigenous peoples (Pineda 1991).

6. I adapted this section title from the title of the provocative article by Eric Wolf and Joseph Jorgensen titled "Anthropology on the Warpath in Thailand" (Wolf and Jorgensen 1970). This article helped to spark debate about professional ethics and the role of anthropologists and anthropological concepts in the cold war.

7. According to a number of Sandinista analysts, however, the existence of these identities could ultimately be traced to class dynamics. Carlos Vilas, a pro-Sandinista Argentine sociologist who spent many years in Nicaragua during the revolutionary period, maintained such a position in his book *State, Class, and Ethnicity in Nicaragua: Capitalist Modernization and Revolutionary Change on the Atlantic Coast* (Vilas 1989; also see Gurdián 1987).

8. Means writes at length about his experiences in Nicaragua supporting the Miskito insurgence in his 1995 autobiography (Means 1995).

9. Sandinista social scientists were quick to point out that institutions such as communal lands, tribal councils, and elders councils had a relatively shallow presence in, if not complete absence from, the ethnographic literature dealing with the region, and therefore the existence and importance of these institutions became a matter of contention (Diskin 1991).

10. To his credit, he began to work with Miskito communities on community development projects after the 1990 elections. To trace the full evolution of his scholarship from less polemical to polemical and back again, see Nietschmann (1973, 1974, 1976, 1983a and b, 1984a and b, 1987, 1989, 1991a and b, 1992a and b, 1993, 1995).

11. In the Iran-Contra hearings, a document, which luckily was saved from the Pentagon's shredding machines, was presented to Congress in which Oliver North outlined his plan of propaganda aimed at winning congressional approval for military aid to the Contras. One memo in this document stated the following: "Request Bernard Nietschmann to update prior paper on suppression of Indians by FSLN (to be published and distributed by April 1)" (Sklar 1988, 262).

12. For articles in *Akwesasne Notes*, see Wiggins 1981; Mohawk 1981, 1983; Akwesasne Notes 1981; W. Ramirez 1982; B. Rivera 1982; Mohawk and Davis 1982; Nietschmann 1983a, 1983b; Barreiro 1984, 1985. For articles in *Cultural Survival Quarterly*, see Macdonald 1981, 1984a, 1984b, 1985; Mohawk 1982; Howe 1986; Morris and Churchill 1987; Nietschmann 1987; Linguists for Nicaragua 1989; Dodds 1989; Wilcox 1993.

13. John Mohawk, a North American Indian leader and intellectual who was involved in the Indian struggle in Nicaragua, expressed this idea clearly: "There

are distinct differences between what is widely accepted as Marxist ideology and the ideologies which comprise the Native People's movements. While both movements are avowedly anti-colonialist, anti-imperialist and anti-capitalist, it will be seen that the two traditions have entirely different roots. The Native People's movement expresses an ideology which is, by definition, primarily anti-colonialist and anti-imperialist and which emphasizes cultural diversity. Marxist ideology, on the other hand, is primarily anti-capitalist and is unquestionably anti-capitalist imperialism and anti-capitalist colonialism [sic] many will be surprised that these two different ideologies have very different objectives. In fact, Marxist-Leninist thought and the ideologies of Native Peoples' movements are so different that the question arises whether the two are in any way compatible at all" (Mohawk 1991, 9).

14. In a subsequent article, Macdonald, backing off from the implications of his previous characterization of the Atlantic Coast as plural society, warned of the dangers of viewing each of the ethnic groups of the Atlantic Coast as culturally isolated. Rather, he emphasized that these ethnic groups should be viewed as "segments of the region's complex socio-political mosaic" (MacDonald 1996, 59).

15. In a section of their 1969 plan of action titled "The Reincorporation of the Atlantic Coast," the founders of the FSLN had proclaimed, "The Popular Sandinista Revolution will put into practice a special plan for the Atlantic Coast, lost in the depth of the greatest abandonment, in order to incorporate it into the national life" (Vilas 1989, 103).

16. I am quoting the late Martin Diskin, an MIT anthropologist who wrote a number of pro-Sandinista articles during the Sandinista-Costeño crisis. He used the term "ethnic discourse" to describe the "new voice" in Costeño politics that emerged in the 1980s. Galio Gurdián, a Nicaraguan social scientist working with CIDCA, used the term "ethnicist" to describe Costeño discourse (Gurdián 1987, 177).

17. It is interesting to note that in the passage in the previous paragraph, Jenkins Molieri not only corrects the Miskito on their mistaken denial of exploitation as laborers but he also claims that Indians were alienated from their land as well. This directly contradicts the claim of most Costeños that the greatest threat to their control of their land came as a result of the very recent integrationism of the Sandinista revolution.

18. This is the title of Diskin's 1987 article condemning the Reagan administration's policy towards the Atlantic Coast of Nicaragua (Diskin 1987).

19. Diskin contrasted this modern state of affairs with the past, when anthropology "traditionally served as the voice of indigenous people and ethnic minorities" (Diskin 1989, 11).

20. Jonathon Hill vigorously criticizes the theoretical framework that Urban and Sherzer (the editors) employ in *Nation-States and Indians in Latin America* (in which Diskin's 1991 article appears) because it assumes that pre-contact Indian societies were isolated and culturally homogenous. They accuse Urban and Sherzer of having "resurrected the ahistorical notion of a fundamental contrast between 'isolated Indian populations' and 'ethnic groups'" (Hill 1996, 8). In contrast, Hill argues that pre-contact Indian societies, linked to other Indian societies through extensive networks along which objects, peoples, and culture flowed, were already multilingual, culturally heterogeneous, and self-aware. My analysis here is in line with Hill's critique of Urban

and Sherzer's view of cultural self-consciousness as a unique product of modern nation-state expansion.

21. Hale considered the village of Sandy Bay Sirpi his principal field site. Apparently due to the war and other reasons, he was not able to live in the village for extended periods of time as is the traditional anthropological practice. Instead, he made periodic trips to the village while working in the Bluefields CIDCA office. Hale considered his contact with government officials in Managua and Bluefields part of his fieldwork, particularly that part of his fieldwork that focused on the Sandinista side of the Miskitu-Sandinista confrontation (Hale 1994, 216).

22. In his literature review, Hale divided writings about the conflict in the Atlantic Coast according to a set of criteria very different from those that I have developed in this chapter. He divided the literature into two groups that he argued crosscut political loyalties (e.g., Sandinista, Contra, or Indian): (1) "structural analysis," which focused on the determinative role played by powerful external actors from either the left or right; and (2) a Miskito-centric approach that relied heavily on what he called the "Miskito perspective" but "tended to caricature the structural determinants of the conflict, to portray Miskitu culture in a vacuum, and to neglect how structural conditions had shaped Miskitu people's consciousness" (Hale 1994b, 18). Hale argued that together these perspectives represented a "dual barrier to a full understanding of Miskitu politics" (ibid., 18). He linked this dual perspective with the theoretical divide in anthropological theory between voluntaristic agency-oriented approaches and deterministic structure-oriented approaches. I do not use Hale's typology here because, despite his claim that the "two emphases do not neatly correspond to political points of view," the Miskito-centric authors that he specifically listed all clearly supported the Miskito in their struggle against the Sandinistas (Hale 1994b, 17). The structural approach that he cited (US Department of State 1984) that focused on Sandinista repression (as opposed to US imperialism) in actuality explicitly attempted to include, albeit in a highly problematic way, a Miskito-centric approach. Thus, Hale's typology obscured the ways in which the political polarization of analysts along cold-war lines directly paralleled the theoretical polarization of the literature.

23. In a review of *Decolonizing Anthropology*, Raymond T. Smith noted the unavoidable contradictions regarding issues of engagement and detachment, which had to be negotiated by the contributors to the volume who had been Sandinista collaborators (Smith 1993, 783).

24. Benedict Anderson argued that the Sandinista attempt at national integration represented nothing less than a typical example of Latin American "Creole nationalism"—a nationalism characterized by the attempt to promote national unity through a program of Hispanicization while simultaneously promoting a hypocritical "indigenist" project that was "necessarily constructed in bad faith and as a kind of political theater" (Anderson 1988, 404). He wrote, "The Sandinista revolutionaries are the unwitting heirs of ladino nationalism; that the Miskitos, whether they speak English or Miskito, block the Hispanic, criollo project; and that, with—perhaps—the best will in the world, Daniel Ortega and his colleagues simply have no idea what to do with the Miskito aborigines, except to Hispanicize, museumize, socialize, and patronize them" (Anderson 1988, 406).

BIBLIOGRAPHY

Abu-Lughod, Lila. 1991. Writing Against Culture. In *Recapturing Anthropology: Working in the Present.* Richard G. Fox, ed. Santa Fe: School of American Research.

Adams, Anna. 1992. Moravian Missionaries in Nicaragua: The American Years 1917–1974. PhD dissertation, Temple University.

———. 1995. Karl Bregenzer: Missionary Martyr-Spy. *Journal of Church and State* 37 (1):121–133.

Adams, Richard N. 1981. The Dynamics of Societal Diversity: Notes from Nicaragua for a Sociology of Survival. *American Ethnologist* 8 (1):1–20.

Adams, Tani M. 1981. Life Giving, Life Threatening: Gold Mining in Atlantic Nicaragua and Response to Nationalization by the Sandinista Regime. Master's thesis, Department of Anthropology, University of Chicago.

Akwesasne Notes. 1981. Miskito Nation: An Indian "Problem" for Nicaragua. *Akwesasne Notes* 13 (1):11.

Allen, James B. 1966. *The Company Town in the American West.* Norman: University of Oklahoma Press.

Alvarez, Sonia, Evelina Dagnino, and Arturo Escobar. 1998. Introduction: The Cultural and the Political in Latin American Social Movements. In *Culture of Politics, Politics of Cultures: Re-Visioning Latin American Social Movements.* Boulder: Westview Press.

Alvarez, Sonia, and Arturo Escobar. 1992. Introduction: Theory and Protest in Latin America Today. In *The Making of Social Movements in Latin America: Identity, Strategy and Democracy.* Sonia Alvarez and Arturo Escobar, eds. Boulder: Westview Press.

Americas Watch Committee. 1984. *An Americas Watch Report. The Miskitos in Nicaragua 1981–1984.* New York: Americas Watch.

———. 1986. *With the Miskitos in Honduras.* New York: Americas Watch.

Anderson, Benedict. 1988. Afterword. In *Ethnicities and Nations: Processes of Interethnic Relations in Latin America, Southeast Asia and the Pacific.* Remo Guidieri et al., eds. Austin: University of Texas Press.

Anuario Indigenista. 1987. Estatuto de la Autonomía de las Regiones de la Costa Atlántica. *Anuario Indigenista* 47:106–117.

Arellano, Jorge Eduardo. 1993. *Historia Básica de Nicaragua (vol. 1).* Managua: Fondo Editorial Cira.

Áviles Campos, Jeannette. 1993. El Pueblo Sumu, Autonomía y Manejo Ecológico. *America Indigena* 53 (1–2):105–146.

Badlato, Margaret P. 2001. Miskitu Discourse. PhD dissertation, University of Texas, Austin.

Barreiro, José. 1984. Miskito/Sandinista War. Brooklyn Rivera Conducts Peace Initiative. *Akwesasne Notes* 16 (Winter):15–16.

———. 1985. The Disappearance of Raiti: A Human Rights Narrative—Interview with Dr. Kenneth Sarapio. *Akwesasne Notes* 17 (3):22–25.

Barth, Frederik. 1969. Introduction. In *Ethnic Groups and Boundaries*. Frederik Barth, ed. London: Athlone Press.

Baudez, Claude F. 1970. *Central America*. London: Barrie and Jenkins.

Belausteguigoitia, Ramón de. 1981 [1934]. *Con Sandino en Nicaragua: la hora de la paz*. Managua: Editorial Nueva Nicaragua.

Blu, Karen. 2001. *The Lumbee Problem: The Making of an American Indian People*. Lincoln: University of Nebraska Press.

Bolland, O. Nigel. 1977. *The Formation of a Colonial Society: Belize, from Conquest to Crown Colony*. Baltimore: The Johns Hopkins University Press.

———. 1992. "Indios Bravos" or "Gentle Savages": 19th Century Views of the "Indians" of Belize and the Miskito Coast. *Revista Interamericana* 22 (1–2):36–54.

Borhek, Mary Virginia. 1949. *Watchman on the Walls—Moravian Missions in Nicaragua during the Last 50 Years*. Bethlehem, PA: Society for Propagating the Gospel.

Bourdieu, Pierre. 1977. *Outline of a Theory of Practice*. Cambridge, UK: Cambridge University Press.

Bourgois, Philippe. 1981. Class, Ethnicity, and the State Among the Miskitu Amerindians of Northeastern Nicaragua. *Latin American Perspectives* 13 (2):22–39.

———. 1985. Ethnic Minorities. In *The Nicaraguan Revolution: The First Five Years*. Thomas W. Walker, ed. New York: Praeger.

———. 1989. West Indian Immigration and the Origins of the Banana Industry. *Cimarrón* 11 (1–2):58–86.

———. 1992. From Marcus Garvey to Mamachi and Miskitu Autonomy: Politicized Ethnicity along Central America's Atlantic Coast. Cambridge, MA: a working paper from the Center for International Studies, MIT.

Bourricaud, François. 1975. Indian, Mestizo and Cholo as Symbols in the Peruvian System of Stratification. In *Ethnicity: Theory and Experience*. Nathan Glazer and Daniel Moynihan, eds. Cambridge: Harvard University Press.

Brooks, David C. 1998. Rebellion from Without: Culture and Politics Along Nicaragua's Atlantic Coast in the Time of the Sandino Revolt, 1926–1934. PhD dissertation, University of Connecticut.

Brown, Nelson C. 1923. *The American Lumber Industry*. New York: John Wiley & Sons.

Brumann, Christopher. 1999. Writing for Culture: Why a Successful Concept Should Not Be Discarded. *Current Anthropology* 40 (February supplement):1–13.

Brysk, Alison. 1996. Turning Weakness Into Strength: The Internationalization of Indian Rights. *Latin American Perspectives* 23 (2):38–57.

———. 2000. *From Tribal Village to Global Village: Indian Rights and International Relations in Latin America*. Stanford: Stanford University Press.

Buvollen, Hans Peter. 1987. The Miskitu-Sandinista Conflict: International Concerns and Outside Actors. *Journal of Peace Proposals* 18 (4):591–601.

CAPRI (Centro de Apoyo a Programas y Proyectos). 1992. *Región Autónoma del Atlántico Norte: El Desafío de la Autonomía.* Managua: Editorial El Amanecer.

Chomsky, Aviva. 1996. *West Indian Workers and the United Fruit Company in Costa Rica, 1870–1940.* Baton Rouge: Louisiana State University Press.

CIDCA (Centro de Documentacion e Investigaciones de la Costa Atlantica). 1984. *Trabil Nani: Historical Background and Current Situation on the Atlantic Coast of Nicaragua.* New York: The Riverside Church Disarmament Project.

CIERA. 1981. *La Mosquitia y la Revolución.* Managua: Colección Blas Real Espinales.

CIERA-MIDINRA. 1985. Poblacion por Etnia—Zonas Especiales I y II. Puerto Cabezas: unpublished manuscript, CIDCA archive.

Coleman, J. M., and Jerry Green. 1976. *Brief History of the Moravian Church: Puerto Cabezas.* Puerto Cabezas: Moravian Church.

Conrad, Robert Edgar, ed. 1990. *Sandino: The Testimony of a Nicaraguan Patriot, 1921–1934.* Princeton: Princeton University Press.

Conzemius, Eduard. 1932. *Ethnographical Survey of the Miskito and Sumu Indians of Honduras and Nicaragua.* Washington DC: Smithsonian Institution Bureau of American Ethnology Bulletin 106, United States Government Printing Office.

Craig, Colette G. 1992. Language Shift and Language Death: The Case of Rama in Nicaragua. *International Journal of the Sociology of Language* 93:11–26.

Crowther, Samuel. 1929. *The Romance and Rise of the American Tropics.* Garden City, NY: Doubleday, Dorant Co.

Dampier, William. 1698. *A New Voyage Around the World.* London: James Knapton.

De Kalb, Courtenay. 1893. Nicaragua: Studies on the Mosquito Shore in 1892. *Journal of the American Geographical Society* 25:236–288.

de la Cadena, Marisol. 2000. *Indigenous Mestizos: The Politics of Race and Culture in Cuzco, Peru, 1919–1991.* Durham: Duke University Press.

Dennis, Philip A. 1981. Costeños and the Revolution in Nicaragua. *Journal of Interamerican Studies and World Affairs* 23 (3):271–296.

———. 2004. *The Miskitu People of Awastara.* Austin: University of Texas Press.

Dennis, Philip A., and Michael D. Olien. 1984. Kingship among the Miskito. *American Ethnologist* 11:718–737.

Denny, Harold Norman. 1929. *Dollars for Bullets: The Story of American Rule in Nicaragua.* New York: The Dial Press.

Diskin, Martin. 1987. The Manipulation of Indigenous Struggles. In *Reagan versus the Sandinistas: The Undeclared War on Nicaragua.* Thomas W. Walker, ed. Boulder: Westview Press.

———. 1989. Revolution and Ethnic Identity: The Nicaraguan Case. In *Conflict, Migration and the Expression of Ethnicity.* Nancie L. Gonzales and Carolyn S. McCommon, eds. Boulder: Westview Press.

———. 1991. Ethnic Discourse and the Challenge to Anthropology: The Nicaraguan Case. In *Nation-States and Indians in Latin America.* Greg Urban and Joel Sherzer, eds. Austin: University of Texas Press.

———. 1995. Anthropological Fieldwork in Mesoamerica: Focus on the Field. *Latin American Research Review* 30 (1):163–175.

Dodds, David. 1989. Miskito and Sumo Refugees: Caught in Conflict in Honduras. *Cultural Survival Quarterly* 13 (3):3–6.

Dozier, Craig L. 1985. *Nicaragua's Mosquito Shore: The Years of British and American Presence*. Birmingham: The University of Alabama Press.

Dunbar Ortiz, Roxanne. 1983. The Fourth World and Indigenism: Politics of Isolation and Alternatives. *Journal of Ethnic Studies* 12 (1):79–105.

———. 1986. *La Cuestion Miskita en la Revolucion Nicaraguense*. Mexico City: Editorial Línea.

———. 1988. *The Miskito Indians of Nicaragua*. London: The Minority Rights Group, Report 79.

Enloe, Cynthia. 1989. *Bananas, Beaches and Bases: Making Feminist Sense of International Politics*. Berkeley: The University of California Press.

Escobar, Arturo. 1992. Culture, Economics, and Politics in Latin American Social Movements: Theory and Research. In *The Making of Social Movements in Latin America: Identity, Strategy and Democracy*. Sonia Alvarez and Arturo Escobar, eds. Boulder: Westview Press.

Exquemelin, Alexandre Olivier. 1685. *Buccaneers of America*. London: Printed for William Crooke.

Fabian, Johannes. 1999. Comment. *Current Anthropology* 40 (4):489–490.

Fagoth, Stedman. 1986. *La Moskitia—Autonomía Regional*. Unknown publisher.

Fernandez, James W. 1994. Culture and Transcendent Humanization: On the "Dynamic of the Categorical." *Ethnos* 59 (3–4):143–167.

Field, Les. 1999. Complicities and Collaborations: Anthropologists and the "Unacknowledged Tribes" of California. *Current Anthropology* 40 (2):193–209.

Fischer, Edward F. 1999. Rethinking Constructivism and Essentialism. *Current Anthropology* 40 (4):473–488.

Floyd, Troy S. 1967. *The Anglo-Spanish Struggle for the Mosquitia*. Albuquerque: University of New Mexico Press.

Foster, George M. 1967. Introduction: What is a Peasant? In *Peasant Society: A Reader*. George M. Foster, May N. Diaz, and Jack M. Potter, eds. Boston: Little, Brown and Company.

Foweraker, Joseph. 1995. *Theorizing Social Movements*. London: Pluto Press.

Fowler, William R. 1985. Ethnohistoric Sources on the Pipil-Nicarao of Central America: A Critical Analysis. *Ethnohistory* 32 (1):37–62.

Friedlander, Judith. 1975. *Being Indian in Hueyapan: A Study of Forced Identity in Contemporary Mexico*. New York: St. Martin's Press.

———. 1976. The Social Scientist and the Indian. *Latin American Research Review* 11 (2):184–190.

Friedman, Jonathan. 1999. Indigenous Struggles and the Discreet Charm of the Bourgeoisie. *The Australian Journal of Anthropology* 10 (1):1–14.

Frye, David. 1996. *Indians into Mexicans: History and Identity in a Mexican Town*. Austin: University of Texas Press.

Gabbert, Wolfgang. 1992. *Creoles—Afroamerikaner im karibischen Tiefland von Nicaragua*. Hamburg: Lit Verlag.

———. 2001. Social Categories, Ethnicity and the State in Yucatan, Mexico. *Journal of Latin American Studies* 33 (3):459–484.

Gámez, Jose Dolores. 1939. *Historia de la Costa de Mosquitos (hasta 1894)*. Managua: Talleres Nacionales.

Gandin, Greg. 1997. To End With All These Evils: Ethnic Transformation and Community Mobilization in Guatemala's Western Highlands, 1954–1980. *Latin American Perspectives* 24 (2):7–34.

García Breso, Javier. 1992. *Monimbó: Una Comunidad India en Nicaragua*. Managua: Editorial Multiformas.

García, Claudia. 1996. The Making of the Miskitu People of Nicaragua: The Social Construction of Ethnic Identity. PhD dissertation, Department of Sociology, Uppsala University, Stockholm.

Geertz, Clifford. 1963. The Integrative Revolution: Primordial Sentiments and Civil Politics in the New States. In *Old Societies and New States: The Quest for Modernity in Asia and Africa*. Clifford Geertz, ed. New York: Free Press.

Gómez, Sandra. 1991. La Tronquera: Una Caracterización—Historia, Población e Infraestructura. In *Como Vamos a Sobrevivir Nosotros: Aspectos de la Pequeñas Economías y Autonomía de la Costa Caribe de Nicaragua*. Ronnie Vernooy et al., eds. Managua: CIDCA-UCA.

Gonzalez, Nancie L. 1988. *Sojourners of the Caribbean: Ethnogenesis and Ethnohistory of the Garifuna*. Urbana: University of Illinois Press.

Gordon, Edmund T. 1995. Revolution, Common Sense and the Dynamics of African-Nicaraguan Politics. *Critique of Anthropology* 15 (1):5–36.

———. 1998. *Disparate Diasporas: Identity and Politics in an African Nicaraguan Community*. Austin: University of Texas Press.

Gordon, Edmund T., and Mark Anderson. 1999. The African Diaspora: Toward an Ethnography of Diasporic Identification. *Journal of American Folklore* 112 (445):282–296.

Gossen, Gary H. 1996. Maya Zapatistas Move to the Ancient Future. *American Anthropologist* 98 (3):528–538.

Gould, Jeffrey L. 1993a. "Vana Ilusión!" The Highlands Indians and the Myth of Nicaragua Mestiza, 1880–1925. *Hispanic American Historical Review* 73 (3):393–429.

———. 1993b. "La Raza Rebelde": Las Luchas de la Comunidad Indígena de Subtiava (1900–1960). *America Indigena* 53 (1–2):199–233.

———. 1995. Review of *Resistance and Contradiction: Miskitu Indians and the Nicaraguan State, 1894–1987* by Charles Hale. *Hispanic American Historical Review* 75 (2):296–297.

———. 1998. *To Die in This Way: Nicaraguan Indians and the Myth of Mestizaje, 1880–1965*. Durham: Duke University Press.

Graham, Laura. 2002. How Should an Indian Speak? Amazonian Indians and the Symbolic Politics of Language in the Global Public Sphere. In *Indigenous Movements, Self-Representation, and the State in Latin America*. Kay Warren and Jean Jackson, eds. Austin: University of Texas Press.

Gudmundson, Lowell. 1995. Review of *Resistance and Contradiction: Miskitu Indians and the Nicaraguan State, 1894–1987* by Charles Hale. *The American Historical Review* 100 (4):1336–1337.

Guerrero, Julian N., and Lola Soriano de Guerrero. 1982. *Las 9 Tribus Aborigenes de Nicaragua*. Managua: Self-published.

Gurdián, Galio. 1987. Autonomy Rights, National Unity and National Liberation: The Autonomy Project of the Sandinista Popular Revolution on the Atlantic Caribbean Coast of Nicaragua. In *Ethnic Groups and the Nation-State: The Case of the Atlantic Coast of Nicaragua.* CIDCA, ed. Stockholm: University of Stockholm.

———. 2001. Mito y Memoria en la Construcción de la Fisonomía de la Comunidad de Alamikangban. PhD dissertation, Department of Anthropology, University of Texas, Austin.

Hahn, Dwight R. 1996. The Use and Abuse of Ethnicity: The Case of the Bolivian CSUTCB. *Latin American Perspectives* 23 (2):91–106.

Hale, Charles R. 1987a. Inter-Ethnic Relations and Class Structure in Nicaragua's Atlantic Coast: An Historical Overview. In *Ethnic Groups and the Nation-State: The Case of the Atlantic Coast of Nicaragua.* CIDCA, ed. Stockholm: University of Stockholm.

———. 1987b. Institutional Struggle, Conflict and Reconciliation: Miskitu Indians and the Nicaraguan State (1979–1985). In *Ethnic Groups and the Nation-State: The Case of the Atlantic Coast of Nicaragua.* CIDCA, ed. Stockholm: University of Stockholm.

———. 1990. Contradictory Consciousness: Miskitu Indians and the Nicaraguan State in Conflict and Reconciliation (1860–1987). PhD dissertation, Stanford University.

———. 1991. "They Exploited Us, But We Didn't Feel It": Hegemony, Ethnic Militancy, and the Miskitu-Sandinista Conflict. In *Decolonizing Anthropology: Moving Toward an Anthropology for Liberation.* Faye V. Harrison, ed. Washington DC: American Anthropological Association.

———. 1994a. Between Che Guevara and the Pachamama: Mestizos, Indians and Identity Politics in the Anti-Quincentenary Campaign. *Critique of Anthropology* 14 (1):9–39.

———. 1994b. *Resistance and Contradiction: Miskitu Indians and the Nicaraguan State, 1894–1987.* Palo Alto: Stanford University Press.

———. 1996. Introduction. *Journal of Latin American Anthropology* 2 (1):2–3.

———. 1997. Cultural Politics of Identity in Latin America. *Annual Review of Anthropology* 26:567–590.

———. 1999. Comment. *Current Anthropology* 40 (4):491–492.

Handler, Richard. 1988. *Nationalism and the Politics of Culture in Quebec.* Madison: University of Wisconsin Press.

———. 1999. Comment. *Current Anthropology* 40 (4):492–493.

Handler, Richard, and Jocelyn Linnekin. 1984. Tradition: Genuine or Spurious? *Journal of American Folklore* 97:273–290.

Harrison, Faye V. 1991. Anthropology as an Agent of Transformation: Introductory Comments and Queries. In *Decolonizing Anthropology: Moving Toward an Anthropology of Liberation.* Faye Harrison, ed. Washington DC: American Anthropological Association.

Hawley, Susan. 1997. Protestantism and Indigenous Mobilization: The Moravian Church among the Miskitu Indians of Nicaragua. *Journal of Latin American Studies* 29 (1):111–129.

Heath, George Reinke. 1913. Notes on Miskuto Grammar and Other Indian Languages of Eastern Nicaragua. *American Anthropologist* 15:48–62.

————. 1927. *Grammar of the Miskito Language*. Herrnhut, Germany: F. Lindenbein.

Helms, Mary W. 1971. *Asang: Adaptations to Culture Contact in a Miskito Community*. Gainesville: University of Florida Press.

————. 1977. Negro or Indian? The Changing Identity of a Frontier Population. In *Old Roots in New Lands: Historical and Anthropological Perspectives on Black Experiences in the Americas*. Ann M. Pescatello, ed. Westport, CT: Greenwood Press.

————. 1983. Miskito Slaving and Culture Contact: Ethnicity and Opportunity in an Expanding Population. *Journal of Anthropological Research* 39 (2):179–197.

————. 1986. Of Kings and Contexts: Ethnohistorical Interpretations of Miskito Political Structure and Function. *American Ethnologist* 13:506–523.

————. 1995. Review of *Resistance and Contradiction: Miskitu Indians and the Nicaraguan State, 1894–1987* by Charles Hale. *The Journal of the Royal Anthropological Institute* 1 (3):658–659.

Herlihy, Laura Hobson. 1994. Review of *Resistance and Contradiction: Miskitu Indians and the Nicaraguan State 1894–1987* by Charles R. Hale. *The Latin American Anthropology Review* 6 (1):62–63.

Herzfeld, Michael. 1982. *Ours Once More: Folklore, Ideology, and the Making of Modern Greece*. Austin: University of Texas Press.

Hill, Jonathan. 1996. Introduction: Ethnogenesis in the Americas. In *History, Power, and Identity: Ethnogenesis in the Americas, 1492–1992*. Jonathan Hill, ed. Iowa City: University of Iowa Press.

Hobsbawm, Eric, and Terence Ranger, eds. 1983. *The Invention of Tradition*. Cambridge: Cambridge University Press.

Hodges, Donald. 1986. *Intellectual Foundations of the Nicaraguan Revolution*. Austin: University of Texas Press.

Holm, John A. 1978. The Creole English of Nicaragua's Mosquito Coast: Its Sociolinguistic History and a Comparative Study of its Lexicon and Syntax. PhD dissertation, University of London.

Houwald, Götz Freiherr von. 1990. *Mayangna = Wir. Zur Geschichte der Sumu-Indianer in Mittelamerika*. Hamburg: Hamburgisches Museum für Völkerkunde.

Howe, James. 1986. Native Rebellion and US Intervention in Central America. The Implications of the Kuna Case for the Miskito. *Cultural Survival Quarterly* 10 (1):59–65.

Incer, Jaime 1985. *Toponomías Indígenas de Nicaragua*. San José, Costa Rica: Self-published.

————. 1990. *Nicaragua: Viajes, Rutas y Encuentros—1502–1838*. San José, Costa Rica: Asociación Libro Libre.

Instituto Nacional de Estadisticas y Censos. 1985. *Anuario Estadistica de Nicaragua 1985*. Managua: Republica de Nicaragua.

Inter-American Commission on Human Rights (IACHR). 1984. *Report on the Situation of Human Rights of a Segment of the Nicaraguan Population of Miskito Origin*. Washington DC: Organization of American States.

Jackson, Jean E. 1994. Becoming Indians: The Politics of Tukanoan Ethnicity. In *Amazonian Indians from Prehistory to the Present: Anthropological Perspectives*. Anna C. Roosevelt, ed. Tucson: The University of Arizona Press.

————. 1995. Culture, Genuine and Spurious: The Politics of Indianness in the Vaupés, Colombia. *American Ethnologist* 22 (1):3–27.

Jamieson, Mark. 1998. Linguistic Innovation and Relationship Terminology in the Pearl Lagoon Basin of Nicaragua. *Journal of the Royal Anthropological Institute* 4 (4):713–730.

———. 2003. Miskitu or Creole? Ethnic Identity and the Moral Economy in a Nicaraguan Miskitu Village. *Journal of the Royal Anthropological Institute* 9 (2):201–222.

Jenkins Molieri, Jorge. 1986. *El Desafío Indígena de Nicaragua: el Caso de los Miskitos*. Managua: Editorial Vanguardia.

Johnson, Frederick. 1948. Central American Cultures: An Introduction. In *Handbook of South American Indians, Volume IV*. Julian H. Steward, ed. Washington DC: United States Government Printing Office.

Karnes, Thomas L. 1978. *Tropical Enterprise: The Standard Fruit and Steamship Company in Latin America*. Baton Rouge: Louisiana State University Press.

Kearney, Michael, and Carole Nagengast. 1990. Mixtec Ethnicity: Social Identity, Political Consciousness, and Political Activism. *Latin American Research Review* 1990: 61–92.

Kearney, Michael. 1996. Introduction. *Latin American Perspectives* 23 (2):5–16.

Keller, Frank B. 1986. *Wiwilí 1980: monografía de un municipio nicaragüense en cambio*. Frankfurt/Main: Vervuert.

Kellogg, R. S. 1914. *The Lumber Industry*. New York: The Ronald Press Company.

Kidd, Stephen W. 1995. Land, Politics and Benevolent Shamanism: The Exnet Indians in a Democratic Paraguay. *Journal of Latin American Studies* 27 (1):43–75.

Kirchoff, Paul. 1948. The Caribbean Lowland Tribes: The Mosquito, Sumu, Paya, and Jicaque. In *Handbook of South American Indians, Volume IV*. Washington DC: United States Government Printing Office.

Laird, Larry. 1972. Origenes de la Reincorporacion Nicaraguense de la Costa Miskita. *Revista Conservadora del Pensamiento Centroamericano* 28 (140):1–57.

Lancaster, Roger. 1991. Skin Color, Race, and Racism in Nicaragua. *Ethnology* 30 (4):339–353.

———. 1992. *Life is Hard: Machismo, Danger, and the Intimacy of Power in Nicaragua*. Berkeley: University of California Press.

Las Casas, Bartolomé de. 1992 [1552]. *The Devastation of the Indies: A Brief Account*. Baltimore: Johns Hopkins University Press.

Lass, Andrew. 1997. The Role of Europe in the Study of Anthropology. *American Anthropologist* 99 (4):713–730.

LeGrand, Catherine. 1984. Colombian Transformations: Peasants and Wage-Laborers in the Santa Marta Banana Zone. *The Journal of Peasant Studies* 2 (4):178–200.

Lehmann, Walter. 1920. *Zentral-Amerika*. Berlin: Dietrich Reimer.

Lernoux, Penny. 1985a. Strangers in a Familiar Land (Nicaragua's Miskitos, Part 1). *The Nation* 241 (14):202–207.

———. 1985b. The Indians and the Commandantes (Nicaragua's Miskitos, Part II). *The Nation* 241 (15):275–278.

Lewis, Laura. 2000. Blacks, Black Indians, Afromexicans: The Dynamics of Race, Nation and Identity in a Mexican Moreno Community (Guerrero). *American Ethnologist* 27 (4):898–926.

———. 2001. Of Ships and Saints: History, Memory and Place in the Making of Moreno Mexican Identity. *Cultural Anthropology* 16 (1):62–82.

Linguists for Nicaragua. 1989. Language Rights on the Nicaraguan Atlantic Coast. *Cultural Survival Quarterly* 13 (3):7–10.

Long, Edward. 1972 [1774]. *The History of Jamaica*. New York: Arno Press.

López, María Antonia, and Walter Treminio Urbina. 2004. Muelle de Bilwi en el ojo de la tormenta. *La Prensa* (newspaper), June 17, 2004.

López, María Antonia. 2004. Demandarán a concesionarios por abandonar puerto de Bilwi. *La Prensa* (newspaper), June 19, 2004.

Lussan, Raveneau de. 1930 [1689]. *Raveneau de Lussan, Buccaneer of the Spanish Main and Early French Filibuster of the Pacific*. Cleveland: Arthur H. Clark.

Macaulay, Neill. 1985 [1967]. *The Sandino Affair*. Durham: Duke University Press.

Macdonald, Theodore. 1981. Nicaragua: National Development and Atlantic Coast Indians. *Cultural Survival Newsletter* 5 (3):9–11.

———. 1984a. Miskito Refugees in Costa Rica. *Cultural Survival Quarterly* 8 (3):59–60.

———. 1984b. Misurasata Goes Home. *Cultural Survival Quarterly* 8 (4):42–49.

———. 1985. Advances Toward a Miskito-Sandinista Cease-Fire. *Cultural Survival Quarterly* 9 (2):38–42.

———. 1988. The Moral Economy of the Miskito Indians: Local Roots of a Geopolitical Conflict. In *Ethnicities and Nations: Processes of Interethnic Relations in Latin America, Southeast Asia and the Pacific*. Remo Guidieri et al., eds. Austin: University of Texas Press.

———. 1996. The Routinization of Protest: Institutionalizing Local Participation. *Cultural Survival Quarterly* 20 (3):57–61.

Magnus, Richard W. 1978. The Prehistoric and Modern Subsistence Patterns of the Atlantic Coast of Nicaragua: A Comparison. In *Prehistoric Coastal Adaptations: The Economy and Ecology of Maritime Middle America*. Barbara Stark and Barbara Voorhies, eds. New York: Academic Press.

Marcus, George E., and Michael Fischer. 1986. *Anthropology as Cultural Critique: An Experimental Moment in the Human Sciences*. Chicago: The University of Chicago Press.

Martinez, Moisés. 2004. Ante invasión campesina Miskitos defienden tierras. *La Prensa* (newspaper), February 8, 2004.

Maxwell, Robert S., and Robert D Baker. 1983. *Sawdust Empire: The Texas Lumber Industry, 1830–1940*. College Station: Texas A&M University Press.

May, Stacy, and Galo Plaza. 1958. *The United Fruit Company in Latin America*. Washington DC: National Planning Association.

Means, Russell. 1995. *Where White Men Fear to Tread: The Autobiography of Russell Means*. New York: St. Martin's Press.

Membreño Idiáquez, Marcos. 1994. *Las Estructuras de las Comunidades Etnicas*. Managua: Editorial ENVIO.

Meschkat, Klaus, et al., eds. 1987. *Mosquitia—die andere Häfte Nicaraguas: über Geschichte und Gegenwart der Atlantikküste*. Hamburg: Junius Verlag GmbH.

Messer, Ellen. 1995. Anthropology and Human Rights in Latin America. *Journal of Latin American Anthropology* 1 (1):48–97.

Ministerio de Economia. 1963. *Censos Nacionales, Volumen III.* Managua: Republica de Nicaragua.

———. 1973. *Anuario Estadistica.* Managua: Republica de Nicaragua.

Mintz, Sidney. 1994. Enduring Substances, Trying Theories: The Caribbean Region Oikoumene. *Journal of the Royal Anthropological Institute* 2:289–311.

Mohawk, John. 1981. Marxism: Perspectives from a Native Movement. *Akwesasne Notes* 13 (1):9–10.

———. 1982. The Possibilities of Uniting Indians and the Left for Social Change in Nicaragua. *Cultural Survival Quarterly* 6 (1):24–25.

———. 1983. Nicaragua: Depressions Cloud the Issues. *Akwesasne Notes* (late winter):11–12.

Mohawk, John, and Shelton Davis. 1982. Revolutionary Contradictions: Miskito and Sandinistas in Nicaragua. *Akwesasne Notes* (late spring):7–12.

Mörner, Magnus. 1967. *Race Mixture in the History of Latin America.* Boston: Little, Brown and Company.

Morris, Glenn, and Ward Churchill. 1987. Between a Rock and a Hard Place. Left-Wing Revolution, Right-Wing Reaction and the Destruction of Indigenous Peoples. *Cultural Survival Quarterly* 11 (3):17–24.

Moscoso, Francisco. 1991. *Los Cacicazgos de Nicaragua Antigua.* San Juan, Puerto Rico: Instituto de Estudios del Caribe.

Mueller, Karl. 1931. *Report of the Official Visitation of the Moravian Missions in Nicaragua.* Bethlehem, PA: Proceedings of the Society for Propagating the Gospel.

Muñoz, Betty. 1992. Comunidades indígenas del Caribe nicaraguense: El caso del barrio El Cocal, Puerto Cabezas. In *Persistencia Indígena en Nicaragua.* German Romero Vargas et al., eds. Managua: CIDCA-UCA.

M.W. 1728. The Mosqueto Indian and his Golden River, Being a Familiar Description of the Mosqueto Kingdom in America. In *A Collection of Voyages and Travels, Some Now First Printed from Original Manuscripts, Others Now First Published in English, in Six Volumes*, Third Edition, Volume 6. Awnsham Churchill, ed. London: Henry Lintot and John Osborn.

Nash, June. 1995. The Reassertion of Indigenous Identity: Mayan Responses to State Intervention in Chiapas. *Latin American Research Review* 30 (3):7–41.

Naylor, Robert. 1989. *Penny Ante Imperialism: The Mosquito Shore and the Bay of Honduras, 1600–1914: A Case Study in British Informal Empire.* Rutherford, NJ: Farleigh Dickinson University Press.

Newson, Linda A. 1987. *Indian Survival in Colonial Nicaragua.* Norman: University of Oklahoma Press.

Nietschmann, Bernard. 1973. *Between Land and Water: The Subsistence Ecology of the Miskito Indians, Eastern Nicaragua.* New York: Seminar Press.

———. 1974. When The Turtle Collapses, the World Ends. *Natural History* 83 (6):34–44.

———. 1976. Drift Coconuts. *Natural History* 85 (9):20–27.

———. 1983a. An Akwesasne Notes Interview. *Akwesasne Notes* 15 (5):6.

———. 1983b. Indian War and Peace in Nicaragua. *Akwesasne Notes* 15 (6):3.

———. 1984a. Nicaragua's Other War. Indian Warriors vs. Sandinistas. *Coevolution Quarterly* 42:41–47.

———. 1984b. The Indian Resistance in Nicaragua. *Akwesasne Notes* 16 (early spring):12–13.

———. 1987. The Third World War. *Cultural Survival Quarterly* 11 (3):1–16.

———. 1989. *The Unknown War: The Miskito Nation, Nicaragua, and the United States.* New York: Freedom House.

———. 1991a. Miskito Coast Protected Area. *Research and Exploration* 7 (1): 232–234.

———. 1991b. Miskito Kupia, Miskito Coast Protected Area: A Project Coordinated by IRENA, MIKUPIA, AC-IRENA. Washington: World Wildlife Fund.

———. 1990. Battlefields of Ashes and Mud. *Natural History*, November 1990, 35–37.

———. 1990. Conservation by Conflict in Nicaragua. *Natural History*, November 1990, 42–48.

———. 1993. The Miskito Nation and the Geopolitics of Self-Determination. In *The Ethnic Dimension in International Relations.* Bernard Schechterman and Martin Slann, eds. Westport: Praeger Publishers.

———. 1995. Defending the Miskito Reefs with Maps and GPS. Mapping With Sail, Scuba and Satellite. *Cultural Survival Quarterly* 18 (4):34–37.

Norwood, Susan. 1987. Mehrsprachigkeit und Amtssprache in Puerto Cabezas. In *Mosquitia—die andere Hälfte Nicaraguas: über Geschichte und Gegenwart der Atlantikküste.* Klaus Meschkat et al., eds. Hamburg: Julius Verlag GmbH.

O'Brien, Thomas F. 1996. *The Revolutionary Mission: American Enterprise in Latin America, 1900–1945.* Cambridge: Cambridge University Press.

Oertzen, Eleonore von, Lioba Rossbach, and Volker Wunderich, eds. 1990. *The Nicaraguan Mosquitia in Historical Documents 1844–1927: The Dynamics of Ethnic and Regional History.* Berlin: Dietrich Reimer Verlag.

Offen, Karl H. 1999. The Miskitu Kingdom: Landscape and the Emergence of a Miskitu Ethnic Identity, Northeastern Nicaragua and Honduras, 1600–1800. PhD dissertation, University of Texas, Austin.

———. 2002. The Sambo and Tawira Miskitu: The Colonial Origins and Geography of Intra-Miskitu Differentiation in Eastern Nicaragua and Honduras. *Ethnohistory* 49 (2):319–372.

Ohland, Klaudine, and Robin Schneider, eds. 1983. *National Revolution and Indigenous Identity: The Conflict between Sandinistas and Miskito Indians on Nicaragua's Atlantic Coast.* Copenhagen: International Work Group for Indigenous Affairs.

Olien, Michael D. 1983. The Miskito Kings and the Line of Succession. *Journal of Anthropological Research* 39:198–241.

———. 1985. E. G. Squier and the Miskito: Anthropological Scholarship and Political Propaganda. *Ethnohistory* 32 (2):111–133.

———. 1987. Micro/Macro-Level Linkages: Regional Political Structures on the Mosquito Coast, 1845–1864. *Ethnohistory* 34 (3):256–287.

———. 1988a. After the Indian Slave Trade: Cross-Cultural Trade in the Western Caribbean Rimland, 1816–1820. *Journal of Anthropological Research* 44 (1):41–66.

———. 1988b. Were the Miskito Indians Black? Ethnicity, Politics, and Plagiarism in the Mid-Nineteenth Century. *Nieuwe West-Indische Gids* 62 (1–2):27–50.

————. 1988c. Imperialism, Ethnogenesis and Marginality: Ethnicity and Politics on the Mosquito Coast, 1845–1864. *Journal of Ethnic Studies* 16 (1):1–29.

Ortega, Marvin. 1991. *Nicaraguan Repatriation to Mosquitia.* Washington DC: Center for Immigration Policy and Refugee Assistance.

Parsons, J. J. 1956. San Andres and Providencia: English-Speaking Islands in the Western Caribbean. *University of California Publications in Geography* 12 (1):1–84.

Pichirallo, Joe. 1987. North "Foot Soldier" Describes Carrying Cash, Data to Contras. *The Washington Post*, May 15, pp.1, 16.

Pike, Frederik. 1992. *The United States and Latin America: Myths and Stereotypes of Civilization and Nature.* Austin: University of Texas Press.

Pineda, Baron. 1991. Nationalism and Ethnic Politics on the Atlantic Coast of Nicaragua. Master's thesis, Department of Anthropology, The University of Chicago.

————. 1998. The "Port People" of Bilwi: Ideologies of Race, Lexicons of Identity and the Politics of Peoplehood in the Mosquito Coast. PhD thesis, Department of Anthropology, The University of Chicago.

————. 2001a. The Chinese Creoles of Nicaragua: Identity, Economy, and Revolution in a Caribbean Port City. *Journal of Asian American Studies* 4 (3):209–233.

————. 2001b. Creole Neighborhood or Miskito Community? A Case Study of Identity Politics in a Mosquito Coast Land Dispute. *Journal of Latin American Anthropology* 6 (1):94–130.

————. 2001c. Cosmopolitan or Primitive? Environmental Dissonance and Regional Ideology in the Mosquito Coast. *American Indian Culture and Research Journal* 25 (4):35–55.

Potthast, Barbara. 1988. *Die Mosquitoküste im Spannungsfeld Britischer und Spanischer Politik, 1502–1821.* Köln: Böhlau Verlag GmbH & Cie.

Ramirez, Sergio. 1988. *Pensamiento Político.* Caracas: Biblioteca Ayacucho.

Ramirez, William. 1982. The Imperialist Threat and the Indigenous Problem in Nicaragua. *Akwesasne Notes* 14 (1):13–16.

Redfield, Robert. 1956. *Peasant Society and Culture: An Anthropological Approach to Civilization.* Chicago: The University of Chicago Press.

República de Nicaragua. 1920. *Cuadros Generales del Censo, 1920.* Managua: República de Nicaragua.

Richter, Ernesto. 1987. ALPROMISU: Die Entstehung einer neuen ethnischen Bewegung. In *Mosquitia—die andere Häfte Nicaraguas: über Geschichte und Gegenwart der Atlantikküste.* Klaus Meschkat et al., eds. Hamburg: Junius Verlag GmbH.

Rivera, Brooklyn. 1982. Interview with Brooklyn Rivera. *Akwesasne Notes* 14 (3):1820.

————. 1988. MISURASTA–FSLN Historical Relations. In *Voices Against the State: Nicaraguan Opposition to the FSLN.* Steven Blakemore, ed. Miami: University of Miami Institute of Interamerican Studies.

Rivera, Virgilio, and Ronnie Vernooy. 1991. El Dama: Una Historia Laboral Costeña. In *Como Vamos a Sobrevivir Nosotros: Aspectos de la Pequeñas Economías y Autonomía de la Costa Caribe de Nicaragua.* Ronnie Vernooy et al., eds. Managua: CIDCA-UCA.

Rizo Zeledón, Mario. 1993. Etnicidad, Legalidad y Demanda de las Comunidades Indígenas del Norte, Centro y Pacífico de Nicaragua. *America Indígena* 53 (1–2):165–198.

Robbins, William G. 1982. *Lumberjacks and Legislators: Political Economy of the US Lumber Industry, 1890–1941.* College Station: Texas A&M University Press.

Romero Vargas, Germán. 1992. Las Poblaciones Indígenas de Nicaragua, 1492–1821. In *Persistencia Indígena en Nicaragua.* Germán Romero Vargas et al., eds. Managua: CIDCA-UCA.

———. 1993a. La Dominación Europea de los Indios de Nicaragua, Siglos XVI al XIX. *America Indígena* 53 (1–2):9–21.

———. 1993b. La Población de Origen Africano en Nicaragua. In *Presencia Africana en Centroamerica.* Luz María Martínez Montiel, ed. Mexico City: Consejo Nacional para la Cultura y las Artes.

———. 1995. *Las Sociedades del Atlántico de Nicaragua en los Siglos XVII y XVIII.* Managua: Colección Cultural Banco Nicaraguense.

Ruiz y Ruiz, Frutos. 1927. *Costa Atlántica de Nicaragua.* Managua: Tipografia Alemana de Carlos Heuberger.

Sahlins, Marshall. 1965. On the Sociology of Primitive Exchange. In *The Relevance of Models for Social Anthropology.* ASA Monograph 1. Michael Banton, ed. London: Travistock Publications.

———. 1968. Notes on the Original Affluent Society. In *Man the Hunter.* Richard B. Lee and Irven DeVore, eds. Chicago: Aldine Press.

———. 1972. *Stone Age Economics.* Chicago: Aldine Press.

Salamanca, Danilo. 1993. Los idiomas indígenas y de la población negra. *America Indigena* 53 (1–2):23–39.

Sánchez, Consuelo. 1994. *La Conformación Étnico-Nacional en Nicaragua.* Mexico City: Instituto Nacional de Antropología e Historia.

Sanchez, Pedro. 1976. *Properties and Management of Soils in the Tropics.* New York: Wiley-Interscience.

Sanders, Douglas. 1985. Mosquitia and Nicaragua: An Incomplete Revolution. In *Native Power: The Quest for National Autonomy and Nationhood of Indigenous Peoples.* Jens Brosted et al., eds. Oslo: Universit ets forlaget.

Sandoval Valdivia, Elba. 1957. *Costumbres y Folklore del Pueblo Miskito.* Managua: Talleres Nacionales.

Schneider, Robin. 1996. *Rebellion der Mískito: Indianische Sozialbewegung und Sandinistische Revolution in Nicaragua.* Berlin: Edition Parabolis.

Scruggs, T. M. 1999. "Let's Enjoy Music as Nicaraguans": The Use of Music in the Construction of Nicaraguan National Consciousness. *Ethnomusicology* 43 (2):297–321.

Shapiro, Michael. 1987. Bilingual-Bicultural Education in Nicaragua's Atlantic Coast Region. *Latin American Perspectives* 14 (1):68–84.

Sherman, William L. 1979. *Forced Native Labor in Sixteenth-Century Central America.* Lincoln: University of Nebraska Press.

Sider, Gerald. 1993. *Lumbee Indian Histories: Race, Ethnicity, and Indian Identity in the Southern United States.* Cambridge: Cambridge University Press.

Sklar, Holly. 1988. *Washington's War on Nicaragua.* Boston: South End Press.

Smith, Carol A. 1991. Maya Nationalism. *NACLA Report on the Americas* 25 (3):29–33.

Smith, Raymond T. 1992. Race, Class, and Gender in the Transition to Freedom. In *The Meaning of Freedom: Economics, Politics, and Culture after Slavery*. Frank McGlynn and Seymour Drescher, eds. Pittsburgh: University of Pittsburgh Press.

———. 1993. Review of *Decolonizing Anthropology: Moving Toward an Anthropology for Liberation* by Faye Harrison. *American Anthropologist* 95 (3):782–783.

———. 1996. *The Matrifocal Family: Power, Pluralism, and Politics*. New York: Routledge.

Smutko, Gregorio. 1983. Historia de la Salvación Misquita. *Boletín Nicaraguense de Bibliografía y Documentación* 26:42–48.

———. 1985. *La Mosquitia, Historia y Cultura de la Costa Atlántica*. Managua: Editorial La Ocarina.

———. 1992. Toward a New Paradigm in Spiritual Formation—One Example: The Miskito Nation. *Missiology* 20 (1):55–68.

Solórzano, Flor de Oro. 1992. La Colonización Inglesa en la Costa Caribe de Nicaragua, 1633–1787. In *Persistencia Indígena en Nicaragua*. Germán Romero Vargas et al., eds. Managua: CIDCA-UCA.

Steward, Julian H. 1948. The Circum-Caribbean Tribes—An Introduction. In *Handbook of South American Indians, Volume IV*. Jualian Steward, ed. Washington DC: United States Government Printing Office.

Stone, Doris. 1964. Synthesis of Lower Central American Ethnohistory. In *Handbook of Middle American Indians, Volume IV*. Robert Wauchope, ed. Austin: University of Texas Press.

Ströbele-Gregor, Juliana. 1996. Culture and Political Practice of the Aymara and Quechua in Bolivia: Autonomous Forms of Modernity in the Andes. *Latin American Perspectives* 23 (2):72–90.

Strong, William Duncan. 1948. The Archaeology of Costa Rica and Nicaragua. In *Handbook of South American Indians, Volume IV*. Julian Steward, ed. Washington DC: United States Government Printing Office.

Talleres Gráficos Pérez. 1941. *Nicaragua: Guía General Ilustrada*. Managua: Talleres Gráficos Pérez.

Taussig, Michael. 1980. *The Devil and Commodity Fetishism in South America*. Chapel Hill: University of North Carolina Press.

———. 1987. *Shamanism, Colonialism and the Wild Man: A Study in Terror and Healing*. Chicago: Chicago University Press.

Treminio Urbina, Walter. 2002. La odisea de viajar a Puerto Cabezas. *La Prensa* (newspaper), August 13, 2002.

United States Department of State Records. Records of Foreign Service Posts. Managua, Bluefields, and Puerto Cabezas. Washington DC: National Archives.

United States Department of State. 1894. *Foreign Relations of the United States: Nicaragua (Mosquito Territory)*. Washington DC: Government Printing Office.

———. 1984. *Broken Promises: Sandinista Repression of Human Rights in Nicaragua*. Washington DC: Office of Public Diplomacy for Latin America and the Caribbean.

———. 1986a. *Dispossessed: The Miskito Indians in Sandinista Nicaragua*. Washington DC: Department of State Publication 9478.

————. 1986b. *Human Rights in Nicaragua under the Sandinistas: From Revolution to Repression.* Washington DC: Department of State Publication 9467.

Urban, Greg, and Joel Sherzer, eds. 1991. *Nation-States and Indians in Latin America.* Austin: University of Texas Press.

Uring, Nathaniel. 1976 [1726]. *A History of the Voyages and Travels of Captain Nathaniel Uring.* London:W. Wilkins (original printing). Ann Arbor: University Microfilms International (modern reprint).

Vail, Leroy. 1989. Preface and Introduction: Ethnicity in Southern African History. In *The Creation of Tribalism in Southern Africa.* Leroy Vail, ed. Berkeley: The University of California Press.

Valle, Alfonso. 1944. *Interpretación de Nombres Geográficos Indígenas de Nicaragua.* Managua: Talleres Gráficos Perez.

Varese, Stefano. 1996. The Ethnopolitics of Indian Resistance in Latin America. *Latin American Perspectives* 23 (2):58–71.

Vilas, Carlos M. 1989. *State, Class, and Ethnicity in Nicaragua: Capitalist Modernization and Revolutionary Change on the Atlantic Coast.* Boulder: Lynne Rienner Publishers.

von Hagen, V. Wolfgang. 1940. The Mosquito Coast of Honduras and Its Inhabitants. *Geographical Review* 30 (2):238–259.

Wade, Peter. 1993. *Blackness and Race Mixture: The Dynamics of Racial Identity in Colombia.* Baltimore: Johns Hopkins University Press.

————. 1997. *Race and Ethnicity in Latin America: Critical Studies On Latin America.* Chicago: Pluto Press, 1997.

————. 1999. Working Culture: Making Cultural Identities in Cali, Colombia. *Current Anthropology* 40 (4): 449–471.

Walcott, Derek. 1992. Nobel Lecture, The Antilles: Fragments of an Epic Memory. *The New Republic,* December 28, 26–32.

Warren, Kay B. 1989 [1978]. *The Symbolism of Subordination: Indian Identity in a Guatemalan Town.* Austin: University of Texas Press.

————. 1993. *The Violence Within: Cultural and Political Opposition in Divided Nations.* Boulder: Westview Press.

————. 1998. Indigenous Movements as a Challenge to the Unified Social Movement Paradigm for Guatemala. In *Culture of Politics, Politics of Cultures: Re-Visioning Latin American Social Movements.* Sonia Alvarez, Arturo Escobar, and Evelina Dagnino, eds. Boulder: Westview Press.

————. 1999. *Indigenous Movements and Their Critics: Pan Maya Activism in Guatemala.* Princeton: Princeton University Press.

Watanabe, John M. 1994. Unimagining the Maya: Anthropologists, Others, and the Inescapable Hubris of Authorship. *Bulletin of Latin American Research* 14 (1):25–45.

Weiss, Wendy A. 1995. Review of *Resistance and Contradiction: Miskitu Indians and the Nicaraguan State, 1894–1987* by Charles R. Hale. *American Ethnologist* 22 (3):672–675.

Whitten, Norman E. 1974. *Black frontiersmen; A South American case.* Cambridge, MA: Schenkman Publishing Company.

————. 1996. The Ecuadorian Levantamiento Indigena of 1990 and the Epitomizing Symbol of 1992: Reflections on Nationalism, Ethnic-Bloc Formation, and Racialist Ideologies. In *History, Power, and Identity: Ethnogenesis in the Americas, 1492–1992*. Jonathan Hill, ed. Iowa City: University of Iowa Press.

Whitten, Norman E., and Arlene Torres. 1992. Blackness in the Americas. *NACLA Report on the Americas* 25 (4):16–22.

Wiggins, Armstrong 1981. Colonialism and Revolution: Nicaraguan Sandinism and the Liberation of the Miskito, Sumu and Rama Peoples. An Interview with Armstrong Wiggins. *Akwesasne Notes* 13 (4):4–15.

Wilcox, Meg. 1993. Miskito Activists Draw the Line on Toxic Wastes. *Cultural Survival* Quarterly 17 (3):6–7.

Williams, Brackette F. 1991. *Stain on my Name, War in my Veins: Guyana and the Politics of Cultural Struggle*. Durham, NC: Duke University Press.

Williams, Brett. 1991. Introduction. In *The Politics of Culture*. Brett Williams, ed. Washington DC: Smithsonian Institution Press.

Wilson, John. 1975. *Obra Morava en Nicaragua: Trasfondo y Breve Historia*. San José, Costa Rica: Seminario Bíblico Latinoamericano.

———. 1983. Resumen de la Vida y Obra de Los Moravos en Nicaragua. *Boletín Nicaraguense de Bibliografía y* Documentación 26:49–57.

Wilson, Richard A. 1995. *Maya Resurgence in Guatemala: Q'eqchi' Experiences*. Norman: University of Oklahoma Press.

Wolf, Eric R. 1955. Types of Latin American Peasantry: A Preliminary Discussion. *American Anthropologist* 62 (3):452–471.

———. 1959. *Sons of the Shaking Earth*. Chicago: University of Chicago Press.

———. 1966. *Peasants*. Englewood Cliffs, NJ: Prentice-Hall.

Wolf, Eric R., and Joseph G. Jorgensen. 1970. Anthropology on the Warpath in Thailand. *The New York Review of Books*, November 19, 1970.

Wright, Robin M. 1988. Anthropological Presuppositions of Indigenous Advocacy. *Annual Review of Anthropology* 17:365–390.

Wünderich, Volker. 1989. *Sandino en la Costa: De las Segovias al Litoral Atlántico*. Managua: Editorial Nueva Nicaragua.

Index

About the Author

Baron Pineda is a cultural anthropologist specializing in race and indigenous peoples in Latin America. He has a bachelor's degree from the University of California at Berkeley and a master's degree and PhD from the University of Chicago. He currently is an assistant professor of anthropology at Oberlin College.